THE LAST REFUGE

HASAN NUHANOVIĆ

THE LAST REFUGE

A TRUE STORY OF WAR, SURVIVAL AND LIFE UNDER SIEGE IN SREBRENICA

PETER OWEN PUBLISHERS
LONDON AND CHICAGO

PETER OWEN PUBLISHERS
Conway Hall, 25 Red Lion Square, London WC1R 4RL

Peter Owen books are distributed in the USA and Canada by
Independent Publishers Group/Trafalgar Square
814 North Franklin Street, Chicago, IL 60610, USA

Translated from the Bosnian *Zbijeg*

First English-language edition published in Great Britain 2019
by Peter Owen Publishers

© Hasan Nuhanović 2012
English translation © Mirjana Evtov and Alison Sluiter 2019

Hardback ISBN 978-0-7206-2041-2
Epub ISBN 978-0-7206-2043-6
Mobipocket ISBN 978-0-7206-2044-3
PDF ISBN 978-0-7206-2045-0

Typeset by Octavo Smith Publishing Services

Printed by Printfinder, Riga, Latvia

PREFACE TO THE ENGLISH-LANGUAGE EDITION

I did not write this book to tell my own story. Nor did I write it to tell my parents' or brother's stories and how their bodies are buried in the Potočari Memorial for genocide victims. I wrote it out of a need to describe the conditions in which one hundred thousand Bosniaks from Srebrenica, Vlasenica, Cerska, Nova Kasaba, Konjević Polje, Žepa and Han Pijesak found themselves in 1992.

The mass killing of more than eight thousand Bosniak men and boys in July 1995 was the last episode in a series of genocidal campaigns conducted by Serb forces beginning in April 1992 on. The number of victims, however, and the manner and speed with which they were killed in July 1995, the presence of UN forces in the field, the media reports that travelled relatively quickly around the world, the raising of an indictment for genocide at The Hague tribunal just a few weeks after the massacre and a number of other factors contributed to the events that occurred from 1992 to 1993, which were just as bloody and awful, being overshadowed only by what two international courts would later term the Genocide of July 1995. It is true that the Serb authorities endorsed mass genocide in the Drina region in July 1995, but the genocide began in April 1992.

It remains to be confirmed as to whether any international court – and the International Criminal Tribunal for the former Yugoslavia at The Hague in particular – will describe the events of 1992 and 1993 as genocide. As I pen these words, this has not yet happened.

This, my second book, is quite different from my first, *Under the UN Flag: The International Community and the Srebrenica Genocide.* (I used the word crime rather than genocide in the Bosnian edition,

5

as at the time it was published no court had ruled definitively that a genocide had occurred.) The previous account took the form of a factual reconstruction of events, with a particular stress on the role of the international community in the events that led up to and followed the fall of the UN Safe Area of Srebrenica. Since its publication in both Bosnian and English versions the book has been used as a source and a reference work by many students on post-graduate courses both within the country and abroad.

The methodology applied was a standard and internationally recognized one for that form of publication – what is known as a case study. In writing *The Last Refuge* I have eschewed methodology, other than to try to follow events chronologically. In some ways one might regard this work as closer to the genre of fiction – although that is not a particularly good analogy, in so far as a novel, even when based on history, includes invented characters and events. Everything set out in *The Last Refuge* really did happen. I have described things I saw with my own eyes and events that took place either where I was or to people I met. Naturally I cannot guarantee that everything other people told me about their experiences happened as they reported, but, still, it is important to recall that all the characters in this book were real – even if, having died during the war or since it ended, not all of them are still among the living. I have changed the names of some at their request.

Before writing this account I spent a long time thinking about its style, including whether the narrative should be in the first or the third person, for example. Should I invent a character through whom to tell the story? In the end I decided to write the book in the first person and to describe events as I saw them. It may be that some day in the future, when they have invented a machine that can project images directly from our minds on to a screen, we will have access to the truth about human suffering. Until then, a part of the truth, at least, will have to be reconstructed in courtrooms, with the aid of forensic science, while, in the case of other events, readers will have to accept the words of those of us who lived through them and have described our individual accounts in books such as this.

Muslim or Bosniak?

The term Bosnian Muslim has problematic connotations that conceal the essentially secular, political and ethnic nature of the 1992–5 conflict. For that reason I should perhaps have preferred the term Bosniak to that of Muslim but in the end decided to use both. I did this for the following reason: I was born in 1968 and was aware from early childhood that in Bosnia and Herzegovina – or, rather, in the former Yugoslavia – nationality, my parents' nationality, was referred to by the term Muslim, the capital M being deployed in my language to distinguish it from muslim without an initial capital, which referred to adherents of the Islamic faith. We learned this rule about when to use the capital or lower-case letter in primary school, and it was built into the 1971 constitution of the Socialist Federal Republic of Yugoslavia. Presumably it was supposed to mean that you could be a Muslim without being a muslim at the same time, and, conversely, you could be a muslim without being a Muslim. Naturally, you could also be both a Muslim and a muslim. So there was an official distinction between Muslim and muslim which was not easy to explain to foreigners in 1992, once the United Nations international forces arrived in Bosnia and Herzegovina, not to mention viewers of the English-language CNN or BBC television channels.

Until war broke out – until my twenty-fifth year, that is – I thought of myself as a Muslim, or, rather, I knew that I was a Muslim and also considered myself a Yugoslav, while at the same time thinking of myself as muslim to the extent that I was somewhat observant – which is to say very little or hardly at all, like almost all my Muslim peers in my home town. Of course, when it came to relationships with people from other republics in Yugoslavia – as my country then was – I thought of myself primarily as a Bosnian, which was my primary identity. So for me – and I am sure most of my peers would concur – the question of identity always involved layers, and I regarded myself at one and the same time as a Yugoslav, a Bosnian, a Muslim and a muslim. I am not sure that this order of words corresponds to how I would have ranked my various identities, which might, in any case, have differed depending on context. Certainly my Serb schoolfellows (there were only few Croats in the towns of eastern Bosnia where I grew up) viewed me as Muslim, and I was always conscious of this being the case. So, within Bosnia and Herzegovina, my primary identity was Muslim.

These were not the only or, indeed, always the most important forms of identity before the war. In everyday life in Vlasenica, where I spent most of my childhood before leaving for army service and then for university in Sarajevo, we had many other identities: good friends, good colleagues, tall, short, handsome, musician, athlete, drinker, liar, honest, good student, working-class, highlander, farmer and so on. But when my Serb neighbours from Vlasenica started taking people from their homes in the spring of 1992 to the Sušica camp and falling upon them and slaughtering them, the sole identity that mattered to them was Muslim. It didn't matter whether you were a good friend or colleague or honest; it wasn't even important whether you were muslim.

In 1993 the term Bosniak was brought into official use instead of Muslim, and it has been enshrined in the Constitution of Bosnia and Herzegovina (Annexe 4 to the General Framework Agreement) since the Dayton Agreement in 1995. I have got used to the term and now consider it a better fit for the identity of the people to whom I belong. I have no desire retrospectively to change the terms used to designate our identity during wartime, just as I have no desire to change history or the truth, so I use the terms Muslim and Bosniak interchangeably in this book.

Hasan Nuhanović
Sarajevo, 2019

EDITOR'S NOTES

BiH Bosna i Hercegovina (Bosnia and Herzegovina)

Dayton Agreement The General Framework Agreement for Peace in Bosnia and Herzegovina, the peace agreement reached at Dayton, Ohio, USA, on 1 November 1995 and formally signed in Paris on 14 December 1995, putting an end to the Bosnian War

JNA Jugoslavenska narodna armija, the Yugoslav People's Army (1945–92)

OZNA Odjeljenje za zaštitu naroda (the Department for People's Protection), the Yugoslav security agency between 1944 and 1952

Potočari Memorial The Srebrenica–Potočari Memorial and Cemetery for the Victims of the 1995 Genocide, a memorial cemetery set up in 2003 to honour the victims of the 1995 Srebrenica genocide

SAO Srpska autonomna oblast (Serb Autonomous Region), a number of which were set up within Croatia and Bosnia and Herzegovina in 1990–1

SDA Stranka demokratske akcije (Party of Democratic Action), a Bosniak political party in Bosnia and Herzegovina founded in 1990

SDS Srpska demokratska stranka (Serb Democratic Party), a Serb political party in Bosnia and Herzegovina founded in 1990

TO Teritorijalna obrana (Territorial Defence), civilian reserve forces in Yugoslavia

UNHCR The Office of the United Nations High Commissioner for Refugees, a UN agency mandated to protect refugees and resolve refugee problems

UNMO United Nations Military Observer

UNPROFOR The United Nations Protection Force, a peacekeeping force in Croatia and Bosnia and Herzegovina between 1992 and 1995

A NOTE ON PRONUNCIATION

C, c like the 'ts' in cats

Č, č like the 'tch' in match

Ć, ć a softer version of č, like the 't' in future

Đ, đ between the 'j' of jam and the 'd' of duke

J, j like a 'y'

Š, š like the 'sh' in push

Ž, ž like the 's' in measure

COMRADE TITO,
WE SWEAR TO YOU

In the spring of 1988 I was undertaking military service in a small town in the Republic of Serbia, Yugoslavia. I was nineteen, and the hardship of the first six months of military training was behind me. I would spend the next six months as a seasoned soldier of the Yugoslav People's Army, the Jugoslovenska narodna armija (JNA).

On 25 May, Youth Day and Tito's official birthday, I stood proudly on the stage of a packed JNA hall to sing with a local amateur band. The group had heard me at a military band rehearsal and, impressed by my voice, they invited me to sing with them. I guess they had an affinity for Bosnian rock music; I did my best to project my voice and occasionally roughen it to sound like Tifa, a popular Bosnian rock singer. They seemed to like that. 'Come on, Bosnian,' they would say, 'sing like Tifa.'

After some discussion we agreed to perform 'Comrade Tito, We Swear Allegiance to You' ('Druže Tito, mi ti se kunemo'), a song by the Yugoslav pop star Zdravko Čolić.

In true rocker fashion I had my bass guitar slung around my neck. The JNA uniform I was wearing was a kind of a dress uniform for going out. The local Serbs didn't know who I was or where I came from, nor did they know what I was going to sing. My friend the guitarist winked at me, signalling that we were about to start, the drummer clicked time with his sticks and we began.

> The years of ordeals behind us.
> Many died for freedom;
> Silently, or singing instead of moaning.

Comrade Tito, we swear allegiance to you!
Comrade Tito, we swear allegiance to you!

I gave it everything. The sergeant-major seemed pleased with my performance. A professional soldier and the leader of our band, he gave me a nod of approval. I do not remember his name, but I do recall the way he smiled at me.

I was surprised by how good we sounded. But as I was singing I observed that the audience barely reacted. In fact, I got the impression they didn't like the song. But my resolve didn't waver, and I sang with even greater gusto. I couldn't help noticing the frowning faces, especially at the mention of our former leader Tito. I presumed they didn't like my singing or the style of music. Eventually we got some applause, but it echoed in my head for days afterwards. Somehow it didn't feel genuine. Something was missing.

Deep down I knew what it was, but I must have repressed it as an ominous sign. I would recall this moment many times during the war in Bosnia, in the cold winter of 1992. By then I had figured out that for these Serbs watching me perform in the JNA hall – as for many others – it was not only Tito who had been laid in his grave in 1980 but all that they had ever had in common with him. He had been erased from their minds because of what had been happening in Serbia for some time. Only I wasn't able to see it. They must have hated him. The song I sang on that spring day in 1988 must have been the last song about Tito ever sung in that town.

We celebrate in the streets,
Now we walk the country freely.
Beware of our song, evil people.
Comrade Tito, we swear allegiance to you!
Comrade Tito, we swear allegiance to you!

Four years later JNA tanks were razing Muslim homes in Žepa and Srebrenica where I inadvertently found myself – together with my parents and my brother, together with tens of thousands of other Bosniak refugees. Hungry, barefoot, empty-handed, we fled through the woods of eastern Bosnia like wild animals. We were scattered all over, in shelters in the forest, before converging on the Srebrenica valley where we thought we would be safe. As it turned out, the Serbs would follow us there, too, and come for our lives.

SPRING 1992:
SARAJEVO STUDENT
ACCOMMODATION

I was woken by the sound of military trucks rumbling in the street. I kept my eyes shut, hoping the noise would stop. But it didn't. I lifted my head off the pillow. My room-mate Hamid – we called him Hans – was still asleep. I got up and looked out of the window. Milošević's JNA, 'Serbianized' by then, was transferring all kinds of war machinery from Croatia to Bosnia.

My room was on the eighth floor of a student accommodation in Sarajevo. Aged twenty-four, I was a fourth-year student of mechanical engineering. I had spent the previous night solving problems in fluid mechanics. Everybody said that this was the most difficult subject and that after passing this examination everything else would be a piece of cake – well, apart from thermodynamics perhaps.

My girlfriend Mirza's room was located two floors below mine. I had serious intentions with regards to her, but I knew we had to wait until graduation, meaning another year, maybe two, before we could consider formalizing our relationship. I assumed we would marry, and I guess she was thinking the same.

'What *is* that?' Hans finally joined me at the window. The two of us watched the scene on the street. Below us, a hundred metres from the building, a huge column of military vehicles was passing towards Lukavica – tanks, trucks, jeeps, armoured personnel carriers (APCs), all kinds of transport. For a long time the convoy passed by; it seemed endless. The JNA was pulling out of Croatia and transferring all its weapons to Bosnia. As if there weren't already enough weapons there; as if the Serbs weren't stockpiling an enormous arsenal already.

We could see artillery mounted on some of the vehicles, but

neither of us said anything. I felt sick to my stomach, but I kept watching silently. I was one of the many Bosnian Muslims who had long ago stopped seeing the JNA as 'my' army. I watched the television news regularly and had seen JNA soldiers fire on a Tuzla mosque. This horrified me, but I knew there had been other incidents, some reported on television and others just rumours.

My family in Vlasenica, my home town, had for some time seen drunken Serb militia in the streets and bars. Although they wore JNA uniforms, they didn't look anything like JNA soldiers. Even without the characteristic insignia they looked to us like Chetniks – Serb nationalists. They would stick two fingers and a thumb up in a familiar salute and sing Chetnik songs. They would walk around town shooting their guns into the air, goading locals and crowing drunkenly. The word was that the soldiers were volunteers from the villages around Vlasenica and that they had returned from the Croatian front on leave. Normally I would spend almost every weekend with my family there. But by the end of 1991 I no longer felt safe. I didn't feel particularly safe in Sarajevo either for that matter, but somehow the accommodation block seemed safer than Vlasenica. I worried about my parents and my brother, though.

In 1991 there weren't any 'mixed' rooms in the accommodation any more. When the war in Croatia began, the students of Croat ethnicity refused to share rooms with students of Serb ethnicity and vice versa. They also refused to share rooms with Muslims. The mood was very tense, and it was getting worse with each passing day. The situation would reach boiling point every evening at about 7.30 when an ethnically mixed crowd of around a hundred students gathered to watch the news in the common room.

On the news one evening we watched a crowd of several thousand protesting in Split. Some of the participants jumped on a JNA APC. We watched a man strangle a soldier on top of the vehicle; the perpetrator wrapped his hands tightly around the soldier's neck, and the man seemed lose consciousness. I was appalled. There was no way of knowing the soldier's ethnicity. It didn't matter anyhow, not to me. I was fearful, to my stomach – fear mixed with sorrow for what was disappearing in front of my eyes at that moment. Sitting in the common room in front of the television, we witnessed dreadful scenes of the collapse of Yugoslavia, the state that had belonged to all of us.

The Serb students started shouting slogans and offending Croats by calling them Ustaše (after the Croatian ultra-nationalist movement that operated between 1929 and 1945), while Croat students shouted slogans against the JNA. I was worried that someone would pull out a knife or a gun and trigger a massacre. Both Serbs and Croats had bouncers guarding the common room door, and some of those individuals were over two metres tall.

That evening I left the common room for my room, opened my textbook where I had left off and returned to my studies in fluid mechanics. I had no illusions about the situation we were in – every one of us, the city of Sarajevo and all of Bosnia and Herzegovina. But I carried on studying as if nothing unusual was happening. April examinations were approaching, and I wanted to be sure that I would be admitted to the next semester. That semester would never come. I would be in the hell of Srebrenica by then. But I had no way of knowing that.

In the meantime some of 'our guys' (by 'our' I mean Bosnian Muslim students) started wearing fezzes. Not all the time, but on the night of 7 January 1992, Orthodox Christmas Day, a number of troublemakers donned fezzes and strolled through the halls in 'their' part of the dorm, while other students, Muslims and Croats alike, listened in fear through the open windows as several hundred Serbs sang 'There, Far Away', a song regarded as an expression of Serb nationalism. They also shouted 'This is Serbia!' and fired guns into the air. But along the corridors where the guys in fezzes strutted no Serb student sang that night. They were as quiet as mice.

That was how bad it was, if not worse, in my Sarajevo student accommodation at the beginning of 1992.

It's not as though I hadn't been aware of the inter-ethnic animosities among my fellow students by then, but in the spring of 1992, as a result of the tense situation in the country, these animosities threatened to escalate into open conflict between students. Three years earlier I had seen Serb students separate themselves from the rest of us. As a freshman I had seen hundreds of students hurry out the front of the building where around ten buses were waiting for them. They were

Serbs off to celebrate the six-hundredth anniversary of the Battle of Kosovo. I wondered who had invited them, who had sent the buses, why the students wanted to go and how it was organized when the rest of us had no idea about it.

Anyway, Hans and I had been silently watching the military convoy through the window for quite some time.

'Hans, if this kicks off, we're screwed. Look at this massive army! Who could fight against this?'

'I know what you mean, but our people have guns, too,' Hans replied. By 'our people' he meant the Bosnians from the predominantly Muslim-populated villages in the Vlasenica and Srebrenica municipalities, including his own village. 'You know how it is. You sell a cow, get 1,500 Deutschmarks for it and buy an automatic rifle.'

'Yeah, but what if you don't have a cow or don't want to sell it?'

'Well, people do have guns – at least, in every other house or maybe every third – you know, hunting rifles, shotguns or carbines. The people won't give up that easily.'

He gave me hope; if there were to be a war, perhaps we wouldn't be slaughtered just like that after all.

But the next day I kept imagining the five or six men from Hans's village standing in the road waiting to confront a Serb tank with their rifles. No matter how hard I tried I couldn't figure out how we could fight a war at all. How on earth would it be possible for these people to defend themselves?

Then a different image came into my mind. I remembered my Uncle Ibrahim who lived in Sweden. I could visualize clearly the yellow and blue of the Swedish flag. I had seen it on my uncle's Volvo often enough. I thought we should go there and decided to suggest it to my parents. The four of us should leave for Sweden and let anyone who wanted to stay and fight do just that. It was fine by me. We would return when the war was over.

At this time many among us naïvely and perniciously saw the war as a kind of game. It's two–one to them, then we level the score, then it's three–two – and on it went . . . And, while some people in Bosnia thought of it as a game, houses were being burned down in Croatia, Vukovar was in flames, people were being killed, terrible crimes were being committed. One Muslim student asked me, 'Do you know what the score is when two Croats and two Serbs kill each other?'

I said I didn't.

'Four–nil to us!' he retorted, bursting into laughter as he walked off down the hall.

I didn't find it remotely funny. I was terrified.

But Bosnian Muslims would not stay referees or spectators of the Serbo-Croat wars for long. We would become collateral damage, not only in the conflict between two nationalist polities but through the unpreparedness and disorientation of our politicians. We would become victims of genocide.

And so we continued to study diligently in our rooms. We were preparing for the April examinations while a bloody war was being fought across the river Sava in Croatia, not two hundred kilometres north of Sarajevo. And just outside Sarajevo, on Mount Trebević, the Serb JNA was digging in.

BLOODY BAJRAM

On 2 April I finally managed to convince Mirza that we should get out of Sarajevo. The plan was for her to go back home to Sandžak, a district of Serbia proper some distance south-east of the city, and for me to go to Vlasenica. From there we would figure out how to meet up in Sweden as soon as possible.

I walked her to the bus station. I wanted to kiss her before she boarded, but she wouldn't let me. Apparently the bus driver knew her father – at least, that's what she told me – and so we parted without saying a word. That morning we had woken up together in my room – Hans had gone home for the weekend – but Mirza wouldn't look at me, much less listen to my concerns that we get out of Sarajevo as quickly as we could.

'You're a coward!' she said. Rolling over, she turned her back to me and closed her eyes again.

Already exasperated that she was refusing to stick to our plan, the insult only made me angrier. I lifted the bed with all my might and shoved it hard against the wall with her still lying on it. Mirza's head appeared from behind the upturned bed. She didn't say anything but looked at me with a serious expression on her face. Evidently she finally understood that I would do anything to make her leave Sarajevo. She got up and packed her things.

Once her bus had left the station I took another to Vlasenica via Olovo and Kladanj. I avoided the route through Sokolac and Han Pijesak, which, in autumn 1991, had been declared part of a Serb Autonomous Region, or SAO (Srpska Autonomna Oblast). None of my Muslim friends had used that route since. Vlasenica was, in fact, part of another SAO, the Birač Oblast. A few months earlier, when a map of the autonomous regions had appeared in a newspaper, my father and I had analysed the SAO borders and saw that our apartment was located near the border between two SAOs.

It seemed to me that my father wasn't paying much attention to all that was going on. As the director of a timber yard, a job he had done for many years, he had more important things to think about. The company employed around five hundred people, mostly Muslims and Serbs. Timber was something Bosnia had never been short of, but each time I went home I would overhear him telling my mother about the company's problems. For some time the loggers hadn't been able to reach the logging sites at several locations near Serb-populated villages. The locals had set up barricades on the roads and weren't allowing them to do their job. Once I had heard him mention that the villagers intended to declare Serb ownership of the woods. The company was struggling, and my father faced serious problems paying the workers – half of whom were Serbs.

After I arrived home from Sarajevo I started following the news closely. My mother and brother Braco didn't comment much on current events. Both of them were waiting to hear what my father would say. He was adamant that he would not leave Vlasenica, let alone go abroad. My plan for us to escape to Sweden was not on the table.

'I can't leave the workers like this,' my father kept saying. 'What kind of message would I be sending them if I, the director, simply left? They haven't been paid, and I've just managed to call in a debt from some friends in Serbia for the wood we've already delivered, which should cover their salaries when it comes in.'

One day I learned that he had a gun – a 7.65-mm Zastava pistol, brand new, licensed – which he had started carrying at all times. He wasn't at home much, and the three of us – my mother, my brother and I – would spend our days watching the news.

And so the holidays arrived. Almost every year at Bajram (Eid al-Fitr) we would visit my mother's parents in Zvornik, where both she and I had been born, and that morning, the first day of Bajram, my parents decided that we would be going as usual.

'But haven't you heard the Serbs are saying this Bajram is going to be a bloody one?' I asked my father anxiously. 'You know we have to pass through Milići and near Kravica and many other Serb villages to get there. What if they stop us? You heard what happened in Bijeljina!' We had seen on the news that JNA and Serb paramilitaries, led by the notorious Željko Ražnatović, better known as Arkan, had entered the city of Bijeljina and, although the news reported a 'skirmish between Muslim fighters and the JNA', rumours had reached us of a massacre of Muslims.

But my parents paid no attention to my warnings. Gifts for my grandparents were packed, we all got in the car my father had bought the previous year – a Zastava Skala 55 – and we set off for Zvornik.

A KNIFE

We didn't encounter a single car on the road between Vlasenica and Zvornik that morning. Passing by the Serb houses in the daylight was frightening enough, but the thought of the return journey after dark was my main concern.

Zvornik seemed pretty lively – it might have been because of Bajram – but there was definitely an atmosphere. People were rushing about and looking over their shoulders. I couldn't help but wonder what was happening behind the scenes.

My grandparents were thrilled to see us. After our festive lunch we went to my Aunt Mina and Uncle Muhamed's house. Aunt Mina was my mother's sister. She and her husband were also close friends of my parents.

Uncle Muhamed was the director of a firm in Zvornik, and everyone in the town respected him. He told us he was on the committee of the group that would defend Zvornik if Serb forces approached it from neighbouring Serbia. Apparently there was a plan to blow up the iron bridge over the Drina. He said that there was a lorry parked somewhere in town that was loaded with barrels of petrol and explosives. The plan was to leave the truck in the middle of the bridge and, at a prearranged signal, blow it up. In addition to the iron bridge, there was a railway bridge and another bridge for traffic in Karakaj, and then there was the road over the dam. Muhamed didn't mention any of those, but I was comforted none the less by the thought that there was a group of people with a plan, any kind of plan.

I told my parents I was going for a walk, but what I really wanted was to see what was going on outside – for all I knew the war might already have started. I wandered around, hands in pockets, carefully watching the passers-by and trying to read their facial expressions. Were they afraid? Or worried? I wanted to know what was going on in their heads. I couldn't tell who among them was a Serb or who was a Muslim – well, except for those wearing the French beret characteristic of older Bosnian Muslim men and the women wearing headscarves, but that was it. Everyone else looked the same.

It was getting dark – that was what worried me most. How were we going to make it home safely? I started to think about my childhood in Zvornik and how I would occasionally stand in front of a kiosk near the local hospital, window-shopping for pocket knives and hunting knives. They looked just like the knives I'd seen in comic books that I, like all my peers, would devour: *Il Comandante Mark* and *Il Grande Blek*. They were trappers, hunters, freedom fighters, protectors of the poor and weak.

I went to the kiosk.

'Good evening,' I greeted the shop assistant. I hesitated for a moment wondering which nationality she might be.

'Good evening,' she said. 'How can I help you?'

'I'd like to buy . . .' I stopped because I was too embarrassed to utter the word. She waited patiently. 'I'd like to buy a knife.'

'What kind of knife?' she asked.

'Well, a hunting knife.'

'You won't believe it, but I've sold out of hunting knives today,' the assistant explained.

I stared at her as questions started lining up in my head: why, who . . . ?

'Thank you, I'll try elsewhere.' I knew they sold hunting equipment in the local department store. I suddenly imagined everybody rushing there to buy a knife, and I picked up my pace so I wouldn't be too late to get one myself.

A middle-aged salesman was watching me as I approached the counter.

'Excuse me, do you have any hunting knives?' I asked, trying not to look overly excited.

'Hello, young man. You are the hundredth customer who's asked for a knife today,' he said with a crooked smile. 'And you won't believe it, but there is one left.' He opened a drawer and pulled out a small knife with black handle and a leather sheath.

'I'll take it!' I stashed the knife in the inside pocket of my jacket and hurried back to my Aunt Mina's. My father was waiting for me rather anxiously. It was dark, and we should already have been on our way. I said nothing about the knife, but I found myself holding it tight inside my pocket on the way back to Vlasenica.

During and after the war I would often recount my knife story. The only way I could explain the shortage of knives in Zvornik was that ordinary Muslim people had tried to arm themselves, just as I had. You would think that no one had a decent kitchen knife at home, let alone a rifle.

WAITING

After our trip to Zvornik my parents no longer hid their anxiety from me and my brother and started discussing what should be done. I begged that we leave Vlasenica to go to Tuzla or Sweden or at least to Sarajevo, although we had seen on television that the capital was in chaos.

I went to a video rental shop and took out a copy of *The Battle on the Neretva*, a famous Yugoslav movie set during the Second World War. I played the video over and over, always in the evening, making sure my father was there to see. I rewound it repeatedly to the scene in which the Chetniks find some wounded Partisans and slit their throats. Every time I played that scene my father would give me a dirty look and say, 'Enough now. You're going to frighten your mother and brother.'

'I want the three of you to remember this,' I said, 'because this is something that might happen to us, too. We have to get out of here!'

My brother made no comment. He was being his usual self, an ironic smile plastered on his face as if to say he didn't expect anything different from me. There was nothing I wouldn't have done to convince them to leave, but there wasn't much chance of that since my father was hardly ever at home. He went to the office early in the morning and came back late at night. I persuaded my mother to reason with him, and I know she tried, but it was clear that she was going to respect his decision, whatever that might be.

When I woke up early each morning I would see Serb families leaving our neighbourhood. They packed their belongings into their cars and went who knows where. Later in the day those cars would come back, but only men would get out of them. Some of them were in uniform and some were openly carrying automatic rifles.

We didn't know our neighbours well because the apartment block was new. Our next-door neighbour was Rajko Dukić's sister, the same Rajko Dukić who was one of the leaders of the SDS and one of the closest associates of Radovan Karadžić. (After the masked SDS members had blockaded Sarajevo, it was Rajko Dukić who, on 3 March 1992, seated in the SDS headquarters in the Holiday Inn, read the ten infamous SDS conditions for lifting the blockade.) Each time I heard someone coming up the stairs and along our landing I would look through the peephole in our door, and on several occasions I'd seen armed men in camouflage uniforms entering Dukić's sister's apartment.

The day after we visited my grandparents the Serb JNA attacked Zvornik. My father was in his office when it happened. When the telephone rang my mother answered, and I saw a look of panic on her face. She was speaking to her youngest sister, Azra. I heard Azra screaming and crying, begging my mother to do something. I heard her shouting that the Chetniks were coming down the hill near my grandparents' house – where Azra also lived – and that they were banging on the door.

The telephone connection was lost. Never in my life had I seen my mother in such a state. She was shaking all over, crying and screaming, 'Leave my children alone, leave my children alone!' By 'children' she meant my brother and me, of course. She was saying things that made no sense at all. She opened the door to our flat and ran out, still screaming, 'Leave my children alone!' The landing echoed with her cries, and the neighbours opened their apartment door and came out to see what was happening. They were Serbs. Seemingly concerned about my mother, they came out and tried to calm her down. Braco and I stood there speechless. I saw tears in my brother's eyes – he'd hardly ever shown much emotion. 'Leave my children alone!' my mother repeated.

One of our neighbours helped her into their apartment and on to a sofa. Somebody, maybe Rajko Dukić's sister, brought her a glass of water. I was sure by then that our Serb neighbours saw us as a threat. Perhaps they thought we were stashing weapons in our flat. Perhaps they thought my father was somehow connected to the SDA in Sarajevo, connected to the President of BiH, Alija Izetbegović, or who knows who or what else. We knew nothing about each other; we had moved in only a few weeks ago.

After a while my mother collected herself. Once she had calmed down she understood the seriousness of the situation. We were sitting in the apartment that SDS leaders – or, at least, their associates – used for meetings. Although I didn't know how much they feared us I did know how frightened we were of them. When my mother started to apologize profusely for her behaviour, Braco and I brought her back to our apartment.

There was no doubt in my mind that we shouldn't delay our departure from Vlasenica for another minute. That evening, after my father learned about the day's events, even he considered the option of leaving. The following day we decided to move to my father's nephew's house, about three hundred metres from our place. Some fifteen people from three or four families were gathered there. Everyone agreed that in the event of attack our chances were better if we all stuck together. There were many Muslims who, like us, had fled from ethnically mixed buildings; word was that hundreds of Muslims from the wider neighbourhood had already left Vlasenica for Kladanj in the west.

It looked as if only Serbs were staying in town and the surrounding Serb villages. Muslims were fleeing *en masse*. On television we'd seen hundreds of people arriving in Tuzla – Muslims from the Vlasenica Municipality had fled there when news broke that Bijeljina and Zvornik had been attacked, although not a single bullet had been fired in Vlasenica itself. The question was, which town would be next on the hit list: Bratunac or ours? You didn't have to be clever to work out that Serb attacks were happening along the Drina. There was no question of *whether* they would attack; the only question was whether it would be today or tomorrow.

I kept insisting that we should go, it didn't matter where, so long as we left town. My father finally agreed. He told us to pack our things and said that we were going to go to Sarajevo. 'We have no one in Tuzla,' he said. So on 12 April we were on the move again, the four of us driving to Sarajevo. Once again our Zastava was the only car on the road.

At a crossroads on the outskirts of the city we came across a parked JNA transporter and a group of armed soldiers standing beside it. It was raining, and the soldiers wore military ponchos. I wondered who the people inside the ponchos were and whether they would harm us. We passed without being stopped and finally arrived at my Uncle Emin's house in Bare, near the city cemetery.

My father stayed only for lunch. He told us that he was going back to Vlasenica. He said he couldn't leave his colleagues in trouble. I thought I would never see him again; I was sure it was only a matter of time before Vlasenica would be attacked.

Sporadic explosions could be heard as my cousins Zijad and Sead filled me in on the situation in Sarajevo. The Muslims in the neighbourhood were trying to organize themselves – there was an open invitation for men who had weapons to report for duty. Firearms were essential. My cousins had no weapons except for Uncle Emin's pistol; I had only the hunting knife I had bought in Zvornik.

Reports on the radio stated that commercial flights were still taking off from the local airport and that buses were still going to a number of European destinations. The cost of a bus ticket to Germany was one hundred Deutschmarks. I asked my mother for the three hundred marks to get us there, but she said we couldn't leave as long as my father remained in Vlasenica. We couldn't leave without him. I must have crossed some imaginary line because, no doubt for the first time in my life, the presence of all four of us no longer seemed a prerequisite for our salvation from the war, and I insisted that the three of us should go without him, but my mother simply refused. I didn't consider the fact that none of us had a passport. My father was the only member of our family who had ever been abroad.

I asked my Uncle Emin to come with me to my university accommodation. I wanted to pick up some documents and an album of photographs I had left in my room. At first he wouldn't even consider the idea; he thought it was too dangerous. But my uncle had always been fearless (later, he would be formally commended for his bravery in the war), and in the end he agreed to accompany me. We waited for a bus in front of the Presidency Building. All of a sudden a terrible explosion resounded through the air – my first experience of shelling. The ground shook, and people fled in all directions. My uncle and I were the only ones who remained at the bus stop.

'Let's go home,' he said. 'I don't think this bus is coming.' However, to our surprise, a tram appeared just across the street. We boarded, but just as we arrived at the next stop there was a second explosion. The door opened, and the passengers ran out, once again scattering every which way.

'We'd better go home,' Uncle Emin said. 'I doubt we can make it today.'

'I wonder who's holding the building now, our lot or theirs,' I said out loud. This was the first time I had distinguished between 'ours' and 'theirs', but it was something I would continue to do throughout the war and long after it had ended.

We walked back to Bare. My mother was again attempting to call her parents in Zvornik, as she had for days to no avail. Zvornik had been cut off from the rest of the country. Although she hadn't said anything I knew she was convinced that all her family there had been killed. The only thing she cared about now was that her sons were alive and out of danger. I was pretty sure that even my father's security was no longer a top priority.

And priorities *had* shifted – we were all aware of that. We began measuring our loved ones against each other: 'Whose life is the most valuable?' 'Which of us has the greater right to life?' For my father, my mother and myself, the answer was obvious. We had tacitly agreed that person was Braco. I was sure that we managed – as if by telepathy – to communicate this to one another. I was also sure that Braco resisted the conclusion, having intercepted our telepathy. His seventeen-year-old face now wore an expression that was much manlier, so to speak, than before, as if it said, 'Don't you worry. I can take care of myself.'

Although the weather was very cold I spent most of my time outside walking around the neighbourhood, but sometimes, in pursuit of anything that might be significant, I wandered to the centre of Sarajevo or up the hill at Kobilja Glava. I wanted to take the pulse of the city. I was looking for signs of the war, the real war. Killing and shooting. I wanted to establish the vulnerability of our position in Bare in relation to possible weak points in the city's defences in case the Serb forces entered it. In the evenings I would walk up the hill to look at the city lights and guess which parts were controlled by the Serbs and which ones by 'our' side. There were no lines yet, only sporadic exchanges of gunfire across the city. My greatest worry was whether my father would be able to join us, whether the road to Vlasenica remained clear.

On 18 April a red Peugeot pulled up in front of my uncle's house. It was my father's company car. My father got out, followed by Relja, his driver. Relja was a Serb. That was all I knew about him.

'Come on. We're leaving,' my father said. 'Back to Vlasenica.'

My mother obviously couldn't wait to end our six-day experience of refugee life and had everything packed within minutes. We loaded the bags and got into the car. My father sat in the front passenger seat, and the three of us sat in the back. Relja drove. He didn't say a word the whole time. He was doing his best not to look in the rear-view mirror. It was as if he were afraid to look the three of us in the eyes. I had a feeling he thought my father had made the wrong decision, but, perhaps because my father had been his boss for so many years, Relja just couldn't bring himself to say, 'Ibro, for God's sake, don't take your family back to Vlasenica. The Serbs will kill you.' Of course, only Relja knows what he was thinking. He must have had an idea of what was going to happen in Vlasenica, and he must have known it wasn't safe for Muslims to stay there any longer.

Years later, when the war was over, Uncle Emin told me that he took my father aside before we left his house that day and suggested to him that we stay in Sarajevo. He said he told my father to take the Peugeot and send Relja on his way, to leave him to his own devices. If I had heard him say that then I would have wholeheartedly agreed that we shouldn't return. My father's decision left me outraged and terrified; I couldn't understand his logic. Braco remained silent as usual. Still unaware that home is where you're safe, even if you don't have a roof over your head, my mother seemed pleased that we were going back. My parents had worked their whole lives to buy and furnish our apartment in Vlasenica, and they could not give it up just like that.

At some point during the war my father revealed that while he'd been back in Vlasenica he'd tried to 'calm things down' between the Serbs and Muslims there. He had spent those six days inviting notable Vlasenica Serbs into our flat for food and drinks and had done his best to reason with them. One of the guests was Milenko Stanić, the Mayor of Vlasenica and the local SDS party president. He had complimented my father on our beautiful home, saying that he would love to have one just like it. He didn't have to look too far for one, though, as he moved into ours at the first opportunity and lived there with his wife and daughter for the duration of the war, moving out only in 2001.

My father seemed unaware that local Serbs weren't interested in the concerns raised by prominent Muslim citizens – or maybe he was but naïvely persisted in his efforts. As it later transpired, marauding Serbs would often single out prominent Muslim citizens, intellectuals, people much more influential than my father, for detainment, torture and execution.

A certain Branko, the director of the sawmill in Milići, was also among those my father entertained in our home during that week. He had warned my father, 'Ibro, get your family out of Sarajevo. Sarajevo is going to be razed to the ground', and so my father had decided to come and do just that – but he should not have brought us back to Vlasenica.

As we passed through Kladanj I pleaded that we take the turning to Tuzla. My father said nothing. I could see small drops of sweat on Relja's forehead, but he, too, was silent.

A few kilometres from Vlasenica we passed a group of about fifty armed soldiers in camouflage standing on the right-hand side of the road. This was the first time I had seen the Serbs fully armed and, obviously, ready to strike. I was terrified by the sight of them and all the more certain we would meet our deaths in Vlasenica.

When we arrived in front of our building my father, principled as ever, told Relja to leave the car in the company car park. Relja drove away, and that was the last we saw of him.

'Pack your things,' my father said as soon as we entered the apartment. 'We're leaving for Stoborani in half an hour.' Stoborani was my father's village. In the Žepa area, it lies twenty kilometres from Han Pijesak, towards the Drina.

If I'd thought it was impossible to be more embittered than I already was I'd have been wrong. 'Why Stoborani?' I cried. 'There's nothing there! Nobody will know what happens to us!'

This, again, was a decision my father had made after his colleague Branko had warned him of Sarajevo's destruction but had neglected to mention it when he collected us. We were to run away to the mountains and hide in the forest until the madness was over. And that was that.

Instead of packing our best things we chose old and well-worn clothing and footwear; we didn't want to ruin our new clothes hiding in the forest. We were not alone in thinking this way. It was one of the many stupid things those who fled believed, that we were undertaking some kind of drill, that the whole thing would be over in a few days or weeks and we would return home.

Like hell we would.

Some tinned food, instant soups, a few potatoes; we got into the car and off we went to Stoborani. We didn't think it then, but it was at this precise moment that we truly became *refugees*. But, unlike refugees who try to seek safety in another country, we went instead to the mountains of eastern Bosnia to hide from the war. As if a forest could shield you. The war flies, reaches you in a second and brings fear along with it. It runs through walls, over mountains and rivers. It enters your mind, your heart and your soul. It sits there and refuses to leave.

STOBORANI

After ten kilometres up a winding mountain road we came to a motel, where men in blue uniforms were standing on the road armed with automatic rifles and wearing caps known as *Titovke*, Tito-caps, only where the red star used to be there was a red, white and blue flag. I was terrified, but my father showed no sign of fear. They asked us if we had any weapons, and my father said he had a licensed pistol. They asked him to open the boot. One of them looked inside it and finally, to my great astonishment, saluted us with two fingers. 'Have a safe journey,' he said.

I couldn't believe we'd got through just like that – a checkpoint manned by the Serb police, if that's what they called themselves. They certainly weren't regular police of the Republic of Bosnia and Herzegovina; in their blue fatigues they looked more like a militia.

We passed through Han Pijesak and carried on towards Stoborani. We were headed to my grandfather's old house. The only person who had lived in the house since the death of my grandparents was my Aunt Krivačka. Her given name had been Mejra, but custom demanded that all new wives married into the village be named after the village of their birth. Mejra was born in Krivače, hence Krivačka. I had aunts with some very funny names.

Stoborani – which means One Hundred Pine Trees in English – was a peaceful mountain village surrounded by forests, hills and mountains. As a child growing up in the early 1980s I was lucky enough to spend my summers there – and what a treat that was for a kid from town! I had a load of uncles, aunts and cousins in the village; my favourite cousins were Haso and Huso, who were my principal playmates during childhood. Come September I would recount my summer holidays with Huso and Haso to my schoolmates in Vlasenica. They thought I was joking about these names, that I'd invented them. My friends and our neighbours (mainly Serbs, by the way) would also tell me that I'd grown a bit taller. I thought it strange then, but who knows? Maybe I did grow taller each time I visited.

The smell of the village and its surroundings was like nowhere else: a sweet mix of meadows and mown grass, wild flowers and pine trees, of sheep, cows and the dung from the stables, and the boiled milk, fresh cream and bread baked in wood-fired ovens . . . And the stillness of this remote mountain settlement was extraordinary; you could hear the wind in the trees, the buzzing of insects, the tinkling of sheep's bells. The deep silence was only rarely disturbed, mainly when Huso turned his music up so loud that the voice of the popular folk singer Šaban Šaulić echoed through the hills: *It's wilting . . . my white daffodil* . . . Šaban's voice travelled across Stoborani from the Nuhanovićs' hamlet of Lazovi to the other end of the village.

One summer after Huso had started high school in Sarajevo he brought back an album by AC/DC. His father, who was living in Sweden, had sent him a cassette player, which was not something everyone could afford. I'd never listened to AC/DC before. Huso slotted *Back in Black* into the player, and I have never forgotten the effect on me of hearing the tolling of the bell and the powerful guitar in 'Hells Bells' for the first time. The sound of the stereo blaring through the whole village annoyed Huso's mother – 'Turn it down! May God put some sense in your head, Huso!' she would shout – but Huso didn't take any notice of my aunt's complaints until, really furious, she'd chase him with a stick and make him go to fetch the cows from the pasture.

As we got older Huso, who was a couple of years my senior, became less willing to hang out with me. Then, unexpectedly, he went to visit his father in Sweden and, like several other Nuhanovićs before him, never came back. Some of them had been living in Malmö for years; the Swedish city would become the meeting place and final destination for many of our relatives who were able to flee Bosnia during the war and those who survived and subsequently left.

Haso and I were the same age, and we were inseparable. To avoid confusion between the two Hasans, he was called Haso and I was called Hasko. A separate book would be required to describe all our adventures in Stoborani and the surrounding woods. As a young boy and teenager Haso was a giant and much stronger than me. He was this huge highlander, and I, Hasko, was a pale boy who used to bring cartons of milk and tinned foods from Vlasenica because I couldn't stand the taste of fresh milk and most of the dishes that were prepared in the village.

This time the circumstances of our arrival at Grandpa Hasan's house were very different, however. My aunt's son Ismet, his wife Ajkuna and their two children, Armin and Irma, had also arrived from the nearby town of Rogatica, so we took the top floor. Braco and I had the room where Huso used to stay during the summer. We unloaded the meagre provisions we'd brought with us, which were rationed from the very start. We survived on thin potato stews my mother would cook with just a trace of carrot and onion, occasionally a bean broth and, while our flour lasted, some white bread. We had left home with 1,200 Deutschmarks – I'd overheard my parents talking about it – but we soon learned that money was of little use in Stoborani because there was no food to buy. Naturally, the villagers, including our numerous relatives, had plenty of food, especially flour – they used to buy it in twenty-five- and fifty-kilogram sacks. But nobody knew what to expect or how long the crisis would continue, so people had begun hoarding food as early as April 1992 and were unwilling to share or sell their supplies. Whenever we would ask the answer was the same, 'Honest to God, we've run out of everything. We have no coffee, no sugar. Even the flour is almost gone . . .'

Curiously, the village shop was still open, but the only items on its shelves were tins. The Yugoslav dinar was still in circulation, but that would soon cease, and in no time we would realize that piles of cash hidden under mattresses had become worthless. The Deutschmark became the only valid currency.

We'd heard that a number of Muslims, mostly from the Zvornik area, had made it to Hungary – through Serbia of all places. I pestered my parents to attempt the same journey, and on 21 April, three days after we had arrived in the village, my parents finally agreed.

My father had somehow managed to arrange a meeting with

Fadil Turković, commander of the police station in Vlasenica. He had escaped with his family to his wife's village, which was near by. Fadil had promised to wait for us near the motel we had passed with the police checkpoint. Seeing us preparing to leave my cousin Ismet decided to join us with his family. Early in the morning, when we were ready to go, a third car appeared – my cousin Haso and his wife Esma who had recently got married.

We arrived in Han Pijesak in a convoy of three cars, terribly afraid and anxious, but nothing extraordinary happened. We proceeded to the motel where Fadil was supposed to be waiting for us in his police Lada, but there was no police car there. Ismet and Haso watched through the windows of their vehicles to see what my father would do. Police escort or no, my father continued towards Vlasenica from where we would aim for the border of Bosnia and Serbia in Zvornik. We were alone on the road once again.

What we feared might happen did happen a few kilometres before we reached Vlasenica. We were passing through a Serb village when five or six armed men appeared in front of us out of nowhere. They were not in uniform, but each had a rifle. Some of them sported the fur caps and white armbands worn by the fascist Chetniks during the Second World War. We stopped, and they encircled the three cars. We were paralysed with fear; nobody so much as moved a muscle or raised their eyes to look out of the window. I was amazed that my father had the courage to speak to a grey-haired man who approached our car. The man didn't appear to be armed but was gesticulating and, when my father wound down the window, he stooped to shout into the car, 'Go back, go back. It's impossible to go any further.'

Ismet and Haso turned their cars around as soon as they understood what the man was saying. My father reversed ours, and we tried to put aside the fear of being detained or shot. The grey-haired man, who was apparently an acquaintance of my father's, had told us we couldn't proceed because Muslims had occupied the city and were shooting at anyone who came close. This was a lie, but we had no way of knowing that – neither did we care to explore the truth. We drove off and soon caught up with Ismet and Haso, who let us drive in front of them once again. We debated what could be going on in Vlasenica, agreeing that whatever was happening there had to be happening in Han Pijesak as well as it was only twenty kilometres away. Not sure what to do next, we parked back in front of the motel. The four of us got out and headed towards the entrance. Our relatives stayed in their cars looking frightened. They were waiting for my father to decide what to do.

I had a strange feeling when we entered the motel's restaurant, and what happened in the next half-hour was like a scene from a spaghetti western – only it wasn't at all comic. We said good morning and sat at the nearest table. Five Serb policemen were sitting at two tables drinking coffee and smoking cigarettes. I recognized the men who had let us pass through the checkpoint four days ago. None of them said anything, but all of them watched us attentively. Some had their rifles strapped around their shoulders; others had them on the tables in front of them. A man was standing behind the counter. Another man, somewhat overweight, was sitting alone at a table in the corner. He had a moustache and long hair pushed under a hat. I wanted to say to my father that we should leave at once, but I couldn't because everyone else in the room would have heard. I had the distinct impression they were measuring me up. I was the right age for military service; maybe they thought I was armed.

It was my father who finally broke the silence. I don't remember what it was that he said exactly, but I think he just wanted to start a conversation. He mentioned Fadil, the police commander. He said something about 'meeting your colleague', even though he must have known they no longer considered Fadil to be their colleague. Nobody had seen Fadil that morning, they replied.

To our surprise, a police Lada pulled up at that very moment, and we watched as Fadil got out and entered the restaurant. He said hello to the Serb policemen and sat at our table. He was in uniform and had his gun on him. At first we felt relieved by his smile; we thought Fadil would be able to accompany us to the border after all. Once in Serbia my father would contact his Serbian friends who would help us get to Hungary or somewhere else – anywhere else.

I don't know whether what followed was staged or not – it certainly didn't feel right. One of the Serb policemen answered his walkie-talkie and then put it on speakerphone for us all to hear. The voice coming through the radio presented himself as the 'deputy commander of the police station in Vlasenica', Fadil's deputy in other words. He spoke directly to Fadil and informed him that the Serbs had taken over the police station. 'Fadil, come down here to surrender your weapon and car. That would be best for you. That's the only thing you can do,' the voice said.

Fadil's demeanour changed at once. His confidence drained away, and I was sure I saw tears in his eyes. Different scenarios raced through my mind as I tried to signal to my family the peril we were in. I thought it would be logical for them to arrest and disarm Fadil and take him to Vlasenica or even to kill him. I thought that we, too, would be killed because we were witnesses.

Fadil exchanged a few words with his now former deputy. His anxiety grew by the second. He looked at the Serb policemen as if he expected them to offer a solution to this awkward situation.

And then one of the policemen spoke. 'Listen, Fadil, I wouldn't go down there if I were you.' The rest of them agreed with him as the deputy's voice rang out from the walkie-talkie to say that Fadil should come to Vlasenica and surrender immediately.

'Fadil, you'd be better off not going down there!' the Serb policeman repeated.

We watched the exchange in disbelief.

'And what are *we* going to do?' my father asked.

Fadil turned to him. The poor guy was sweating bullets. 'I can't take you anywhere, as you can see. You'd better go back to Han Pijesak.'

We didn't need to be told twice, although I was pretty sure each of us thought Fadil would either be killed or arrested the second we left. We stood up and cautiously headed towards the door. Ismet and Haso were waiting by their cars, both of them as pale as ghosts. They wordlessly looked at my father, as if asking, 'And now what?' My father signalled to them to head to Han Pijesak, so we all jumped into our cars and drove off. I looked back, and the last thing I saw was Fadil's Lada. I was certain that the poor man was not going to survive the day, and I thought about how readily we had deserted him to save our own necks.

When we arrived in Han Pijesak my father pulled the car over in front of the Forestry Office, a business where he had colleagues and friends. Ismet and Haso protested; they wanted to get to Stoborani while it was still possible. But, surprisingly, nothing unusual was happening in Han Pijesak despite the fact that the town was mainly populated by Serbs. In fact, that might have been the reason why nothing unusual was happening there, but we couldn't understand the situation rationally. Still in shock, we entered the offices and were met by a man who welcomed my father warmly and invited us to sit down. My father briefly recounted what had happened. The man, a Serb, said he had no idea what was happening in Vlasenica, but he suggested that if we really wanted to leave we ought to take the old road to the town of Olovo. If we had only listened to him we could have reached safety only twenty or thirty kilometres away, but Ismet and Haso were against the idea. My own family couldn't agree on what to do. Somebody said that the old road was not a good idea because it was a village road, which went mainly through the forest and occasionally through Serb villages. The majority was for going back to Stoborani.

That was our last chance to get out of an area that would soon be under the complete control of Serb forces like those we had briefly encountered, an area that would soon be terrorized by their new government. Unwilling to take the risk, we went back to Stoborani, and this was a crucial mistake, one we would discuss often during the war that followed.

And so it happened that the Serb forces seized Vlasenica the very same day my parents finally agreed to escape from Bosnia. As we learned later, a JNA detachment had crossed the Serbian border as we had intended to – only in the opposite direction. The troops that entered Vlasenica soon withdrew, leaving the local Serbs in charge, fully armed and organized well enough to control the situation and terrorize the local Muslims. During this time the Sušica concentration camp was established; thousands of Muslims from Vlasenica and the surrounding municipalities were detained there. We were lucky enough not to fall into the hands of the Chetniks at the very beginning of the war, but throughout the conflict we would hear about the horrors these people were put through.

There were no more opportunities for us to escape. Višegrad, Foča and parts of Sarajevo were already in flames, but in our part of Bosnia the war was slow to erupt. In Stoborani at the beginning of

May we still had electricity. Every evening we would gather, about ten of us, in front of the television. Our horror grew daily as we saw the rising numbers of dead in Sarajevo. We also learned about plans to blow up the Višegrad dam and watched the Serb forces entering Srebrenica. But one evening in mid-May the electricity went off. Here come the Chetniks to slit our throats, we thought. Everybody jumped, startled, colliding into one another in the dark, and, as if by unspoken agreement, we all ran into the woods. But after half an hour, when it became clear that the electricity had just stopped working, we all went back to the house, relieved and embarrassed. From that day until the end of the war in 1995 we would be without electricity.

Our days went by in waiting. The coffee was getting weaker and weaker while my father's anxiety was growing – which had as much to do with the realization that he would soon run out of cigarettes as anything else. He was a chain smoker, and it was very hard on him.

The village shop closed down. First I heard that the shopkeeper was selling the supplies from home at a much higher price but later that he had actually given away much of his stock before closing the shop.

My parents were getting increasingly concerned about the lack of food. My aunts used to send us bottles of milk and bowls of cottage cheese from time to time, and that was our lifeline. But flour was something nobody felt they could share, so one morning my father decided to go to Vlasenica and collect the twenty-kilogram sack of flour from our garage. We couldn't believe that he was intent on this, but he was deadly serious despite the awful news we had seen on the television before the electricity had packed in. But he went and returned that evening. He had managed to obtain a kind of permit from the Vlasenica police that allowed him to get home. 'Ibro, this is a one-time-only pass,' they'd told him. On the way back he had stopped at the post office to call his firm. In front of the building a woman had opened his car door and screamed at him, 'He's here! Serb killer!'

'Man, you should thank God for saving your life against all the odds,' I said to my father.

To make the call he had then tried the post office in Han Pijesak. A colleague answered, one who'd always been on good terms with my father. 'It was a strange call,' my father said. 'My colleague was silent for a while, but then she whispered, "Ibro, don't come back here", and hung up.'

My mother set aside some flour and tins of food in case we had to hide in the forest, and this stash was completely off limits. In the meantime we started skipping meals, and the meals we did have were getting increasingly meagre by the day: small portions of potato soup, sometimes with a piece of bread.

Braco spent his time mainly with our cousin Aljo. They were the same age. Aljo was the son of my father's late brother Munib. His mother, our Aunt Đula, thought Aljo would be safer in the village, given that he looked older than his seventeen years. In April 1992 Aunt Đula had gone back to Vlasenica, taking her younger son Muamer with her, and Aljo was left on his own with no adult to look after him. When he didn't eat with us he would have a meal with some of our other relatives in Stoborani. Aljo's mother had gone back home believing that the Serbs – should the town fall into their hands – wouldn't harm women and children. She wasn't alone in believing that, but Aljo's mother and brother were among numerous Vlasenica Muslims taken from their homes. It was rumoured that they had ended up in the Sušica camp; it was also rumoured that they were later seen in the village of Pelemiš, where there was apparently a detention camp for women. Various rumours filtered through to us of their whereabouts over time until, eventually, we heard nothing more.

I once heard Aljo whispering to my brother that he was hungry. We were all hungry. Our food supplies had almost run out. I suggested that we visit Aunt Mila, as she would probably offer us something. Aunt Mila had several cows, and she also kept chickens. She had milk, cheese, cream and eggs. Although my parents were hungry, too, they told us to go without them so there would be more food for us but also because it would seem pushy if we all showed up together at my aunt's door.

Everybody knew Aunt Mila could make *burek*, what Bosnians call *pita*, in fifteen minutes. She would roll out the dough into translucent sheets of pastry, using the rolling pin incredibly quickly, then toss the dough in the air, turn it over, oil it, then turn it over again and oil the other side. And so it went on, layer upon layer of dough sandwiching a mixture of cheese and eggs. The whole thing would then go into the oven, and you would be eating *pita* in no time at all.

When the three of us arrived on that mid-May day my aunt immediately offered us the pleasure of this very spectacle.

'Come on in, boys! The *pita* will be ready before you know it!'

We could have jumped for joy. While we sat on the sofa salivating, imagining a *pita* swimming in cream and butter, the transistor radio on the windowsill – tuned to BiH Radio, the government station and the only we listened to in those days – was reporting on the day's events in Sarajevo. When my aunt finally put the *pita* in front of us we took a few moments to admire the beauty of her creation before we began to devour it. I could feel my strength returning with every bite. Braco and Aljo were beaming at each other with their mouths full. The *pita* was gone in a flash, but Aunt Mila reappeared from the kitchen with a pile of pancakes, put the plate in front of us together with a jar of jam and went back to make more pancakes for us. Heaven on earth, the three of us thought as we looked at one another.

At the same time the voice on the radio was reporting:

The aggressor's shells rained down on every neighbourhood in Sarajevo . . . the number of victims has not been confirmed . . . the population has appealed for the urgent delivery of humanitarian assistance . . . shortages of basic foods . . . city water supply interrupted . . .

We noticed that Aunt Mila had slowed down her pancake production. When the voice on the radio named one of the neighbourhoods as having a shortage of basic foodstuffs she stopped in her tracks. 'Ah, sweet mother, my child is starving! What am I to do? What am I to do? What is my Jasmin going to eat?' she cried in shock. Jasmin was her grandson, and he must have been her favourite. What could we say to her while jam was trickling down our chins?

I leaned towards Aljo and whispered, 'Turn the radio off.' Aljo did as he was told, and Mila brought a new batch of pancakes and put it on the table without saying a word. We finished these off, thanked

Aunt Mila and left. That was our last decent meal for the next twelve months.

We went down the path through the village. The weather was warm. The sun was setting. Our stomachs were full. We were all in a good mood. I looked towards the west, towards Sarajevo, where the sky was red.

THE ULTIMATUM

Stoborani's villagers organized lookouts to monitor the surrounding area for Serb troop movements, and a rota was devised for several dozen men to stand guard around the clock. The most critical lookout point was to the west, towards the Serb village of Jelovci and on towards Han Pijesak. Those covering that area had rifles, mainly hunting guns, but I'd heard that a couple of them had automatic rifles.

We, the Nuhanovićs, had a designated lookout of our own around Lazovi, but several family members, my father included, still had to take shifts with the rest of the villagers in the Jelovci area. At Lazovi we only had two shifts, from twilight to midnight and from midnight until dawn. More often than not I ended up on the second shift.

Although it was hot during the day, the nights were cold, and we had to dress warmly; we were in the mountains, after all. Whenever our shifts didn't coincide my father would give me his pistol. Two men always kept watch together. Sometimes I shared my watch with Ismet and sometimes with Hamdo, but most often I was with my Uncle Hasib, the eldest of the eight Nuhanović brothers. Hasib was sixty-five at the time and in excellent health for his age. The teenagers, Braco and Aljo, were excused duties.

At first we would sit by the fire through the night, listening and staring into the darkness. Clearly, there wasn't anything we could have done if an attack came, apart from warning the others to run to the woods. But after a few days it was decided we should patrol the area instead of just sitting by the fire. We would walk across the field towards the village, then up the hill where we would meet the men patrolling from the opposite direction. So we had to walk up and down the whole night, from Lazovi towards the village and back again. That was fine under the bright moonlight, but on cloudy nights it was pitch black and we couldn't see a thing in front of us. We would stumble around and fumble in the dark for the fences we had to clamber over. Torches were useless as we had no batteries.

When I was on watch with Hasib I would usually have to wake him up. His house was very close to the woods, so I had to walk about a hundred metres through the dark alone. I'm not sure whether I was more afraid of the Chetniks, bears or ghosts. The sound of owls hooting wasn't particularly encouraging, and it gave me the creeps every time.

'Hasib! Hasib!' I would shout, banging on the door. But his snoring would be the only answer I would receive. I had to bang on the door and shout his name at least ten more times, clutching my father's pistol, which was tucked into my belt, and casting worried looks in all directions. 'What is it? I'll be there in a sec,' I would finally hear and then silence. And then more snoring.

It would always end with me standing under his window and shouting his name until he got out of bed – a whole hour past midnight. When he finally appeared in his black fur cap he resembled a Chetnik more than anything else. With his hunting gun slung over his shoulder he would rummage through his pockets along the way, mumbling something to himself. About halfway to the village he would stop, take out a cigarette paper and get rolling. I knew if I asked for one the answer would be that his tobacco was all gone.

On several occasions we heard the distant sound of gunfire from the Serb villages. Shots fired from a large-calibre weapon, usually in a *ta-ta-ta-tatata* rhythm. This went on repeatedly.

'Listen to that, Haso. They have ammunition to waste,' one of the villagers at the lookout once said. 'They're fooling around, if you know what I mean. That guy won't stop . . . He sits there at his machine gun, canon or whatever it is and plays it like an instrument. Me, on the other hand, I've got four cartridges for this shotgun of mine. If they attack, we've had it. What are we going to fight them with? Tell me.'

I listened and shrugged.

My Uncle Hasib and Uncle Pašan spent their days building

makeshift shelters deep in the woods on Mršić Hill. Simple, wooden shed-like constructions. The planks and beams had been cut with my Uncle Avdija's machinery while there was still electricity in the village. The oxen had then dragged the timber to the top of the hill. You could hear the noise of chainsaws all day long. They planned to build shelters for every household in Stoborani. The shacks were built only a kilometre away from the village itself, some even closer, but they were well hidden in the thick pine forest. The trees were half a metre thick. I'm not sure whose idea it was originally, but it turned out to be the best possible plan under the circumstances. For days we cut down tall trees and loaded them on ox-carts. We built a whole new settlement and left clothing, food and blankets there. Several Nuhanović families filled a fifty-litre plastic barrel with food and buried it a metre underground, concealing the spot with twigs and leaves.

The villagers, almost all of them, ploughed their plots and planted potatoes, even though that meant less food in the shorter term. With no rescue in sight, we tried to prepare for a long stay in the forest. We regularly listened to the radio. The news was mainly about Sarajevo, and not once did we hear any mention of us, the people stuck in a corner of Bosnia that the Chetniks hadn't occupied yet. We were the forgotten people. It felt like there was an encoded message in all this, one we were able to decode pretty easily: 'You are on you own. You'll just have to make the best of it. Expect no help from us.' With the Chetniks besieging Sarajevo the government there surely had too many problems of their own to think about us. After all, what could they possibly do to help?

News reached us by other means. Shocking reports that the residents of Slap, a village near Žepa, had been pulling corpses out of the Drina for days. At the end of May my uncle Ahmet made it to our village. Ahmet told us that the Chetniks had been attacking Muslim villages on the left bank of the river Jadar for a whole month and had burned them down. Many people were missing, and many had been killed. My aunt and her children had also disappeared. Uncle Ahmet said that Chetnik tanks and artillery had ploughed through everything, even the graveyards.

Only we, Stoborani and other villages around Žepa, were left on this side of Mount Javor. We started hearing about Muslim villages in the Bratunac Municipality being burned down and the long lists of the missing and the dead from around Bratunac and Srebrenica. I wondered what had happened to Ćamil and Fahro, my friends from university. They were both from villages in the Bratunac Municipality. Had they stayed in Sarajevo, or had they decided to go home and spend Bajram with their families?

At the end of May news reached us from Han Pijesak that the local Chetniks had set an ultimatum for all the Muslim villages in the area between Han Pijesak and Žepa. They wanted us to surrender all our weapons in two days or face the consequences. They expected 3,500 rifles to be handed in. What a crazy notion. How could they imagine we had so many weapons? All the pistols, hunting rifles and those few illegally obtained automatic rifles put together wouldn't come anywhere close to that number.

But that didn't come as a surprise. There had been signs that worse was yet to come. Before the electricity went off permanently many employees at the sawmill in Han Pijesak, including those from Stoborani, had decided to go back to work. Off they went one morning, just as they had done for years. Several buses packed with loggers made it as far as the Serb checkpoint just outside Han Pijesak where they were ordered to get out. While disembarking they recognized some of their Serb colleagues among the heavily armed uniformed men. The workers were sent home because the sawmill had been closed down – or so they were told. Their buses were driven off, and they had to walk home. At least they were sent home and not to a concentration camp, which is what might have been expected given the news of displacements, persecutions and ethnic cleansing reportedly happening all around us. At that time news still reached us relatively quickly. But the Serbs of Han Pijesak had sent us a clear message: 'What's mine is mine, and what's yours is yours – and you have no business in Han Pijesak.' Its underlying meaning was that we were trapped. The thousands of inhabitants of Muslim villages in the area were completely blockaded. We were besieged.

And there was something else, too . . . A helicopter started flying over the village almost every day but never at the same time. It came from the direction of Han Pijesak and flew so low that we could see the pilot – we often thought that it would hit the treetops. Its destination was a mountain peak with an underground military installation – a communications station of the former JNA – with a staff of twenty, soldiers and officers of the Serb army, given that the JNA, as such, no longer existed. The helicopter was apparently delivering food to the station in addition to performing its regular reconnaissance duties. Zlovrh Peak dominates the area and, from a military perspective, it had always been one of the most important points in the region. There were no Serb villages below it since the area had always had a Muslim-majority population. None of the villagers knew what exactly was going on up there, and civilians had been denied access to the whole area.

'There's a meeting above the shop at eight o'clock tonight,' my father told me. 'We'll discuss the ultimatum. All adult villagers are to be present, and we will all have a vote. We have to decide what's to be done.'

All the villages around Žepa had agreed, through messengers, to hold meetings at the same time and then declare whether they intended to surrender their arms. It was raining that day, and there were thunderstorms. It was a dark day in every sense, which made the tense atmosphere surrounding the ultimatum even more terrifying. Since we had no power, only a few oil lamps lit the room. There were more than fifty men sitting on wooden planks and on the floor, while some stood. The room was full of cigarette smoke. The mood was understandably downbeat. The ultimatum was discussed in small groups, and then the local commander of the Territorial Defence reserve force (TO) addressed us.

'The ultimatum has to be answered tomorrow. Tonight we must decide if we are going to surrender our weapons or not.'

My father whispered to me that he thought it was madness to try to fight the Serb army, but he didn't dare say it out loud. I stared at the faces around the room, trying to figure out how many of them were for giving in, which was what I secretly hoped for. If anybody was for doing so, they didn't dare speak up, however. It is not impossible that they might actually have been a majority, but saying so in front of everybody else was a totally different matter. To do so would almost certainly mean being accused of cowardice and being a traitor.

'They'll kill us all, that's what they'll do. We're powerless against such an enemy. What can we fight them with?' an elderly man shouted from a corner.

Then everybody started arguing until another man shouted above the noise. He was about sixty years old. His hair was pure white, but he still looked vital and strong. He wore a black French beret like many older Bosnian Muslim men. He stood up, holding his rifle.

'No surrender to the enemy! No way I'll surrender this rifle of mine,' he said, banging the butt on the floor. 'What would that mean? Keeping your arms at your side while they slit your throats? No different from a ram slaughtered at Bajram!'

Then Salko stood up; I'd known him since we were children. He was a few years older than me and rather short but wiry and strong. 'Listen, we're not handing in our arms. I certainly won't surrender mine. To each his own, but nobody can make me do that. I know every inch of this mountain. There's no way the Chetniks are ever going to catch me. I could hide here for years. What are you so afraid of? If they do come, here's the forest, here's my rifle. Let's see who wins.'

A profound silence fell over the room, with people looking from one to the other. The silence was broken by the voice of the commander. 'Let's vote. Who thinks we should surrender our weapons?' Not a single hand went up. 'Who thinks we should *not* surrender our weapons?' Everyone in the room raised a hand. I looked at my father, and he looked at me. We silently agreed that we should do the same as everybody else and raise our hands. So it was unanimous. The meeting ended soon after the vote.

The next day we learned that all the villages around Žepa had voted the same way.

THE CHETNIKS ARE COMING!

Uncle Hasib and I had just got back from keeping watch, me with my father's pistol and Uncle Hasib with his double-barrelled shotgun. It was seven o'clock in the morning and a lovely summer's day in June. I went straight to bed, and just as I was about to fall asleep my father rushed in.

'We have to run!' he shouted. 'The Chetniks are coming!'

The moment we had been dreading had finally arrived. In my imagination I had always seen myself crazily running into the forest, but that's not how it happened. Instead, I went to the bathroom and washed my face. Outside, Aljo was shouting, 'They're on the road coming this way!' Then I grabbed all the bags I could find in the house and made for the woods.

A very peculiar scene in front of my Uncle Avdija's house stopped me in my tracks. There was a sofa stuck in their window. My uncle was standing outside trying to pull it out, and my aunt was pushing from inside the house. I couldn't believe my eyes!

'What do you think you're doing?' I shouted. 'The Chetniks are coming!'

'Where do you think we'll sleep when they burn the house down?' they shouted back in unison.

'You have to get out of here. They'll kill you!' I cried, as I turned and ran only to be halted again, this time by my mother. She told me to take two buckets of fresh milk instead of the bags – necessities first. I ran backwards and forwards a couple of times, each time carrying different things. I had put on all my shirts and sweaters so that I wouldn't need to carry them in a bag and looked double my actual size. Glancing back to see if the Chetniks were in sight I tripped and twisted my ankle. I was sure my leg was broken. The milk I was carrying spilled around me, but nobody noticed – they were all sprinting towards the forest. I yelled, but nobody heard me. Left on my own I stood up and hopped to the nearest tree.

THE FIRST CIGARETTE I EVER SMOKED IN FRONT OF MY FATHER

After rushing headlong into the woods, the four of us hid from the Chetniks behind the pine trees. When the shooting started I couldn't believe the intensity of the noise. An infinite number of war movies couldn't have prepared me for the rumbling, booming thunder of the guns and the whistling of bullets, shrapnel, shells . . . I simply couldn't believe such noise and destruction were possible. I subsequently learned that more than 350 Chetniks had arrived with two tanks, three armoured transporters and a total of forty-two trucks and various smaller vehicles.

About fifteen other Nuhanovićs were with the four of us on the hill. Overwhelmed by a feeling of helplessness, we expected to be killed at any moment. We looked around us for the rest of our family. Where's your father? Your mother? Your brother? I saw my father truly scared – the man who had been looked up to as an authority on so many issues by so many people for such a long time! All of us – his family, his employees – had always believed him capable of finding a solution to any problem. Seeing him as bewildered as everyone else somehow made things even worse.

We began to run in all directions because we couldn't tell where the bullets were coming from. The Chetniks were firing at will from anti-aircraft guns mounted on armoured transporters. They were shooting blindly into the woods – from the village road, I guess – firing projectiles that exploded all around us.

Somebody cried out that Aunt Mila was missing. She had gone down to the village to get her cow. My father immediately decided to go to look for her, to go back to the village straight into the hands of the Chetniks! I ran after him but then back again, back and forth, confused by fear like a hunted animal. Scurrying between the trees I eventually found my father. He was with Aunt Mila. Mila was crying. She had made it to the stable but found that a tank had run over her cow's head.

'Never mind the cow,' I said, trying to console her. 'Soon we'll all be dead.'

It seemed as if the Chetniks had been given the whole JNA arsenal to fire at us for as long as they liked. It never occurred to me that anyone would dare fire back at them – and yet someone *had* dared, although I didn't find out about it until later.

Meanwhile, after running from tree to tree, from cover to cover, for two or three hours, the four of us found shelter amid the exposed roots of a large pine tree. My mother began rummaging through her handbag. Finally she fished out a packet of cigarettes. She handed one to me and then one to my brother. We had never smoked in front of our father before, but my mother didn't want to deny us a last cigarette; she was convinced we were going to die that day. My father looked the other way.

As the sun appeared from behind the clouds the shooting and shelling decreased slightly, and we heard the sound of distant rumbling from the direction of the valley below the hill. 'That's our guys fighting the Chetniks,' somebody said.

Later that afternoon a neighbour from Stoborani appeared on Mršić Hill, and we couldn't believe our eyes. He came up the slope holding an automatic rifle in one hand and some kind of sack in the other. He was sweaty and dirty, and the first thing he said was 'Give me some water!'

I asked him whether any of our people had survived the skirmish we had heard, believing he might be one of the few. After gulping down the water and taking some time to catch his breath he started telling us what had gone on in the valley. Several of our men had been killed, and three were wounded, but, he said, a lot of Chetniks had been killed, certainly more than a hundred.

I'm not sure about the others, but when I heard this I got butterflies in my stomach and an adrenaline rush in my veins. Elation and horror came over me at the same time, but I was more frightened than joyful. Thoughts were racing around my head. The Serbs are not going to let us off easily for this. There's no way back for us. It's all or nothing! There will be no negotiations now. At the same time I was thinking that there really might be some people out there who were courageous enough to thwart the Chetnik thugs after all.

'But how did you do it? What with?' I asked him. 'Where did you get the weapons, the ammunition?'

'I've got around three hundred rounds in here,' he said, nodding at the sack he was carrying. 'I got them just in time. The people down there mostly have hunting rifles, but they're keeping up all right. The Serbs are trapped in the valley. Their tank can't go forward because the road is too narrow. Can't turn around either. There's a cliff on one side of the road and a wall of rock on the other. It was a serious error on their part. Our men fired down on them. Several of our people were wounded. It didn't last more than an hour. Now they're sticking to their vehicles, and our men are holding their initial position. It all happened quite quickly. People just appeared on the slope, running from their villages with any weapon they had to hand. If that tank pushes through, though, nothing will stop it from getting all the way to Žepa.'

While he was talking my mind kept flitting between jubilation and fear. How is this going to end? I was thinking. They'll surely send a whole division after us. They'll kill us all and burn all the villages to the ground. But hang on, they'd do that anyway, that's what they're trying to do right now. Why else would they have come here? All the soldiers, all the weapons, all the tanks . . . There are no Serb houses here, not one Serb house within ten kilometres or more. Just then a shell whizzed over our heads, and we all ran for cover. I felt the heat of the explosion on my face.

It grew dark, but the thunderous noises coming from the valley were unrelenting. My God, I thought, this is a real war. There's no quarter. Kill or be killed. And look at us! We're scattered around the forest like frightened sheep, totally and utterly bewildered. Just waiting for shells to blow us to bits.

Rain poured down throughout the night, and eventually the gunfire and explosions became less frequent. When another fighter appeared we learned that the military convoy had been almost destroyed. There was only one tank and one armoured transporter still resisting. Our men could not get close to them, and even if they could there was nothing they could do without the right weapons and ammunition. It was stalemate. The man also said that about thirty Serb soldiers had been captured and were being held in a school in the village of Gođenje a few kilometres down the road.

I was forced to spend the night outside in the rain, as the shack was full. I was convinced that the next day was going to be worse. The Chetniks had more tanks, as many as they wanted, and they were not going to make the same mistake again. What would the new day bring?

The radio reported that a major unit of the Serb army (although they were still calling themselves the JNA) had left the barracks in Sarajevo earlier that day. They were allowed to leave Sarajevo fully armed. We can expect them here. It's less than a hundred kilometres away, across Mount Romanija, which the Serbs control, I thought.

That night I took a nap beneath a spruce tree while the rain poured through its branches and down my back. I woke up to the sounds of moaning and crying. First, I made sure that my father, mother and brother were still alive and in one piece. At some point during the night the shells had stopped falling on the hill. I heard a number of explosions in the valley. I couldn't yet distinguish between the different sounds of firing – between launch and detonation – or between tank grenades and mortar shells. But soon we would all learn to differentiate them.

Several more men arrived from the battle, some with rifles, some without. They were panting, tired after fighting and walking uphill. I tried to find signs of fear on their faces, but they showed none. They clearly hadn't slept much the night before. They sat down to smoke and explained how the Chetnik military convoy had got stuck trying to drive over the barricade of tree trunks and boulders that the villagers had thrown from the top of the cliff down on to the road below. They confirmed that several of our people had been killed and that the Chetnik forces were in complete disarray and panic. They also told us about a Serb officer who had blown himself up together with a truckload of ammunition, ostensibly so that it wouldn't fall into our hands. They listed the weapons they had captured: M84 machine guns and hand-held rocket launchers such as the M80 Zolja and M79 Osas. I vaguely remembered the names from a high-school course called 'General People's Defence and Social Self-Protection', but I didn't recall much beyond the title.

Our people would fight on at the valley pass for as long as was needed to destroy the entire Chetnik formation. These men from Stoborani had been sent back to the village to hold the position in a clearing by the reservoir to stop Chetnik reinforcements from getting in. Easier said than done, I thought. The Serb reinforcements could arrive at any moment. There was neither time nor reason to relax, although the enemy breakthrough to Žepa had been prevented. But I felt it would be inappropriate to say anything given that they'd just come from the battle, which was still raging, while I'd been hiding up on the hill with the women, children and old people. I felt ashamed, although I was pretty sure that none of us had any weapons we could use. My father had his pistol – which had never been fired – while I had just my knife.

As a JNA soldier I had been issued with a semi-automatic rifle, a PAP as we called it. I had participated in firearms practice only two or three times – that is to say that in twelve months of military service I had fired ten, maybe fifteen, shots at a fixed target. That was it, and that had been back in 1987. In twelve months of military service I hadn't seen a single tank or armoured transporter. I had been in a signals regiment – we were trained to use communications equipment. Most of my time in the army had been spent cleaning toilets, floors, boiler rooms. Seeing how those five or six guys handled their rifles and automatic weapons I realized that, as a soldier, I was completely out of my league.

They left for the reservoir. About half an hour later I was also on my way there. My father was not pleased with my decision, but he didn't try to stop me, so I left my family in the forest and went to join the Stoborani fighters. It was June, true, but I knew how cold the summer nights could be in the mountains. I wore a woollen sweater under my windcheater. I also had on my yellow winter shoes.

Our village was utterly deserted but intact. The Serbs hadn't opened fire while passing through. They must have thought there wouldn't be any resistance and that they could reach Žepa without any problem. It was a beautiful day with just a breath of wind. The forest, meadows and hills were covered with lush June vegetation, but the noise of explosions from the valley could still be heard. What a combination of beauty and death, I thought. Over the next three years that same thought would often cross my mind.

At the reservoir I greeted the group. 'What's up?' Some responded, but most did not. The majority recognized me, but some of them didn't know me at all. I sat on the ground with my back against a spruce tree and looked around. Yesterday's battle was being discussed. Those who had managed to capture weapons proudly showed them off: an automatic rifle, a semi-automatic rifle, even a machine gun. A JNA olive-coloured crate with it lid open caught my attention. It was full of shells. I couldn't tell whether they were anti-tank grenades or mortar shells, but standing next to the crate didn't seem like a good idea. The whole scene felt somehow unreal.

I asked if anyone knew what kind of shells they were. The fighters shrugged. A voice shouted that they were mortar shells, but nobody had managed to capture a mortar launcher. I wondered why then they had bothered to bring the crate all the way up here.

Emin, whom I knew, was sitting beside a tree. There was a long rifle on the ground next to him. A sniper's rifle! I had seen those in movies. When we were kids playing Germans and Partisans we went for the longest pieces of wood we could find – I would often get a broomstick for the role – and shout, 'I'm a sniper, I'm a sniper!' What a powerful weapon it had seemed to us! You target someone so far away they can't even see you, you shoot and – whoosh, they're gone. A make-believe victim would usually start yelling, 'You didn't kill me, you didn't kill me! I'm only wounded!' while the make-believe sniper would demand that the other boy lie down and play dead. A bitter quarrel would follow, usually ending in 'I'm never gonna play with you again!'

But Emin's rifle was the real thing. I asked him if I could take a look. He smiled, happy to oblige, handed me the rifle and leaned against the tree, puffing on his cigarette. I must have picked it up clumsily because the guys around him sniggered. I looked through the sight, but I couldn't see a thing.

'Not like that, mate! Move the scope away from your eye.'

Then the rifle was taken off me because some more men had arrived who were curious to see it. Emin had spent all the previous day and night in the valley. He was the fighter who had managed to capture the most important weapon – and he was treated accordingly. I say *fighter* because that's what he had become. All of them had become fighters overnight.

They confirmed once again that a group of Serb soldiers who had surrendered the previous day were being held in the school in Gođenje. 'About *thirty,*' somebody stressed. Unbelievable. Thirty captured Chetniks! What was going to be done with them now?

Despite being in a state of post-victory euphoria I felt a dull ache in my stomach – a growing sense of foreboding. It all seemed way too easy. The Chetniks had already taken a huge chunk of the country's territory by brute force – Zvornik, Višegrad, Bratunac, Vlasenica, Srebrenica. Everything was in flames; there was killing all around. Was it really possible that they'd been captured down here on the very first day of fighting?

Around noon I decided to go back to check on my family. I'd better talk to them, I thought, and see what we should do next.

I headed back into the woods.

HELL ON THE HILL

Families had congregated around their makeshift shelters and lit fires to cook lunch. A bad idea, I thought. The Chetniks would see the smoke and find us. I hurried towards our shack. My father was evidently not happy that I'd separated myself from them that morning.

My mother was looking through the things we'd brought from the village, and my father was standing beside the fire supervising the bread baking. None of us had eaten anything since the previous day – we'd been too frightened. My brother was quiet. I wondered what he made of all this horror; he was still a teenager. His stubble was more noticeable than mine, his shoulders were well developed, and he may even have been stronger than me – I felt somewhat underdeveloped after four years sitting around in university reading rooms – but his face betrayed his age.

That distant thunder from the valley – it was still there but not as loud as earlier that morning or the day before, almost as if the tank and transporter were breathing their last.

But all of sudden: *Swoosh – Boom! Swoosh – Boom!*

I was on my feet in a flash and just as quickly threw myself to the ground. All my senses came alive at once; my instinct for self-preservation was up and running and had carried me over to a sizeable tree. Hissing sounds and explosions shook the entire hill. I realized that this had nothing to do with the ongoing battle in the valley. The Chetniks were shelling the hill from somewhere else and doing so mercilessly. It was impossible to determine where the shells were coming from; we didn't know where to seek cover among the trees. We were learning the difference between mortar and tank shells fast. This time we were definitely dealing with mortars, and they were huge.

'Braco, Braco!' I screamed. 'Mother, let's run!'

I looked around for my father. I saw him running back towards our shack. I yelled to him, but he just kept running in the opposite direction.

'Where are you going! Come back!' I cried.

'Go back. Don't follow me! We've left the bread behind. Don't follow me!' he shouted to me and ran towards the fire.

I hid in some bushes and waited for him. In the meantime I'd lost track of my mother and Braco and the rest of the Nuhanovićs. Everyone was trying to save themselves. As soon as someone had found a place to hide they just stayed there silently, not answering the calls of others. It was as if they we were all thinking, I've found shelter and I won't call out and give myself away. I waited there in the bushes for what seemed like an eternity, distressed at how quickly my family had become separated in the chaos. Then I saw my father running back with the bread, which was obviously very hot – you could tell by the way he was juggling it that it was burning his hands. Mortar shells were falling near by. I saw him trip and fall, dropping the loaf and picking it up again. By the time he had reached me I felt like cursing the bread, but I couldn't, of course. Not the bread and not in front of my father.

'Where are they?' my father asked.

'I don't know.'

'What do you mean you don't know?' he cried.

'Let's go and find them.'

We ran through a thicket. I instinctively protected my face with my hands, while my father instinctively protected the bread.

'Braco! Mum! Braco!' I called, but I could hardly hear my own voice over the sound of the exploding shells. Several trees erupted at once. The sound of heavy-machine-gun and rifle fire left no doubt in my mind that the barrage was coming from Stoborani.

Then I heard my mother. 'Hasko! Here! We're over here!' she shouted.

The two of them were huddled in the bushes along with Aljo,

Uncle Pašan, Aunt Ramiza, Uncle Rizvan, Aunt Mila and some others from our group. Some were lying on the ground. Then a voice came from deeper in the forest, shouting that our men had fled from the reservoir.

A moment later Osman Šošić – Šošo as we called him – approached us looking oddly serene. Crouching down beside us he said that those at the reservoir had scattered at the sight of the Chetnik troops approaching. Osman had run into one of them, who had counted ten armoured transporters and as many tanks and guessed that a thousand Serb infantry had arrived. Šošo supposed the troops were reinforcements for the stranded Serbs battling in the valley. There was no convoy formation this time. They had spread out wide and advanced across the field, turning it black with their uniforms and shooting as they came.

Then he told us Stoborani was on fire – the Serbs were burning everything in their path. If they bypassed us on the hill, I was thinking, which they have to do to get to the valley, they will pass through Gođenje and burn that village down with its two hundred households. As soon as that happened we would be surrounded. That was my greatest fear. And that's exactly what happened. Within the next hour they'd burned Gođenje and relieved the troops in the valley.

None of us believed we were going to survive that day under the continued shelling. We all thought we'd soon be dead. Our greatest fear was that the Chetniks would enter the woods, hunt us down and slaughter us like lambs.

The Nuhanovićs hiding on the hill were fifteen in number, no more and no less armed than the other families in the woods. My father had a pistol, my Uncle Pašan a shotgun and a carbine, my Uncle Hasib had a pistol and a shotgun and my Uncle Rizvan, who was sixty-something years old, had a shotgun.

I couldn't figure out why – this would interest psychologists – but the different family groups kept apart. It seemed that people didn't trust each other. It's quite possible that everybody reasoned in more or less the same way: it was better to remain separated because there was less chance of everyone being slaughtered if only one group were to be discovered. At the same time, if the Chetniks had indeed entered the forest and discovered a single group then they could expect little help – not that there would have been any way to help. But even within our wider group of Nuhanovićs, only immediate families stuck together at critical moments. It's not like people act that way on purpose; it just happened. I guess some instinct kicked in.

Apart from the knife I had bought in Zvornik I also had a rusty old bayonet – and that bayonet was a story in itself. My Aunt Krivačka had found it while digging up potatoes. Shaking the dirt off it she told me that I should have it. 'You might need it,' she'd said. She'd forgotten that my cousin Huso had buried it a long time ago. That was a pretty strange moment. I took the bayonet, cleaned it off and let it dry. I mused over it, wondering how old it might have been. Maybe it was from the Second World War. It had a sheath that could be attached to a belt. If ever I get to use it to defend myself, I thought, if I ever get caught, I will have to stab someone before they stab me. I tried to imagine being in a situation like that and wondered whether I'd actually be able to do such a thing. I attached the bayonet to my belt. Now, hiding in the woods, I felt a fraction safer whenever I touched it. But it was twice as long as my hunting knife and made walking, let alone running, problematic. Despite its inconvenience, for much of my time in the forest, every time we were under attack I kept it there on my belt.

For the whole day the shelling didn't let up. We ran through the woods, hoping to find a better place to hide. The sun was only halfway across the sky. We were surrounded by fir, pine and spruce, which were tall and a deep green in colour. If you dropped down on to the moss you felt like you were sitting on a luxurious carpet. I cursed nature's beauty, which could only offer us limited cover but which would cover all trace of us.

It was dark by the time the shelling and machine-gun fire showed any sign of letting up. When we dared return to our shacks everything around us was pitch black. If it had been just a regular night in the woods I would have been afraid of bears, wolves or apparitions. Now, all these things seemed harmless, even funny, when compared with the Chetniks. Just now darkness was my friend. I felt like an animal hiding from hunters. The Serbs could do whatever they wanted. They could just pull the trigger and open fire on us *Baliya*, as they called us (a derogatory name for Muslims) for as long as they wanted. It's not as if there was a shortage of ammunition or weapons; Yugoslavia had been stockpiling weapons for fifty years! Just bring them here and fire on the *Baliya*. Who cares? Kill them all – a shell doesn't distinguish between a fighter and a child.

Later, in the autumn of that year, once we'd arrived in Srebrenica, I found a four-volume illustrated series on the Second World War. Somewhere in those four volumes I read that the ratio of shots fired to soldiers killed kept diminishing as the end of the war approached. Towards the latter part of the twentieth century more and more bullets were fired, from several hundred to several thousand, to kill one soldier. At the same time the civilian percentage of war-related deaths multiplied.

But I didn't know any of that as I was hiding on Mršić Hill. At that point I thought that every shot was going to be the fatal one. So did everyone else. With time we would learn from our own experience that this was not the case.

Paša approached me. Paša and his brother Nefis were part of our group. Nefis's two boys – who were only three and five years old at the time – were the youngest members of our company. I'd noticed that their mother and grandparents kept sheltering them from the mortar rounds with their bodies. They would hug each other and put the little boys between them. The boys had been struck dumb, and their mother and grandparents were even more distraught. What were the little boys thinking? How could they understand what was going on? Did they imagine that a great evil was falling from the skies all of a sudden? Their parents' and grandparents' eyes expressed the sort of desperate powerlessness that people feel when they know they cannot protect their own family members, not even at the cost of their own lives.

Paša stood next to me and didn't say a word. We both looked at the sky in the direction of Stoborani. Ten days earlier he and I had counted all the descendants of our Grandpa Hasan and Grandma Muška, who were both born around 1910. Now that there were grand-children to take into account, the number of their direct descendants was anywhere between seventy and a hundred. Their graves faced up towards the trees on the hill where we were hiding.

'Paša,' I said, 'what's that crackling sound? Can you hear it? Are those gunshots?'

'No, they're not gunshots,' he said.

After listening for a bit longer we realized it was the sound of a conflagration. We couldn't see the houses in Stoborani because of the trees, but we could see a faint orange glow in the sky above it – it took a big fire to cast such a glow.

Others joined us, and a woman started weeping. 'Sweet mother, what am I to do now without a house? It's all gone!' she cried. The others tried to shush her – 'The Chetniks will hear us!' And perhaps we were all remembering and, where memory couldn't reach, imagining a point in the Nuhanovićs' two-hundred-year history in the area, from the founding of Stoborani during the Austro-Hungarian occupation to the Partisan struggles of the Second World War.

I fell asleep to that crackling sound. It was a short, fitful sleep among the shelters we had constructed for ourselves. We took turns keeping watch throughout the night.

MRŠIĆ HILL

I woke up early. Brushed the dead leaves and twigs from my hair. My mother and Braco had slept in the shack, but my father had spent the night outside, too. Unlike me he hadn't slept a wink. His fatherly instinct had kicked in, and I could tell he was trying to come up with a solution. There was no solution, but he couldn't admit that to himself. We were where we were, and there was nothing to be done now.

My father smoked in silence, gazing into space. He was thinking deeply. I'd seen him do that my whole life. This was what I used to call his musing pose. If you said anything while he was deep in thought he would give you a kind of ironic half-smile. That was also how he used to express his agreement or disagreement – mainly disagreement – with what you might be saying. Irony, of course, was totally out of place in our current situation. We were all terrified, and nobody was trying to hide their fear any more except, to some degree, parents in front of their children. But the fear was impossible to hide. You could smell it because the smell was real; we learned that fearing for your own life and the lives of those dear to you makes you sweat profusely. But we weren't embarrassed by the unmistakable odour any longer; the only thing that mattered was survival.

The Nuhanovićs slowly awoke and shuffled around in the shelters. Braco and my mother were as pale as ghosts. Uncle Pašan and Uncle Hasib were cutting down a small withered tree for firewood.

We're completely surrounded, I thought to myself.

I could hear sporadic shots of gunfire from the valley but no shells. It seemed strange. There hadn't been any explosions since last night. What was going on this morning?

Someone turned the transistor radio on; it was tuned to BiH Radio news. A band came on playing a song, the lyrics of which ran:

> Thomson fires, Kalashnikov and Papovka, too . . .
> Throw a bomb, chase the gang away from Sarajevo . . .
> Hey, you soldiers, hey defenders from all parts of Bosnia . . .
> Sarajevo will never forget you . . .

Aljo, Braco and I agreed that it was a good song, but it was about chasing a gang away from Sarajevo. What about us? Nobody cared about us. Was there anyone in the world who cared about what would happen to us in these dark woods surrounded by mountains a hundred kilometres from Sarajevo?

Making sure my father wasn't looking I waved to my mother and made a gesture to ask her for a cigarette. I was sure she had more hidden somewhere; she was saving them for my father because she knew how hard it was for him to go without, especially given the situation we were in. She shook her head. She didn't have any for me. Hasib said that he had run out of cigarettes at the end of April. Pašan had never smoked. Hamdo didn't have any – for real, I was sure of that. I thought I might try asking around some of the other shacks, but that would have been like begging.

I looked up through the branches and saw the beautiful morning sky. The sun was just emerging, so I couldn't see it yet, but sunbeams were shining through the leaves. The woods were so thick that hardly any light reached the ground, but I could feel the sun on my face. It was mild and caressing.

And then all hell broke loose.

Badaboom. Baroom. Boosh. Bwoom.

This time the earth really shook.

Boom.

'Planes! Planes! Run!'

I hugged the nearest tree and shut my eyes tight, but it was no use. When I opened them again nothing had changed. I saw my mother hugging a tree, too. Her eyes told me how frightened she was. I felt the same. Our eyes locked, and we both thought the same thing: this is the end.

'Oh, sweet God!' I heard Esma wail.

The squeal of a diving aeroplane was unlike anything I could have imagined. It was grunting, too, as if a gigantic pig were flying over our heads. Later somebody would tell me that that was actually the sound of the cannon. They were shooting at us from the sky with a cannon. I didn't even know that was possible!

The planes ripped through the sky above, first coming from one side and then from the other.

'Do they hate us that much?' I asked myself. 'I know they want to kill us, but to send planes to fire into the trees . . .'

We didn't know it then, but the warplanes had apparently dropped most of their bombs on the Luke valley, which was only a kilometre or so from Mršić Hill. Quite a few had landed very close to where we were hiding, and the impression was that these winged cannons along with all the evil of this world had been unleashed directly upon us.

'What else? Really? Air-raids on civilians . . . !' I shouted as soon as I gathered enough courage to part with my tree trunk. A thick line of smoke was billowing up above the trees.

Within ten minutes the sound of the planes grew fainter, but almost immediately a fierce artillery bombardment began. Then I heard the sound of infantry fire coming from across the reservoir, from where all our fighters had fled the day before. Šošo appeared again.

'Where are our fighters now?' I asked him.

'How should I know?'

At that moment a family hurried past, informing us in haste that the Chetniks had stormed the shelters not far from where we were hiding and had slaughtered everyone they had found, including thirteen women and children.

'They have no intention of leaving a single Muslim alive. If they find us we're all as good as dead.'

Men from several families gathered around to discuss what was to be done. Some asked whether anyone knew what was happening in the valley, whether our men were still down there fighting. If they weren't, then where were they? Nobody knew the answers to any of these questions. It was generally believed that the Chetnik reinforcements were trying to pull their men out of the valley. We figured that our fighters had been scattered and that no one was putting up any resistance any more. But it was all a guessing game. We couldn't know what the Chetniks intended to do next or where our people were. The only thing we knew for sure was that several injured fighters had been brought from the valley and placed in one of the nearby shelters.

'This is what I think,' I said. 'The gunfire is coming from around the reservoir. You can hear that it's getting closer. I'm afraid the Chetnik infantry will penetrate deeper into the woods, and if they do they'll kill us all. If they see there's no resistance from the forest – and there won't be any since our fighters have run away – they'll surround us. As it is, we can't go down to the valley because their forces are on the road. I think we should head towards the reservoir, slowly sneak up on them and open fire with any weapons we can collect here to make them think it's our fighters.'

As I went on my father's expression grew increasingly grim. He was standing a little way away and sending me warning looks. He wanted me to shut up.

But the rest of them nodded in agreement. 'Let's do it. Let's get some weapons together,' Osman Šošo said.

'Will you give me your pistol?' I asked my father.

He looked at me without knowing what to say. Then he grudgingly took his pistol out and handed it to me. 'You shouldn't have done that,' he said under his breath.

'Let's go!' Osman Šošo shouted. There were five or six men with him. I'm pretty sure I was the youngest among them.

I cocked the gun as soon as we set off. I had three men on each side, some armed with pistols, some with shotguns. The sun was already high in the sky, and its rays were shining through the thick forest. We walked through the ferns, taking care not to step on anything that would snap and give us away.

The further we went the more afraid I became. Was this a good idea? Maybe we'd better stop. Why had I suggested it? Well, some-body had to. And it was a good idea. But could we pull it off? So ran my internal monologue as we walked through the forest.

I glanced to my left – there was old Šošo, puffing and panting. His forehead was covered in sweat, either because he was afraid or because he was out of shape. Nobody spoke. We began stepping more cautiously. It would have taken just one Chetnik and a single burst of fire from his Kalashnikov to kill us all.

'Hasko,' Šošo called to me. The rest of them stopped immediately. Everybody was silent. 'Hasko, can you hear anything? Seems like the shooting has stopped,' Šošo whispered, clutching his rifle. We all listened for the sound of gunfire. It was true. The shooting really had stopped. We couldn't hear anything, at least not from the direction of the reservoir.

'Should we go back?' someone whispered.

'Let's go back,' I said.

We did so with a spring in our step. We couldn't wait to reach the shacks. We were almost there when it began raining shells on Mršić Hill again, as if they had been waiting for us to return.

I ran like a madman. When I reached the shelters I couldn't see my family. To make matters worse, real rain had started to fall, too. We were in the middle of a thunderstorm. Running through the forest I desperately shouted the names of my family members. I had never called my father Ibro before, but it felt stupid to shout for him by calling him Dad as I always had done.

I found them in a kind of gulley. They were all there, huddled together like sheep. The light shower had become a downpour, and we were all soaking in a matter of minutes. Shells were coming in from all sides. Twenty of us squatted in this dip in the ground. Everything had become grey; colours disappeared and everything was drenched in water: the trees, the dead leaves under our feet, us.

The gulley was about a metre deep. If you stood up, you could see what was happening around it, but if you were squatting down you could see only the tops of the trees. Nobody spoke. The rain was relentless. So was the artillery fire. The ground shook with explosions all over the forest. Something whizzed over our heads.

'It's shrapnel,' I cried. 'It can chop your head off just like that.'

We all ducked down and covered our heads with our hands. I flinched at every explosion and looked for something to bury my head in like an ostrich. But my uncles stood upright the whole time. Hasib had his rifle slung over his shoulder and kept a lookout. Pašan was doing the same thing, but he held his rifle in his hands. And what hands he had – they were as big as shovels! The rifle looked like a toy. Hasib had his black fur cap on. Pašan was bareheaded, his hair thick and black. Pašan always looked as if he were smiling, even when he was deadly serious. Maybe it was because of the sizeable scar he had by his mouth.

With each explosion Pašan would duck for just a moment and then stand upright to observe. I knew they were both doing it so they could warn us if the Chetniks came our way. But, honest to God, there wasn't much to see given how heavy the rain was and how dense the forest. Even if they had seen the Chetniks it would have been too late to run away. And where would we run anyway?

A shell exploded close by. I threw myself to the ground by a tree with a hole under its roots. I'd noticed it as soon as I'd arrived. I'd had my eye on it for just such a moment – I was fairly sure my head would fit in that hole – but Aljo had the same idea and was quicker. I slammed my head pretty hard against the tree, only to land on top of Aljo, who had beaten me to the relative safety of the hole. I practically covered him with my body.

'I'm sorry,' I whispered in his ear. 'I didn't mean to hurt you.'

'No worries,' he replied. 'Feel free to stay where you are.' He wasn't joking. As a shield against bullets I was as good as a rock or a tree. But knowing that shrapnel can tear through the air at a velocity of two kilometres per second I was happy to keep my head down.

The hissing and whizzing over our heads went on for hours, and I lost track of time. At one point I crawled to the tree that my mother was leaning against. She may have been crying, but it might have been the rain. She said nothing. I held her hand. I held her hand for quite a long time, feeling totally helpless, miserable.

Braco was lying under a tree the whole time. He never said a word to anyone. I thought he didn't want anyone to see how frightened he was. Whatever he felt, he kept it all inside.

'We'll all die down here,' I said to Hasib. 'I think we'd better move somewhere else.'

All eyes turned to me. They all looked at me as if I had a hidden agenda. They looked at me with contempt.

'Hasib! We will almost certainly die here!' I spoke to Hasib as if he were the one with all the answers.

'No, Hasko, we will not. No we will not,' Hasib said kindly, almost tenderly, repeating it several times. 'See how tiny our shelter is? Nobody can see us through the forest.'

'But shells are falling from above!' I wouldn't let it go, even though I knew they all thought I should back down.

'So, what do you think we should do?' Hasib asked me calmly. 'Tell us.'

'Let's go somewhere else,' I said. 'Maybe the shelling isn't so heavy on another hill.'

I thought of the beautiful plain on the top of the pass between Mršić Hill and Mount Javor. I had gone there on my own while we were identifying sites to build the shelters. I was convinced we'd be safe there because I was sure the Chetniks had not yet gone up Mount Javor. I thought we could get there in around fifteen minutes. We would have to cross a road, enter the forest on the other side and climb the mountain. But the Chetniks were somewhere along that road; we would have to cross without being spotted.

We waited another ten minutes, then we ran out of the shelter, and the group split in two. The four of us started running in one direction, everyone else went in another. Families kept together as before.

We ran through the forest. The shelling didn't let up. The ground was wet, and the mud stuck to our shoes. We stumbled upon Šaban's little grandsons hiding in the bushes. Šaban and his wife were sheltering the boys with their bodies as they had done the previous day. It was a touching but terrible scene. The little ones were totally speechless.

The rain slowly died down. Soon the shelling stopped. We emerged from the woods into a clearing. The clouds had disappeared. All of this happened almost simultaneously.

No explosions, no rain. The sun was shining.

The birds started to sing; the forest came back to life.

The sun was so hot that steam started rising from our jackets – what a sight! Everything was steaming after the rain, the whole forest.

My father finally spoke, having said little for several days. 'I promise that if we survive this we'll go to Australia. I promise. One day more in Bosnia would be a day too many.'

Standing in the dreamy oasis of calm after the day of hell I watched the steaming forest, but all I saw in front of me were the sandy beaches of Australia.

OUR FOREST LIFE

Somewhere beyond the forest, from the direction of Stoborani, I could clearly hear helicopters. Judging by the sound, two large-bladed aircraft landed and, after a short time, took off again. The Serb casualties had probably been evacuated. Much later, after the war, I heard that the mothers of the dead soldiers had surrounded Karadžić when the bodies arrived in Pale. They spat on him, called him names and apparently asked, 'Why did you send our children to their deaths for no reason? And where is this godforsaken place? Where is this Žepa?'

We were not sure if the Chetnik attack was definitely over – maybe the sudden quiet was just a lull before the next onslaught – but we welcomed it, no matter how long it lasted. Their weapons had finally fallen silent.

We built a fire because we needed to dry our sodden clothes and whip up a meal. Later in the evening, while we were sat around the fire, the mortars resumed. This time the explosions didn't make the ground shake, and we wondered what this distant, dull rumble meant. It came from somewhere far away in the Žepa valley. The shells were passing over Mršić Hill. First we would hear the shells whistling over our heads and then a distant explosion. The Chetniks had planted a mortar battery somewhere around Jelovci and were shelling Žepa.

That was the first of many occasions I would be overwhelmed by this strange sense of relief. I felt I was safe, if only for a brief moment. It was strange because it came from knowing that the shells were falling somewhere else. I don't think it ever occurred to me that the shells flying over my head might actually kill someone in Žepa; the only thing that mattered was that they weren't going to kill me or any of my immediate family. That's the way the human survival instinct operates. Each time I heard a shell being launched I would listen to the type of whistling it made, hoping that the whistling wouldn't stop halfway, hoping that the shell wouldn't land on us.

Nobody counted the number of shells fired on Žepa, but the bombardment continued throughout the night and over the following days. The Chetnik land offensive had ended, but the shelling seemed to be their revenge for the failed plan to reach the town and for the casualties caused by the Žepa locals. This would become a pattern over the following three years; it happened every time the Chetniks lost a battle.

At dawn I asked Paša if he wanted to sneak away with me and go down to Stoborani to check on the state of the Nuhanovićs' houses. We went from tree to tree and approached the clearing above the village, stopping every now and again to listen out for any unusual sounds. Standing behind a thick tree trunk we saw the charred ruins of the houses. Neither of us had ever seen anything like it before. All that remained of the five buildings that made up our family's property was the retaining wall of Hasib's house, the stone basement of Ismet's house and the outdoor latrine that he had built out of concrete blocks. Somebody suggested that the Chetniks must have saved the toilet for their own personal needs.

We saw traces of tank tracks on the ground; it had obviously made a U-turn there. The sight of trees riddled with bullets and shrapnel terrified me even before I discovered that some of the bullets had gone all the way through forty-centimetre-thick trunks. No way, I thought. What kind of weapon could do that? Up to that point I had never heard of anti-aircraft cannons. When I ventured into the clearing I noticed a big pile of empty shell cases left behind by the tank crew. Unbelievable, I thought, picking one up. It was at least half a metre long and weighed more than five kilograms. I was afraid to imagine what the projectile looked like. I put the empty shell case over my shoulder like some kind of trophy and brought it back.

'Hey, look, this is what the Chetniks are firing at us,' I said.

My father's face became tense. 'Throw that away!' he yelled at me. 'Don't show it around! Are you insane? Why did you bring it here?'

I threw the case to the ground in front of me. It landed with a thud.

'I wanted everyone to be aware of this,' I said, justifying myself to my father, although everyone else could hear me. 'There's tons of this stuff down there.'

Later that day we heard the story of the thirty-two Chetniks who were being detained in the school in Gođenje guarded by six of our fighters. They had been well looked after and hadn't been mistreated in any way. On the second day of the shelling, however, the school was hit several times, and some of our men were injured. It was decided that all the Chetniks should be released. So the thirty-two Chetniks headed towards Stoborani on foot. Passing through the village, I later found out, they met an elderly woman on the road. The old woman was frozen with fear when she saw them, but the soldiers greeted her with 'Good morning', and she returned their greeting.

So, while the battle in the valley raged on and Serb tanks were furiously bombarding the area and the dead and wounded lay all around – including the thirteen women and children killed in the shelter not far from where we were hiding – the Chetniks wished a regular 'Good morning' to this old woman, she greeted them in return and they moved on. Not a hair on their heads was harmed, and not a hair on hers either. Fancy that.

The six fighters who had guarded this group and released them from their makeshift prison were not so lucky. While trying to escape the beleaguered village they went the wrong way, got lost in the forest and were killed by the Serb forces who, on their way to the valley, burned Stoborani, Gođenje and several other villages to the ground.

Some years later, after the war, when information gathered through personal conversations, statements and investigations shed some light on the events of the time, I would find out what had happened to Muslim detainees in Vlasenica on 4 June, the day that Žepa was attacked. The person who provided the most information was one of the butchers, Predrag Bastah, also known as 'the Czar'. According to this butcher's statement during his war-crimes trial, on 4 June the

Chetniks took twenty-eight Muslims out of the Sušica concentration camp, which had been set up several weeks earlier, and drove them by bus to a place not far from Vlasenica where they were executed. According to Bastah they were all shot by a Serb woman while the rest of the Chetniks just stood watching. The woman's brother had apparently been killed in combat that very day, possibly in the attack on Žepa. And so it happened that on the same day our fighters released thirty-two Chetniks prisoners the Vlasenica Serbs killed twenty-eight Muslim detainees.

On 11 June, exactly a week after the shelling started, my family decided to take a risk and flee Mršić Hill for Mount Javor on the other side of the valley. My Uncle Pašan and Aunt Ramiza decided to join us. They were sure we would find other refugees there and that it would be possible for us all to shelter in the shepherds' huts for a while.

We left the forest and descended into the valley. We crossed the road, which until recently had been full of Serb tanks and APCs. We had been shelled from that location, so it was an eerie feeling. We were on edge, walking in single file through the dewy grass. All that remained of our earthly possessions was in our hands and on our backs – about twenty kilograms of flour, some salt, sugar, a few tins, some pots and pans, some underwear and the clothes we were wearing. Braco and I carried most of it. My mother was barely able to walk. She had health issues she refused to talk about, but clearly she wasn't well. My father, for some reason, wrapped his head in a scarf, pirate-style, which was something he usually did when he had a headache. None of the men had shaved for ten days or so, but who cared? We hadn't bathed either, and we all stank. I had managed to wash my hair and clean myself up a little the day before with a small pot of water heated over an open fire.

My Uncle Pašan was the only one with a rifle. As we walked through the valley my Aunt Ramiza broke the silence. She said it was Kurban Bajram (Eid al-Adha) that day and, with any luck, we might get some mutton to eat up on the mountain. She knew some people up there; maybe somebody had sacrificed a ram; she mentioned someone called Blatnjak. I thought that was highly unlikely. I found it hard to imagine that anybody was still living up there or keeping sheep or sacrificing them for Eid. Hadn't everyone fled, people and sheep alike?

And then, once again, I was seized by that damn feeling of being surrounded by such beauty. I was overwhelmed by the loveliness of green pastures and the sweet smell of dewy grass. I couldn't help but enjoy it – that is, until the moment the village of Luke appeared before my eyes. I was presented with a sight I had already seen in Stoborani. All the houses had been burned to the ground. We picked up our pace, passing charred beams and scorched bricks. We reached the foot of Mount Javor and swiftly began our ascent, following the course of a brook.

MOUNT JAVOR

That was my first time on Mount Javor, although Haso and I had hiked the length and breadth of the other side of the valley. The mountain dominates the landscape, and I would see it when I was in and around Stoborani. It is only a few kilometres from the village, and yet I had stayed well clear. I had always admired from afar the meadow at its highest elevation at around 1,500 metres. Zlovrh Peak, where the JNA communication post was sited, lay east of the meadow.

We were ascending the section of the mountain that we believed to be held by our fighters. I felt full of energy, as though I could actually run uphill despite the forty-kilogram load on my back. We started to climb briskly. The pass was formed of a narrow ravine, and we had to walk over the rocks and occasionally wade through water. There was no other way. I walked ahead of the others, and my father kept warning me to stick with the group. I took a part of the load from my parents so that they could walk faster, but I had to go back several times and help my mother.

After two hours we were halfway up the mountain and decided to take a break. Almost immediately we heard a sound resembling that of tanks rumbling along the road – although we couldn't actually see them because of the tall trees.

'We escaped just in time. If we had stayed we would be surrounded by now,' I said. We felt sorry for the people hiding in the woods, but at the same time we were greatly relieved that we had already crossed the road. The thought of the Chetnik infantry heading up the pass spurred us to move on immediately, and we climbed even faster than before. We didn't know what to expect at the top of the mountain.

A few hours later we arrived at the first clearing. Chetniks or no Chetniks, I couldn't help but stand in awe of the enormous green pastures full of wild flowers of a thousand colours surrounded by a dark and dense coniferous forest. The sky was clear, blue and wonderful. There was not a breath of wind. What a picnic spot it would have made if only we had time and the Chetniks hadn't been trying to kill us.

There were several huts at the top of the clearing, and we headed towards the largest. On the way it became apparent that at least a hundred people had arrived before us. We were not sure if we would be welcome, but we put down our bags all the same. I was hoping that my father might know someone or that someone might recognize him – he was widely respected throughout eastern Bosnia. In my childhood memories everyone we ever met addressed my father as 'Director'. I had rarely been called anything but 'Ibro's son', and I don't recall anyone even asking my actual name let alone remembering it.

I was hungry. I asked Braco if he thought there was any chance our mother might make us something to eat. But how could she? We were sitting on the grass in this meadow that seemed to be our new home, but we weren't invited into any of the huts. My father sat down on a stump and lit a cigarette in his thinking pose. My mother was obviously embarrassed. She realized that we had nowhere to sit let alone spend the night.

Near by, a group of young men was gathered around a big ruddy-cheeked fellow, bursting with strength, who was throwing a knife into a tree trunk. Every time he threw the knife into the tree he would slowly walk up to it and wrench it from the trunk; when he missed his friends would burst out laughing and tease him. As I watched this scene all I could think was that these brave highlanders could laugh and joke no matter what.

Then someone shouted from the edge of the clearing, 'Chetniks, Chetniks!' The voice seemed to echo across the mountain. This was followed by a scene I will never forget, one which demonstrated how determined these highlanders were. Dozens of young men appeared from the forest. The guys throwing the knife instantly grabbed their rifles, which I had not seen until then, and, leaving the knife embedded in the tree, ran down in the direction of the brook. From all sides men both armed and unarmed were appearing and just as quickly disappearing down the mountain.

I felt ashamed that I was not among them. We refugees were hanging around hoping to find shelter while those courageous men went down to intercept the Chetniks and defend us. What I did not know is that the Chetniks would never dare set foot anywhere their tanks could not move ahead of them, but I was yet to learn about that distinctive feature of their strategy. The process of learning about war and survival skills had only just begun for us.

In an hour the highlanders returned. At all times they kept a man on watch down by the brook.

Smoke was rising from the chimney of a nearby hut. Noticing that my mother wasn't well, the inhabitants had let her in and told her she could use the stove to prepare a meal. Someone gave her a piece of Qurbani meat from a ram slaughtered in the neighbourhood, and she quickly made a *pita* – my first *pita* with meat in a long time. It was gone in two minutes.

In the early evening I met some fellow refugees and asked one of them to show me around. I wanted to know exactly where we were in case we had to get away quickly. Planning an escape route was something I would do every time we arrived in a new place while fleeing from the Chetniks. I was led to a point from which you could see for miles around you – the broadest view was to the west, towards the peak of Veliki Žep, Han Pijesak and Vlasenica. The Drina was a few kilometres to the east and on the far bank was Serbia.

We were trapped. That's what I thought while standing on the highest mountain peak in eastern Bosnia. Everywhere I looked I knew there were Chetniks. They controlled everything to the north, south, east and west. At that time the Serb forces also held Srebrenica. I knew that the Bosnian Territorial Defence forces held Kladanj, but the mountains screened my view of it, so my eyes dwelled on the lights of Vlasenica and the villages around it. I thought about the detention camp where hundreds of Bosnian Muslims were being held – perhaps even thousands. The landscape was full of atrocities: concentration camps, firing squads, burned villages . . . I was greatly troubled by the thought of what could have happened to us had we stayed in Vlasenica. The possibilities horrified me.

A part of me thought that the four of us should be grateful we had escaped in time. We were free despite everything, despite the fact that we were roaming the woods and mountains; despite the fact that the free territory was shrinking and the Chetniks were getting closer and closer, we were still free. But we had nowhere to go. It seemed the sky was the only way out, and I began daydreaming of being rescued by a helicopter. There was enough space for a helicopter to land, if only . . .

But who was thinking about the thousand Muslims trapped on that mountain? Nobody. Listening to the radio we heard Žepa fighters praised for inflicting the most serious losses on Chetnik forces to date. The Chetniks' defeat was celebrated in Sarajevo, and yet we didn't know what to do with ourselves. We didn't know where we should go, where to spend the night, what to eat.

Not all the villages around Žepa had been incinerated, and those that survived would accommodate refugees for the next three years; those who had fled from Višegrad, from across the Drina, streams of refugees from the municipalities of Rogatica, Vlasenica and Han Pijesak and even further afield, poured into the few villages around Žepa that the Chetniks hadn't managed to reduce to ashes.

It was already dark, and we still didn't have a place to spend the night. I went back towards the huts. Although it was 11 June it was so cold that I had to put on all the clothes I owned to stay warm. I couldn't risk getting a chill, so it was two pairs of trousers, both of my jackets, a woollen sweater and a shirt for me. There were at least fifty people in the building with the stove. Its owner was Blatnjak, the man my aunt had talked about on the way up. Blatnjak had welcomed my aunt and uncle inside. The four of us stood outside with our teeth chattering with the cold until one of Blatnjak's relatives asked my mother in.

'Ibro,' he said, 'you and your sons can sleep in the stable. Come with me. I'll show you.' We followed him to the stable. There we found a big horse and several cows tied to a manger. 'Best to go up to the hayloft. You'll be warmer there.'

Up we went. The floorboards were so far apart that my foot fell through several times. We made three piles of hay, and we each crept into one. I imagine it was worse outside, but I was freezing even though I had covered myself with so much hay that I could hardly breathe. Sleeping in hay was something I had only seen in films. There's a first time for everything, I thought as I tried to lull myself to sleep. But I couldn't sleep because the horse below kept waking me up. I could see it through the floorboards, stamping the ground with its front hoof and whinnying every few minutes. I cursed the horse, the stable, the mountain and our destiny. I wondered about the twists of fate that had led us from the tranquillity of our comfortable apartment in Vlasenica to this stable with the cows and the horse that wouldn't let me sleep. I wondered how we would survive the next day. I managed to fall asleep just before dawn.

The flies buzzing around the horse woke me up. The sun was shining through the wooden boards of the roof. We got up, brushing off the hay and insects, and went out. It was yet another beautiful day. The planes that bombed us up until March 1993 enjoyed clear skies. I would often curse such weather and pray to God to send us some clouds.

ZLOVRH PEAK

While we were standing in front of the stable and trying to warm up a little in the sun, a man approached us with an outstretched hand. He, of course, recognized my father.

'Hey, Ibro, what's up?' he asked. 'I couldn't believe it was you. How come you haven't gone to Tuzla or abroad somewhere? I thought all the smart people had pulled their families out in time.'

My father recounted our odyssey since leaving home. The man said that his family had escaped from Žepa as soon as the Chetniks attacked on 4 June. His children were small, and he had wanted to get them to safety. 'But', he continued, 'it hasn't been as safe as I'd hoped. We watched the battle from here, you know. We could see everything. On the second day the planes arrived from across the Drina, from Serbia. I saw it with my own eyes. First the plane dropped bombs all across the mountain and then it fired some kind of rocket. The rocket had a trail of smoke behind it, hissing and humming before it nosedived into the ground. But it didn't explode. I tell you, the Chetniks mean to kill us all – they've even sent planes, imagine that! I wasn't in the battle myself; I didn't want to leave my wife and children on their own here,' the man went on, 'but soon after that I was called to Zlovrh. My people here told me that I had to go to Zlovrh immediately.'

'And how do you get there from here?' I asked.

'Straight across the clearing. It's only a few kilometres. When I got there I did a double-take – I saw about twenty, maybe thirty, of our men standing in front of an enormous bunker door made of reinforced concrete and with hinges thicker than my arm – like this, I swear,' he said, showing us his forearm. 'The Chetniks had barricaded themselves in the bunker, and we had no idea how many of them were in there. The others, the ones in the valley, they must have wanted to meet up with the guys in the bunker. If they had, if they had taken it and positioned their tanks and artillery up there, we'd have had nowhere to go. You think that all these people could stay here if they had? No way!'

'So what happened to the Chetniks in the bunker?' we asked.

'Well, we could hear that the battle in the valley was still going on, and we couldn't be sure the Chetniks wouldn't break through and reach the peak, so we thought it would be better to disarm them as soon as possible. One of the locals started negotiating with them. He shouted through the door for them to come out and promised they wouldn't be harmed. But they wouldn't leave. One of our lot grabbed a pickaxe and struck the hinges with the sharp end of the head, then, using the handle as a lever, got the hinges to give a bit. The negotiations went on, but the Chetniks still wouldn't give up. We had a few hunting rifles and one automatic rifle. Most of us were carrying homemade rifles.' (By homemade rifles he meant the improvised weapons the Bosniaks made. They'd take a narrow tube and weld a trigger mechanism to it – a strong spring, for instance. The shooter would have to pull the spring, stretch it tight – like a kind of crossbow – in order to insert a bullet into the tube. When the trigger was released the spring would fire the bullet – at least in theory. In practice the bullets would often explode while still in the pipe and blow the shooter's eye out or scorch him badly.) 'One of us had a kilo of dynamite,' the man went on, 'and that was all we had in the way of weapons. But they didn't know that! God only knows how many Bosniak Green Berets they thought had attacked them!'

'So how did it end?' we asked.

'Our negotiator thrust his hand through the hole where the hinge had given and shouted to the Chetniks, "Here, cut off my hand if you don't believe me. I guarantee that we will not harm you!" After a couple of minutes they pushed the door from the inside and started coming out one at a time, all thirteen of them, all of them in uniform. Once their eyes got accustomed to the light and they could see how many of us there were and what arms we had they cursed us and themselves. They had twenty rifles in there, ten automatic and ten semi-automatic, and a rocket launcher, too, loads of ammunition, bombs and food. But it was a done deal, and while they were cursing us we took their guns. Now we were the ones who were properly armed, and they couldn't do a thing! This is one of those rifles. I was asked to give it up for some commander or other, but I refused. I captured it. It's mine, and I'm keeping it. I need to protect and defend my family here.'

'And what happened to your prisoners?'

'First we sent them under escort to Han Pijesak, and then we let them go. One of them was a civilian, and the others were all young recent recruits.'

'Has anyone been killed in bombardments here?' I asked.

'No, nobody has been killed here, but down in Žepa it was a massacre. One bomb took out an entire family. I heard that a piece of rock from the blast hit one woman in the back and killed her on the spot. Many of the victims were refugees from Višegrad – and there were children among them.'

We said goodbye and went our separate ways. Walking across the clearing we found Blatnjak, who was leading the sheep to pasture. If I had met that old shepherd anywhere else he would certainly have made me think I was near a Serb village because, in his fur hat and sheepskin coat, he looked like a Serb shepherd to me. We asked what was on the other side of the mountain, and when he mentioned Luka my father's face brightened up.

'My sister Mina is there! I thought the whole area had been burned down!'

'No, it hasn't,' Blatnjak said. 'Luka is still free. There haven't been any Chetnik attacks there – at least, not yet.'

We went back to the huts. My uncle and aunt told us that they had decided to stay for a few more days and, if and when the Chetnik offensive ended, go back to Mršić Hill. Their son Haso and his wife Esma were still in the woods with the other families from Stoborani. I thought that was a very bad idea. Why go back to an area that was half-surrounded by Chetnik forces, forces that could completely cut them off whenever they chose to? I was convinced I would never see my aunt and uncle again.

The four of us picked up our things and headed through the woods. We walked tentatively past the untenanted military communication installation with its antennas and concrete bunkers. We couldn't be sure the area wasn't mined.

For the first time since the Chetnik attack the four of us were on our own. We had separated ourselves from the others and were headed through the forest to look for a new refuge. We didn't know what to expect behind the next hill, whether we would come across friend or foe. We were entering the Municipality of Srebrenica.

LUKA

I'd never seen this side of the mountain before. A panorama of the Drina valley lay before our eyes. Meadows and thick woodland were stitched together forming a plateau above the gorge. The river at the bottom of the valley could not be seen. On the opposite side was Serbia, the hinterlands of which could be seen in the distance. Further still, Mount Tara, in Serbia, loomed.

Running away from slaughter we had reached the borders of Bosnia. There was nowhere else to go. My father remembered passing this way thirty years ago. He had walked half a day from Stoborani to Luka, but he didn't remember the path. He seemed a little disorientated, so I took the lead, a rare moment when my father left the final word to me.

'All right then,' he said, 'let's see how you'll get us there.' He did not believe I could find my way around in the wilderness, but I've always had a good sense of direction – maybe it was all those three-dimensional drawings I had made as a student. I'd always been good at reading maps, and I'd always loved hill-climbing. My sense of direction would save my neck – and not only mine – on several occasions during the war.

We had been walking downhill for an hour or so when all of a sudden a gravel road appeared in front of us. I gave my father a triumphant look. He said nothing. After an hour we saw some shepherds' huts – we had reached Vukoljin Stan, a summer-pasture camp for the nearby villages of Luka and Krušev Do. Several people came out to greet us, including my father's sister Mina and her husband Asim. There were twenty people in the hut, mainly women with children and a few men. We were all related in one way or another.

My Aunt Mina's face grew pale as she recognized her brother. 'Ibro, for God's sake, how did you end up here?'

'It's a long story,' my father said.

That was the first time we walked into a proper shelter after two weeks of hiding in the mountains. Our hosts told us that they had fled their house in the village several kilometres away a few days earlier when planes had started bombing Luka. They had planned to go back home now that the danger was over – at least temporarily. The little shepherd's hut was built like a small house with all the necessary amenities. We washed, ate and rested, and after a good night's sleep we all headed to Luka. I had been there once before, in the early 1980s, for the wedding of my aunt's eldest son. I had been twelve at the time, and, apart from the car journey there from Vlasenica, I didn't remember much about it.

Luka was part of the Srebrenica Municipality. I'd often heard people speaking of Luka as 'a backwater in the middle of nowhere' or 'the back of beyond'. It took us more than two hours to get there. Descending along the steep slope leading to the village I remembered that Luka's location was often described as being at the bottom of a cauldron. Looking up you could see nothing but the cliffs of the gorge – in some places more than a hundred metres high – and the mountains. The place was surrounded by a massive rock wall and totally isolated from the rest of the world. The only way to reach it from the Bosnian side was the path down the rocky slope we had travelled. Serbia was on the opposite side, not more than two kilometres away. Below Luka there was an unusual-looking valley that led down towards the Drina; appropriately, the locals called it Grđenj, which means 'ugly'. The Chetniks had been firing artillery at Luka from Serbia along the valley, but most of the village remained safe because Grđenj was narrow and orientated in such a way that the gunners couldn't get the right angle.

To me, Luka, surrounded by high cliffs and visible only from the sky, was like a Native American village in a western. There was no way of approaching it because hawk-eyed sentries stood guard on the top of the cliffs. I didn't see the guards in Luka, but I did spot several men with rifles. Luka had its lookouts.

The houses were spread out in groups of five or ten on different levels along the mountain pass. The mosque was not far from my aunt's house, and the main road passed behind it. Where the road forked was the square. About twenty locals met there every evening, and I made a habit of joining them. They passed the time with stone-tossing competitions.

Given how close Serbia was, the first thing I asked about were the nearest bridges. I was told that none of them was very close; the nearest was in Višegrad more than twenty kilometres upriver and the next further downstream. It was known that the Chetniks had been crossing the river over the Bajina Bašta power plant, but that was about fifteen kilometres away. So far the Chetniks hadn't dared descend into the gorge. Should they, however, decide to cross the river by boat or swim across the guards watching Grđenj would raise the alarm. I wasn't at all convinced that we were safe from a Chetnik infantry attack. I needed to see for myself how deep the valley was and if it were really so difficult to cross the river at that point.

A few days later, feeling rested, I asked my relatives if anyone was willing to join me for a trip out to the top of the cliff. Not only was no one willing but they failed to understand why I would want to clamber up the rocky slope in the first place. 'Nobody does that here,' they said. My aunt's family clearly thought I was weird. They kept busy by tending to various agricultural tasks; things unrelated to farming were generally considered pointless. They were right, of course, at least when it came to their daily work. I must have looked like a spoiled city brat who wouldn't dirty his hands with soil. So I rolled up my sleeves and went to help with the hay and collecting firewood. Mina's son Hasan, Braco and I made a bomb shelter in a day. We used a small natural depression in the ground behind the house and covered it with thick boards.

The local forester was my aunt's neighbour, and I befriended his elder son Ćamil Duraković, who was twelve at the time. He was the only one willing to join me on my expedition to the highest point along the valley. We left early in the morning. The slope was very steep and difficult. In half an hour I suddenly felt a wave of cold air, which meant that we had reached the summit. We found ourselves on the edge of an abyss.

I had never seen anything like it before, except maybe in Indiana Jones films. I told Ćamil to stay away from the edge and to get down. We both took in the scenery in front of us on all fours. We could hardly see the Drina, just a faint narrow strip of deep greenish-blue. The cliffs were several hundred metres high on both sides of the river. We could see quite clearly the village of Jagoštica on the opposite side in Serbia, and we had a splendid view of Mount Tara and the surrounding peaks behind it.

And so I looked across to Serbia, not believing my own eyes. I could see houses and farms with cars and tractors parked behind them. I could see men scything grass and haystacks in the fields. Less than five hundred metres away, just across the river, completely normal life was taking place while a mass exodus was under way on the Bosnian side! The planes dropping bombs on us were taking off from the military airport at Ponikve, which was not far from Jagoštica. Just below Jagoštica there was a tank lobbing shells across the river, firing on us, but the people of Jagoštica were happily cutting grass! They were sure there was nothing we could do to harm them.

'Do you reckon', young Ćamil said, 'we could shoot them from here? They certainly shoot at us from there. My father's got a hunting rifle. I could steal it, you know. I say we give it a try. What do you think?'

'Don't be silly,' I said. 'A hunting rifle hasn't the range, and, anyway, it would be a stupid thing to do in the circumstances. All we can do is pray to God that the planes don't attack again and that the tank across the river doesn't figure out how to start aiming more accurately.'

After a short silence I said, 'Do you think it might be possible to cross the river at night, get over to Jagoštica and go on to, say, Sandžak? I was thinking of trying to reach my girlfriend there. We studied at university together.' I thought then about how the war had severed our relationship in the prime of our love.

My stomach started to rumble.

'Let's go back,' I said. 'I haven't had anything to eat since last night.'

We navigated our way down the slope. I would see Ćamil again fifteen years later in 2007; he was then a big, bold, confident man just back from the USA. He would later become Mayor of Srebrenica – but that's a different story for a different book.

A MEAL

I arrived just in time for lunch.

My mother gave me a sharp look. 'You're almost late,' she said. We both knew I'd be hungry and stay hungry if I was late. The food situation was, to put it mildly, embarrassing for us. We four had arrived uninvited at a household with fourteen members. Nobody knew how long we would stay. We had no food of our own, and the other refugees had arrived before us. Besides, those refugees were my aunt and uncle's three children: their daughter Sabera with her two daughters; their other daughter Munira with her two sons; and their son Hasan with his wife and two small children. There was also a cousin of ours with her small daughter. That made for a total of eighteen mouths to feed.

We all had to adjust to house rules and had to show our gratitude, and we did. We had a place to sleep in a house, on foam mats on the second floor, which was more than comfortable given the conditions we'd recently endured. We always ate together.

Two tables would be set for meals – an adults' table and one for the children. A bowl was placed on each, which was a common bowl of thick soup that we all shared. Each of us was given a slice of bread and a spoon, and the race would begin. With everybody scooping from the bowl at the same time, our spoons clashed against each other producing a strange kind of music. My mother would nudge us with her foot under the table to make us eat faster to fight for ourselves. The faster and more skilful you were with your spoon the less hungry you would be. This fight was real – we were all aware of it although we never spoke about it. This kind of struggle had imposed itself on all of us as some kind of natural law – the law of survival. There was no bitterness between us; you could only be bitter at yourself. There were no allies in this kind of struggle. In a few months even the four of us would compete against one another. It's not as though we were able to pinpoint what was happening. A silent imperceptible force was trying to break the unbreakable bonds between father and son, between two brothers, between mother and son. With every passing day, week and month I felt more like an animal and less like a human being. Hunger and the self-preservation instinct had made me become someone else, something else.

I know this will sound strange. I was not myself any more, but, having said that, my love and sense of responsibility for my fellow man was at the same time growing stronger. The more time we spent together, the better I got to know my mother, father and brother. The war was bringing us closer. I began to notice strengths and weaknesses I'd never seen before. I realized that I had been taking my family for granted, as something God given that would always be there. But now my thoughts were on how to protect them, how to keep them by my side. I couldn't bear to think about the possibility of any of them being injured or killed. And yet I knew that was a real possibility, and I was forcing myself to prepare for the worst. Every morning after I awoke I would tell myself to be strong and be ready for anything, for who knew what the day would bring.

OUR HOUSE IN LUKA

Lunch at Aunt Mina's house was always before noon and dinner was always after dusk. There was never enough food for breakfast. Both meals were always either broth or a *pita*, and the system of a common dish that everyone shared never changed. It was easier with *pita* because everyone could see how big their piece was and how many pieces everyone else had. After finishing we would share a bowl of milk or yoghurt, which sometimes had pieces of cornbread soaked in it.

This was enough to keep us alive, but the arrangement couldn't last for ever. After three weeks my father informed us that he and his sister had agreed that the four of us would move to a different house. I knew that, despite his sister's protestations against us leaving, my father didn't want us to take any more food from her immediate family members. He was determined to move into old Abdulah's house right across the street. Abdulah was an old acquaintance of my father's, and he had offered to let us stay in his house while he and his daughter were in his mountain cottage. He found the cottage more practical – it had the advantage of suitable pastures for his cattle. It was also safer, I guess, given the bombardment the village had suffered. Anyway, once again, at least until further notice, we had a new place to stay. It was a wooden house that had been built forty years earlier, but the stone retaining wall was as blackened as its wooden façade and made it seem much older. Inside, we found a burlap ottoman, three creaky old beds and a wood-burning stove. That was quite enough for us.

Through the window of the room where my brother and I were

to sleep we could see Grđenj. Looking along it we had a glimpse of Serbia – and somewhere among the sloping pasture and forests was a Chetnik tank. What a sight, I thought, and every night I went to bed hoping that the tank would not fire a shell through my window. It could easily have done so – it was only a few kilometres away. We knew it was there but couldn't actually see it until Ćamil brought his father's binoculars over and we got a glimpse of it sitting there.

My aunt gave us some flour – I don't know how much, but it was enough for at least ten days. Almost every morning she would bring us fresh milk, and every evening we ate cornbread soaked in milk. Over the next month I began to lose weight noticeably for the first time. There was less and less food every day. We were afraid of hunger almost as much as we were afraid of the shelling.

Although we had moved out of my aunt's house we spent most of our time there. I used to play chess with Uncle Asim for hours. The game would be interrupted when it was time to listen to the news – my uncle had hooked up an old car battery to a radio for that very purpose. Two or three times a day we would gather around the table. During the early days of our stay in Luka we hoped to hear that the war was over, but that hope quickly disappeared. Then we hoped to hear that NATO would intervene in Bosnia. Every day we tried to listen between the lines for hints of a planned intervention. We heard about the daily shelling of Sarajevo, about the hundreds of wounded and killed all over Bosnia, about the first successes of the BiH army, about the Serb army breaking through into towns and villages, about the slaughter of civilians. It was clear that thousands of Muslims were missing or had been killed in mass executions.

We soon realized that Srebrenica was one of the only territories in eastern Bosnia that the Serbs didn't control. Instead, it was held by forces loyal to the Bosnian government – ostensibly, the BiH army. We heard very little about Žepa and not a thing about a godforsaken village such as Luka. Although Luka was formally a part of the Srebrenica Municipality, we felt as though we were part of Žepa, which was just behind the mountain ridge. Srebrenica was far away; you had to cross three mountains to reach it, and, besides, the road was controlled by the Chetniks.

Serb radio also reported that aeroplanes had been sent to bomb ten thousand Bosnian Green Berets fighting in the Žepa area. This was news to us. You wouldn't be able to find that many berets of any colour in Žepa let alone rifles! Evidently the Serbs had found it hard to accept their defeat in the recent battle, and, embarrassed that local villagers, farmers, loggers and shepherds with hunting rifles and shotguns had defeated a professional army, they had decided to explain it to their listeners by inventing ten thousand 'armed and dangerous Green Berets'. I wondered if the perpetrators of that lie would come to believe it in time. I was yet to learn about the special war and the 'big lie' propaganda.

We also heard on the radio that the JNA had formally withdrawn from Bosnia. Milošević had declared that Serbia – or the new Yugoslavia of his – would stay out of the war in Bosnia and Herzegovina. In my memory this declaration came just as a shell from Serbia whistled through the air and exploded near by. We all jumped to our feet at once. The women and children were shaking with fear. My uncle, hiding under the table, asked, 'Where are they shooting from? Where did it land?'

The shell surprised us because it was the first one in days. It was followed swiftly by others; shell after shell fell on the village. One woman was fatally injured while tending to her cow in the fields. The cow was also dying.

My aunt wept because she had known the woman all her life.

TRUE FAITH

After dark, when the artillery fell silent, we gathered at my aunt's house by the light of an oil lamp. We talked long into the night. My father was getting more and more nervous. I knew that his main concern was the shortage of food, but there was also the issue of cigarettes – his supplies were almost exhausted. He had smoked two packs a day before the war; now he was down to a few cigarettes a day. My brother and I hadn't exactly quit either. My mother had given me a few cigarettes. Every time she gave me one I cut it in half and saved half for later.

Presently, my father was lighting one of his remaining cigarettes while my aunt subjected us to one of her monologues.

'We called this upon ourselves when we started behaving like Vlachs. Men drink and gamble; nobody goes to the mosque any more. People eat pork or tinned stuff. And who knows what they put in those cans? We were the worst kind of Muslims. We weren't Muslims at all! And now we are being punished for it. This is God's punishment for us – and we deserve it.'

'Absolutely right!' my Uncle Asim added. 'It's as hard to find a true Muslim as it is a needle in a haystack. The few elders that remain respect our customs, but only them and no one else. At Friday prayers you don't see anyone in the mosque other than men of my generation.'

Although I hadn't been asked to express my opinion I couldn't help myself and snapped rudely, 'What are you talking about? Why would God punish us? It doesn't make any sense. I don't believe it, and I don't accept it. Why doesn't God punish the Serbs? Why are we punished while they are given everything – tanks, aeroplanes, all kinds of weapons – to shoot, kill and slaughter as much as they wish?' They blaspheme nearly every other word. Muslims have never cursed God as much, so why punish us and not them?

Needless to say, my parents were embarrassed because I was being a smartarse in front of everyone. These people were our hosts; we were supposed to be humble.

'Well, maybe God has chosen the Serbs to punish us. But in time He will bring punishment upon them as well, don't you worry. That is something no one can escape from,' Uncle Asim said.

'All right then, but why does God allow innocent children to die? They have no time to become sinners,' I said.

'Listen,' Uncle Asim replied, 'God doesn't punish only adults. When He chooses to punish, it is the entire people that He punishes, not individuals. Have you read the Quran?'

'Yes, I have,' I said, which was only a half-truth.

'Then you know how He completely destroyed two cities by raining down a shower of brimstone on them. Those were Lut's people. Lut was one of Allah's prophets.'

'Oh, I know. Sodom and Gomorrah. It's in the Bible as well,' I said.

'The two cities were completely consumed by fire – men, women and children alike. That's just the way it is. Sometimes children must pay for the sins of their parents or even the sins of their parents' parents. Sometimes children pay for the sins of their forefathers long forgotten. That's just the way it is,' my Uncle Asim said.

I recoiled at the very idea, thinking: We, the children, must pay for the sins of our forefathers long forgotten? How can that be? God would never do that! I believe in God, but that logic is unacceptable. If that's the way it is, then nothing you do in your lifetime can save you from that punishment. And you can't do anything except hope that at least your soul will be saved and go to heaven. What else could you do if you were born sinful because others had sinned long before you were born? I simply could not accept the notion that God was working through the Serbs and that the accounts would only be settled in the afterlife. I thought: Well, justice has to be served in this world first and then in the hereafter. How was I to know whether those people who had shot at us from the tank earlier that day, who had killed an innocent woman, would receive their punishment in the hereafter? How could I be sure that they would end up in hell? And who cared anyway? The only thing we should care about is staying alive.

'Have you heard of the Kremna Prophecies?' Asim asked me. Asim seemed to be talking only to me, although the room was full of people. Maybe this was because he thought I was a rebel or maybe he thought I was a conceited, spoiled city boy. Maybe he thought they had brainwashed me at university in Sarajevo. 'The Kremna Prophecies were made by Mitar the Seer, a Serb from Kremna, which is a village not far from here – over there, in fact. See Mount Tara just across the Drina? He predicted that a time would come when the Serbs would be so few in number that all of them would be able to stand under a single plum tree. Just one tree, that's how few of them there will be.'

'That's right,' everybody confirmed. 'The people have known this for a hundred years.'

'So, there, that is what is going to happen to the Serbs,' Asim said. 'Punishment will befall them eventually.'

'If there are going to be so few of them that they can all stand under a single plum tree how many of us do you think there will be? This Mitar never mentioned the Bosnians, the Muslims.'

'Don't you worry. God will have the last word. But it's prayer time now. Put your trust in Him, in Allah. Do you know how to pray?' Asim asked standing up and leaning on his stick.

I looked first at my mother and my father and then at the rest of them. 'I do,' I said, hoping that that would be the end of it and that I wouldn't be asked which Quran verses I could recite. I could remember some from my childhood that my grandparents had taught me, but it certainly wasn't enough for a prayer. I had forgotten at least half of what I had learned as a child, and I hadn't been inside a mosque since then – and I wouldn't enter another until after the war. This applied not only to me but to all the friends I grew up with who were identified as Muslims by ethnicity or any other ethnic Muslims whom I'd ever come into contact with. However, I wasn't ready to discuss that with Asim.

'There you go. We have completely neglected our faith. And you are not the only one. I know that. When the Chetniks come they don't ask who says their prayers and who doesn't or who is a true Muslim and who isn't. As soon as they hear your name they'll want to kill you. Oh, brother, I wonder if these people will ever come to their senses,' Asim said. 'I'm off now. I am going to pray. Good night everyone.'

And off Asim went to his room on the second floor.

We stayed a bit longer and discussed faith. My Aunt Mina said that the village of Luka had always been known for its men who didn't drink or make *rakija*. The younger generation, however, had started doing both of those things. 'The youth', Mina said, 'drink and gamble and even make *rakija*. They do whatever they want.'

Then my father told us about his first visit to Luka in the 1950s after my Aunt Mina had married. The family had arrived on foot from Stoborani. He remembered how the first thing they had to do when they arrived was to participate in a joint prayer. There could be no exception. They had to recite a prayer first and then dinner was offered. That was a long time ago, and this custom had all but disappeared.

I had learned a lot about our religion from my grandparents. I used to stay with them in Zvornik when I was a small boy before I started school. The old mosque was across the street from their house. When I was five they would wake me up almost every morning to take me there. I would sit in a circle with other children. The imam recited the Quran, and we counted prayers with an enormous *tasbih*, a string of prayer beads, repeating 'Amen, amen, amen'. After the prayer the imam would give us each a hot flatbread, a *lepinja*. I would take it home and eat it for breakfast. That is all I remember. When I was old enough to go to school I went back to Srebrenica and forgot almost everything I had learned.

But maybe I missed the old mosque. Once, when my father took me to a café in Srebrenica, I wandered off without him noticing. He panicked when he realized I was missing, and everybody went to look for me. Right across from the café there was a mosque, an old wooden one. My father noticed that there was a pair of small shoes among all the large ones lined up in front of it and found me inside sitting in a corner and keenly watching the adults praying.

And then, almost twenty years later, as a refugee trying to escape slaughter, I asked myself if that had all been wrong. Had we been leading the wrong kind of life? And did it matter now anyway?

FIRST DESCENT INTO THE DRINA VALLEY

July went by at the very edge of Bosnia, and we were still alive.

Every day the tank on the opposite side of the river fired five or six shells at us with regular pauses in between, as though wanting to remind us that it was still there. Apart from that Luka was relatively safe. To the south, behind the mountain, was Žepa. Its villages were well organized, and the Chetniks were still recovering from their catastrophic defeat in June. The greatest danger to Luka came from the west, where there were a handful of Serb villages. But these were pretty far away, maybe twenty-five kilometres or so. Men from Luka kept watch on that side.

I felt embarrassed seeing groups of them alternate watch duty. They would walk for two hours to reach lookout points on the mountain, spend a night or two there, then another group would relieve them. I felt the urge to go with them, but I wasn't called for duty for some time.

We were almost relaxed in Luka, but the lack of food was becoming ever more life-threatening. When our daily milk stopped coming from Aunt Mina, my mother and I walked up to the mountain several times to scrounge off other villagers. With what milk we were given and what little cornmeal we still had, the four of us were on the brink of starvation. The locals were better off – they were farmers and had sheep, cows and chickens as well as their own supplies of milk, eggs, flour, cooking oil and sugar.

Sometime at the beginning of July my father and I paid a visit to Kadrija Begić, our neighbour in Luka. He was one of the most respected people in the area, and we were not surprised to find that a group of men were already gathered. Several of them had arrived in Luka to visit their families – some had come from Žepa and others from Srebrenica. We learned from them that the Žepa fighters had repelled another Chetnik attack. This time the Chetniks had come with several hundred soldiers and two tanks. The battle lasted a few hours. With what weapons and ammunition they had our forces had put up a strong resistance. The Chetniks had failed to break through and suffered heavy losses. The IDs of the dead Chetniks showed that some of them were from Prijedor in north-western Bosnia. This was alarming, as it meant that Karadžić was sending in an army with soldiers from far away. Well, relatively far away, but the fact was that people had come from the opposite side of the country to kill or be killed in Žepa.

One of those killed was our friend and erstwhile head of the Vlasenica police Fadil Turković. After our failed attempt to escape Bosnia Fadil had retreated to Žepa and assumed command of the town's defences. In the heat of the most recent assault Commander Turković had tried to capture a tank. The tank's machine gun had cut him in half. Despite his death Žepa had proved to be a stumbling block for the Chetniks once again. A quantity of weapons and ammunition had been seized.

'Our forces in Srebrenica were very well organized,' one man said, sitting with a machine gun between his legs. 'We consolidated our positions around the town in no time – and we didn't stop there.' He told us how he'd captured the machine gun single-handedly during a battle, approaching a Chetnik bunker and grabbing the machine gun with one hand while throwing a grenade into the bunker with the other. The soldiers in the bunker were killed, but the machine gun was not damaged. 'We attacked the Chetniks' mortars and artillery positions, and we chased them away. We all respect Naser as our commander. In Sućeska the main man is Zulfo.'

'Zulfo?' I asked a man sitting next to me.

'Zulfo Tursunović,' he replied. 'He's a big man, over sixty but doesn't look his age. Twenty years ago he killed two men in a bar and did time for it. Two brothers jumped him – I guess they were all drunk – but Zulfo had a knife and ripped their bowels open. People were leaping out of the window they were so afraid. That's Zulfo for you.'

'When did he get out of prison?' I asked.

'Oh, not so long ago. They say he was in Foča. They say he did time with Alija.'

'Alija Izetbegović?'

'Yeah!'

'What? He knew Alija?' different voices asked.

'Eh, Zulfo, he's a tough one,' the man continued. 'Nobody dares refuse an order he gives. Zulfo thrashes anyone who refuses to do his duty. People will take any duty rather than the alternative of waiting for Zulfo to pay them a visit at home.'

I thought: What a dangerous man this Zulfo is, but discipline obviously doesn't work without people like him.

Kadrija's wife filled our cups with coffee – which, of course, was not made from coffee but from roasted barley grains. It tasted a little like coffee, though. Some of the men lit cigarettes. I watched as they started rolling their own with newspaper. One of them offered tobacco to my father, and he eagerly dipped his hand into the pouch asking, 'Where did you get this from?'

'It's not impossible to find, you know – people still have it. It seems that in some villages people planted tobacco before the war. You can buy it at the Srebrenica market for a hundred marks a kilo, but it's getting more expensive by the day.'

I wasn't offered a smoke, and I was too ashamed to ask for one. I would have been ashamed to smoke it in front of my father anyway, so it didn't matter. I was glad that my father had had a chance to smoke a cigarette or two. While the rest of them enjoyed their caffeine-free coffee and puffed on their smokes, I was imagining Zulfo Tursunović somewhere in the distance, behind the mountains, establishing in his way order all around him.

'Sorry,' my father said to an old acquaintance from Srebrenica, 'but how did you get here from Srebrenica?'

'Along the river,' the man said.

My father and I exchanged astonished looks.

'What do you mean *along the river*?'

'Well, there's a man with a boat. He brought us along the river to Luka. It took us the whole night.'

We couldn't believe what we were hearing.

'You can't do it by land, you know that? The last group that tried to make it over the mountain – a caravan of women and children – the Chetniks killed them all.'

He was referring to a group that had set off from Luka several days earlier. We had no idea they had been killed.

'The Serbs waited in ambush,' he said. 'They know it's the only land route between here and Srebrenica. The river is safer.'

'Listen,' my father said, 'do you think I could go with you? Is there any room left in that boat of yours? I need to buy some wheat in Srebrenica. We've completely run out of food.'

'Ibro . . .' he hesitated. 'All right, but only because it's you. I swear I wouldn't do it for anyone else. You know you'll have to walk ten, maybe fifteen, kilometres from Klotijevac. You should try the villages around Srebrenica. You're well known there.'

'I've got some money left,' my father said. I knew that more than half of the money we had brought from Vlasenica had gone. We might have had about five hundred Deutschmarks left.

'Two hundred marks will buy you a hundred kilos of corn,' the man said.

'All right, I'll go!'

'We leave at dawn. Be ready.'

My father's decision to embark upon such an adventure terrified me. The three of us spent the whole night trying to dissuade him, but his mind was made up. There was no other way, he said, for us to survive. Something had to be done – we had no more flour and couldn't get any in Luka. Wheat and corn could not be grown in the mountain regions, so Luka and Žepa were doomed to starvation. The lowlands along the Drina, around Srebrenica and Bratunac, had been cultivated with wheat and corn for years, mainly as cattle feed.

Once again we said our goodbyes. Once again we were convinced that we would not see my father return. He must have been of the same opinion, otherwise he would have taken me or Braco with him.

We lived in anguish for four days. On the fifth day he appeared early in the morning. He had managed to buy a fifty-kilogram sack of corn but couldn't carry it up the hill. He was helped by a man who had travelled with him on the boat. I ran out of the house just as the man threw the sack to the ground. He was sweating from carrying it.

His eyes widened when he saw me. 'Ibro,' he gasped, 'this can't be your son, can it?' He turned to me. 'Come on, do I look like a donkey to you? You're lying in, and I'm delivering your corn to your doorstep!'

I still clearly remember his long hair, unkempt and dirty, and his long beard. His shirt was almost completely unbuttoned, and there was sweat running down his chest. His arms were covered in bulging veins and lean muscles. He looked ready for anything. He looked capable of coping with anything and anyone, even under our wartime circumstances. I didn't know what to say to him, and I expected him to slap me at any moment.

'Please, don't be angry,' my father said to him. 'Nobody knew when I'd come back. I had no way of letting them know.'

The man swore at all of us, took up his own sack and left. My father sat down. He was drenched in sweat. It seemed that the adventure had been too much for him. He was twice my age. He had lost more weight in the past few days, and his complexion had darkened. This was no doubt because of the sun, but it seemed to me a symptom of fatigue.

'I was scared to death', he said as he started recounting his unthinkable journey, 'while we were on the river. That was the worst part.'

My father had been fortunate to find an old colleague willing to sell the fifty-kilogram sack of corn for the 'good' price of two hundred Deutschmarks, which was comparatively cheap. 'People didn't really want to sell me any grain,' my father told us. 'If they did they asked for gold not money. Then I had to wait two days for a boat back. The boatmen were waiting for more customers to earn more from the trip. All the while the Chetniks were shelling the place from the opposite side of the river. I took cover between houses, crawled through the grass. I ran into one of the Srebrenica commanders – they call him Lieutenant Nedžad. He used to be an officer in the JNA. He wanted to attack the Chetniks in Serbia! While I was there he was planning to swim across with his men, climb the cliff and shoot at the Chetniks from behind. He would have done it, too, but he couldn't find enough volunteers.'

My father took a tobacco pouch from his pocket and started rolling a cigarette. 'I was given a bit of tobacco for free,' he said as he lit up. 'The journey along the river is terrible. God forbid that anyone should have to go through what I've just been through.'

THE SLAUGHTER IN VIŠEGRAD

One morning during that summer a man we didn't know appeared from the valley as we were sitting in front of my aunt's house. The man was thin, pale and exhausted. He looked only half alive and moved very slowly, leaning on a walking stick. We all jumped up to help him – it looked as though he was going to keel over. He sat on a bench and asked for water. It took him a long time to catch his breath. We waited in silence to hear who he was and where he was from.

He had fled from Višegrad. The Chetniks had locked him inside a house with a group of women and children. They had forced them into the house, locked it from the outside and set it on fire. He had managed to jump out of a window. He thought that one of the women had also jumped out holding a child, but he couldn't be sure if she had managed to escape – he had kept low and not looked back. For three days he hid in the tall grass in a field overlooking the river, too frightened to move. For three days he watched as the Chetniks brought more and more people to the old bridge, cut their throats and threw their bodies into the river.

'My hair,' he stammered, 'my hair turned white watching that.'

On the third day he plucked up the courage to move. 'I crawled through the grass, and when night fell I left the riverbank and entered the forest. I wandered for days along the river, through torched Muslim villages. If I'm alive it's thanks to the many abandoned cows. I milked the cows and have had nothing but raw milk to eat or drink for days.' We gave him some cornbread. After he had rested he said he was going to walk to Žepa. He was hoping to find other Višegrad refugees there.

It was not the only tale of slaughter we would hear. Already by this stage of the war it was clear that we could expect nothing less if we were ever to fall into Chetnik hands.

THE WOUNDED

At the beginning of August the Chetniks launched a new offensive against Žepa, and the whole area was shelled for several days. Our side of the mountain reverberated with the dull echo of detonations, and every now and then the ground would tremble under our feet. I wondered what kind of weapon could shake mountains. The attack had been launched after a small group of our fighters had climbed up to the top of Veliki Žep and surprised the crew of the military installation, capturing eleven of them. They had also taken six ground-to-air missiles.

'They're Strela missiles,' reported a man who had been involved in the raid. Several of the fighters had come to Luka to rest. 'They're portable and fired from the shoulder with a range of 3,500 metres.' He said that the prisoners had been taken somewhere else on the mountain and described the situation in Žepa. 'There are lots of dead and wounded civilians. Heavy artillery fire is coming from all sides. Meanwhile, the eleven prisoners are up on the mountain, alive and well, so we sent a radio message to the Chetniks' commander saying we would start killing them one at a time if the shelling doesn't stop.'

'That's just negotiating tactics,' said another fighter. 'We didn't touch them. Our guys even spit-roasted a lamb for them.'

'So have the Chetniks stopped shelling? I haven't heard any explosions since yesterday,' I asked.

'They did, yes. An exchange is being negotiated as we speak. Twenty tons of flour for the hungry people of Žepa and two tons of fuel, and then the eleven prisoners will be released,' he explained.

A few days later we learned that the exchange had taken place in a Muslim village close to Han Pijesak called Krivače. Despite the great risk, Bosnian Muslims continued living in the area, protected only by means of a barricade on the road that had to be removed temporarily for the exchange. But the Chetniks launched another attack as soon as the barricade was removed. Artillery shells once more began to land all over the Žepa area. Soon most of the villages had fallen.

Panic broke out among the people again. One day a group of refugees appeared in Luka. They had come across the mountain. This time the explosions were not just a distant echo; the shelling seemed to be getting closer.

The men from Luka organized the lookouts, and once more I wasn't called. I wasn't the only one left out, but it didn't feel good all the same. I started to get suspicious looks, or so I thought.

Then, one morning, amid the incessant sound of explosions, several trucks appeared in Luka and parked in the centre of the village. We gathered to see what was going on. The armed Žepa fighters were taking the wounded off the trucks. When they'd finished there were about fifteen wounded men on improvised stretchers on the ground beside the vehicles.

'What happened to you?' I asked.

Some of them scowled at me, but one smiled, saying, 'You must be . . . Nuhanović? From Stoborani?' I said that my father was from Stoborani, but the guy clearly recognized me from somewhere. He looked about twenty. His arm was behind his head as he lay on the stretcher, and he was chewing a piece of straw. He was wrapped with the kind of blanket that peasants call a horse blanket. I thought it odd that he was wrapped in a blanket because, although it was early in the morning, it was warm. Then I realized that something wasn't right with his legs. It took me some time to register that he was missing one of his feet. I was shocked and confused. Nothing in his demeanour suggested the anxiety, fatigue or fear visible on the faces of the other wounded men.

I started wondering how I would act in his situation. His hair looked freshly trimmed – a smart haircut, nothing like what I would have imagined. What I imagined was probably a distillation of images from all the war films I'd ever seen: people with typhus, sweaty, dirty, dishevelled.

'Well, we're kind of related,' he said. 'My grandmother married into a Stoborani family.'

'I'm sorry, I have a lot of relatives around the local villages,' I said, 'and I don't know everyone by name.'

'Listen up, everyone,' a big guy with an automatic rifle on his shoulder shouted over the commotion. 'The wounded need to be carried down to the river urgently! There are boats waiting for them. The doctor did what was possible under the circumstances, but now they're going to the hospital in Srebrenica. Naser Orić has said we should send them all there. Some of them have gangrene. They have to go now or they won't survive. The trucks are going back to Žepa; the wounded down to the river.'

Four men were needed per stretcher, and over fifty volunteered. I volunteered, although there was no time to let my family know. This was my first descent down into the valley. There were Chetniks on the opposite bank, and descents were often made at night. Getting the stretchers across the rough ground wasn't easy, especially not for four inexperienced stretcher-bearers who stumbled all the time. On several occasions I nearly fell, but I used all the strength I could muster to keep the wounded man from tipping off. The further down we went, the more difficult it became to keep him safely on the stretcher. Being a makeshift stretcher its poles were made from rough branches that cut into my shoulder. The terrain became steeper and rockier, and I found it increasingly hard to keep my balance. In some places the descent would have been difficult enough even without carrying anything, let alone another human being. Sweat was running down my back and forehead. I noticed that the other stretcher-bearers could hardly stand.

We had been going for two hours when I heard the man on my stretcher asking, 'How much longer until we reach the river?' His voice was trembling – with fear, I thought.

'I have no idea. I've never been down there before. This is my first time,' I said.

'An hour or so,' my fellow stretcher-bearer put in. 'Normally it doesn't take this long, but now . . .'

'Do the Chetniks shoot from those rocks there?' the wounded man asked.

'They do if they notice someone. But don't worry. It's not as bad as it sounds. We'll manage somehow. We won't all go at once. We couldn't even if we wanted to because . . . You'll see, once we arrive at Grđenj there isn't a path any more.'

'What do you mean there isn't a path?' the injured man asked desperately.

'There are just rocks for a hundred, maybe two hundred metres to the water's edge. Only wild goats can climb down. But we'll manage; we just need to go slowly and watch our step. It's important to tread carefully so we don't slip.'

The man who had explained it all so well was a local; he would know. But instead of calming the agitated mind of the wounded fighter he alarmed him even more. Some of the wounded started crying aloud, whether from pain or fear I couldn't tell.

'Shush! Quiet,' one of the guides chided.

At the end of the steep rocky track Grđenj appeared in all its ugliness. It looked like a big bowl of jagged rocks. You knew there was water at the bottom, but you couldn't see it unless you leaned right over the cliff edge. We put the stretchers down for a few minutes before starting our next descent. We were sitting ducks. I glanced over to the opposite side of the gorge, worried that the Chetniks might start shooting at us.

The big guy with the automatic rifle on his shoulder appeared in front of us again. He and three other men were our armed escort. They went to check the way down and quickly came back. 'This won't be possible with the stretchers,' he said. 'No way. We have to carry the wounded without the stretchers, any way we can.'

The sobbing started again. I could only imagine how terrified they were, and no wonder.

The strongest among us were chosen. I wasn't in that group and was told to go back.

I stood on the edge of the cliff watching a new tragic episode in the exodus of the wretched. I wondered how they would make it to Srebrenica, how much more they would have to suffer. They were trying bravely not to make any noise.

DEATH FROM THE SKY

It took me at least two hours to get back. Just before I entered the village I spotted a spring flowing directly from the rock. Sweaty and thirsty as I was, I kneeled down and let the water flow directly into my mouth. The water was so cold that I felt dizzy and weak for a moment. In a matter of hours my throat was sore, and I felt mucus running down it. I wasn't able to get out of bed for several days. I felt so ill that my mother decided to give me one of the two penicillin ampoules she kept in her purse. She said she'd been saving them in case one of us got injured. I drank the penicillin directly from the ampoule – it was as bitter as poison. I had to lie in bed with a direct view of the meadow where I knew the tank was sitting. At regular intervals it was still firing shells that exploded in and around the village. Once I shouted at it, 'Just you fire, you son of a bitch!' Much of the time I slept – my dreams were feverish – but someone brought me a copy of *Wuthering Heights* to read as I lay there, and for a few days I was transported from war-torn Bosnia to the Yorkshire moors.

As soon as I had recovered enough to stand on my own I went for a walk. I actually dragged myself. My heart was pounding like crazy, but I wanted to find out if the attack on Žepa was still going on. I could hear explosions, but nobody knew how far the Chetniks had got.

I found Uncle Asim in his garden sitting in front of a chessboard. He said, 'You had too long a lie-in. Have you slept enough now? We've almost gathered in all the hay.'

'You know I've been unwell. I was pretty sick,' I said, trying to justify my inactivity.

'It's all right. You couldn't help it. I've lined up the chess pieces, and they're waiting for you. Black or white?'

Between mid-June and mid-August, before I got sick, Asim and I had played chess quite regularly. He was much better than me and led by a large margin, but that didn't mean that he took defeat graciously. On the rare occasions I beat him he became quite angry. His hands would start shaking once he realized that he was going to lose. He would mutter, 'Dear me,' but he never cursed – Uncle Asim was known for never cursing.

So I watched Asim – the black French beret on his head, the walking stick resting against his knee – thinking before making his next move as if his life depended on it. Suddenly I heard a rumble from the sky. When the sound grew louder and more intense we both looked up. I thought I saw a glint of metal between the clouds. Several tiny points were rapidly approaching from Serbia, from across the Drina, moving out of sight behind Mount Javor. We exchanged glances.

'Planes,' I said.

'So it seems,' Asim replied.

'They went to Žepa.'

'I guess so.'

Then it was silent again. We looked at each other and at the chessboard. Asim moved a piece and said, 'Check.'

'You wrong-footed me,' I said.

Asim's face beamed. He was glad that I was cornered. I could see he was preparing to checkmate.

Boom. Boom. The sound of explosions reached us. The sound of an air strike is different from the sound of shells. It's deeper and heftier. It triggers a visceral panic.

'They're bombing Žepa,' I said.

'I think so,' Asim replied, studying the chessboard.

'Good that they flew over us; they won't bomb us,' I said, delivering a variation of the utterance so often heard during the war: *good that it's them and not us.* This reveals the self-centred nature of humans: I come before everything and everybody else.

'I guess they won't,' Asim said, thinking about how to deliver the final blow. All of sudden all hell broke loose. A deafeningly loud noise filled the air as a bomb struck somewhere very close to the village, raising a cloud of dust and smoke. The ground trembled beneath our feet, and all the chess pieces scattered across the grass. We jumped up and ran behind the house. Everywhere people were scattering, seeking shelter. Asim and I went inside. While he was praying for our salvation I dared to open the door and look up at the sky. The aeroplanes circled above the village dropping the deadly 250-kilogram 'krmače' ('pigs'). After half an hour they flew back to Serbia – for a fresh load, I guessed – and then returned to bombard us for another half an hour.

I am not sure whether it was more frightening just standing there waiting for them to come back or listening to the ear-splitting explosions. We felt totally powerless.

When they'd left after the first thirty-minute bombing the village was painfully silent. Every time we began to hope that it was over, the thunder of the planes came back along with a new series of explosions that lasted for exactly half an hour. This was followed by another half-hour of blood-curdling silence, and then it began all over again. They came six times that day, which meant we suffered three hours of intense bombing. During the breaks we had to run to the latrine. As soon as you entered someone would come banging impatiently at the door.

Afterwards it was suggested that the villagers should retreat to the caves above the village if they returned the next day. I remembered someone pointing the caves out to me in the distance. They looked like holes drilled in the rocks.

I sat on the wooden fence above the village and looked out towards Serbia, from where all this violence was emanating. I wondered whether the Serb pilots hated us. I assumed they could see where their bombs were falling. Did they ever think about those on whom those bombs would fall? Did they know that little children were among us? What had they been told about this in their military bases in Serbia? What kind of hatred could cause this? What kind of propaganda?

During the night I heard people shouting outside, but with no electricity I couldn't see a thing in the moonless night. Roaming in the dark I ran into a group of men heading to Šarena Bukva where the barricades were located and lookouts posted. They expected an attack from the Serb village of Podravanje, given the air strikes and the major attack launched against Žepa's villages. 'If they pass that way', somebody said, 'there will be nothing to stop them from entering Luka. They just have to go down the hill. We'd have nowhere to run.' Someone else noted that the river would be our only escape in that case. He laughed as though it were a joke, but no one found it funny. They told me that every man in possession of a weapon was to join them, but I noticed that half of them were empty-handed.

I snuck back into the house. My parents were still awake.

'Will you give me your pistol?' I asked my father. He looked at me in silence.

It was my mother who asked, 'Hasko, why do you need a gun?'

'I'm going to keep watch with the others at the barricade.'

'You want to get killed? What if they attack from Podravanje?' my father asked.

'You know what,' I replied, 'it's much likelier I'll get killed here if the planes come back tomorrow.'

'We'll be safe in the caves. People used to hide there during the war,' my father said, referring to the Second World War. 'We hid there from the Chetniks before; we'll hide there from the Chetniks again.'

'Yes, you'll be safe there,' I said. 'You should take enough food for a few days and blankets and warm clothes. Come on now. Give me that pistol. I have to be up at five.'

My father relented and gave me his handgun, which was wrapped in a piece of cloth. My mother gave me a piece of bread and a tin of sardines that she had been hiding since April. She also added a piece of *pita*.

Not so much as a 'Take care' was said. I knew why. They didn't want to jinx me. I was glad that Braco was going to stay with them and hoped I was right about the caves being safe.

ŠARENA BUKVA

Early the next morning I met two other guys in the village, and together we hurried up the steep hillside in the direction of the barricades. Every so often I would look back at the Drina valley behind us. If the planes came back they would not see the three of us up here. We'd be safe, but they'd bomb the village. The thought of my own safety was set against the thought of everyone else in harm's way. It was possible that I might never see my family again. They might be thinking the same about me.

After nearly two hours of hiking we came upon a few huts and decided to take a break. We were still a kilometre from the barricades. I was hungry, but, unsure of how long I would be away, I was saving my food. Then we heard the planes. We rushed into the woods, convinced that the thick forest of pine, spruce and fir would conceal and protect us. Judging from the sounds the planes split into two formations. We soon heard explosions coming from Žepa. We thought that our side of the mountain was safe and that the few huts here wouldn't be considered a worthwhile target.

We were wrong. A group of planes, or maybe it was just a single pilot, decided to unload its deadly cargo on us. We ran deeper into the forest thinking that we would be safer there. I lost sight of my two companions. When the first explosion shook the ground I hugged the nearest tree and closed my eyes. *Fizz.* Please God, please God, don't let it fall on me. *Wham.* The entire forest shook. So there were two, I thought to myself. How many more has he got? Maybe two or three? I scanned my surroundings for shelter. There was a hollow in a nearby rock. It was cramped, dark, damp and probably crawling with insects. There was no way I would have ever entered it before the war, but now I ran and crawled inside feet first. I covered my head with both my arms and closed my eyes again. *Wham.*

'How many bombs have you got, you bastards!'

A squirrel scurried across the ground beside me. It stood upright and made short work of an acorn in its front paws. What did this small creature think of the bombs?

'Hasko! Hasko!' Somebody was calling my name. One of my companions found me. 'Look at him!' he laughed. 'He's found himself a hole. Are you a man or a mouse?'

I pulled myself out of the hollow and brushed the dirt off my jeans. I listened for the sound of the planes. Nothing.

'Come on, let's go. The planes left half an hour ago,' my companion said.

'I was so afraid I didn't even notice I couldn't hear them any longer,' I said.

'I was afraid, too. Who wouldn't be? But we have to be at the barricades at nine.'

We came to an assembly point. There were around fifty men waiting. Except for a few middle-aged men and one who looked like he was about sixty, we were all under thirty years old. I was impressed because throughout the whole summer the villagers hadn't been able to agree on where best to position lookouts or the number of people needed to keep watch. Most of the men were locals. They were leaning against trees or lying beside the gravel road. There was a tarpaulin tent, the only indication of a place of assembly for guards. On the right-hand side of the road the earth suddenly disappeared. As I would see later, this was the edge of a precipice with a drop of several hundred metres. Crni Potok, or Black Stream, lay at the bottom. Mount Tara was opposite. On the left-hand side of the road a steep forested slope led to a plateau on top of the mountain. The gravel road, winding through the woods, led to the Serb villages and on to Srebrenica.

'You're here,' said a big guy who was clearly in charge. 'You'll be in my group. Now, fall in and let's see how many we are and how many weapons we've got.'

We formed two lines. The commander read our names from a list, ordering us to state, one at a time, whether we had a weapon and, if so, what type.

'A pistol, a CZ 7.65,' I said when it was my turn. 'It's my father's gun,' I added.

Half the group didn't have a weapon of any kind, just as I had expected.

'All right,' our commander said. 'Those who arrived this morning will stay here until the day after tomorrow. The rest of you are relieved.' Then he passed by both lines, taking weapons from the men who were leaving and redistributing them to those about to go on watch. 'Anyone without a weapon, here, you'll take these. You two take the shotguns. You take the automatic rifle and you take the semi-automatic. The shotguns take two cartridges, and each of you will get two more. The automatic rifles have one magazine apiece.'

I looked around. There were about fifteen of us with five weapons and no ammunition to speak of. What could we actually do in case of an attack?

'You're Hasan if I remember correctly?' the commander asked me. 'Given that this is your first time you'd better come with me.'

He told me he wanted to show me something and led me down the road. The barricades came into view around the bend. About two hundred metres of the road was blocked with enormous trees.

'Well done,' I said. 'It would take them at least two hours to clear this for the APCs and tanks to pass.'

'Don't count on it, mate,' the commander said. 'They're well equipped and quick. They bring chainsaws. Don't count on this stopping them. Besides, the infantry would get to you before that. But this is what I wanted to show you . . .' He disappeared behind a tree and came back carrying a small box wrapped in black foil. 'This device stays here at all times. When the Chetniks arrive you're to hide behind a tree, and when a tank or an APC comes close enough you throw it at them. But first you have to activate it. See this?' he said showing me a string hanging from the device. 'This is the fuse, you have to light it, but don't wait too long to throw it or it'll explode in your hand.'

While he was explaining this to me I was thinking: No way am I going to wait for a tank behind this tree, let alone throw an explosive from two metres away. My dear commander, I sincerely doubt you'll find anyone crazy enough to do it. If the Chetniks attack the trees on the road will slow them down just enough for us to run to the village and warn everyone to flee into the forest.

'OK. Got it,' I said.

'That's it then. I'm going back to Luka now. I'll see you in two days. And, oh, that's a nice weapon you've got,' he said, looking at the pistol stuck in the waistband of my jeans.

'It's my father's handgun; never been fired. He let me borrow it for a few days. I have to give it back,' I said.

'OK. Tell your father to let me know if he ever wants to trade it for food. I have wheat, potatoes and prunes,' the commander said and left.

Pistols were highly appreciated during the war – something I didn't know at the time but would learn later. People were ready to pay top money for a good handgun.

We had a quiet night. The clear summer sky was beautiful and full of stars. We could hear the rumble of the Serb multiple rocket launchers firing bursts of missiles at the Muslim villages on the other side of the mountain. A fierce battle was going on. People were being killed. I wondered whether I should consider myself lucky that I was here and not there. My fellow fighters had built a fire, and half of them fell asleep before midnight. I asked them if the fire might give away our position to the enemy, but they said that the Chetniks surely already knew we were here and that the nights were very cold on the mountain. They were right. Although it was August it was so cold I had to stay by the fire. I didn't really sleep much.

Far away to the east I could see a glow across the valley, somewhere over in Serbia. I was told the light was coming from the memorial to the Partisans of the Workers' Battalion killed during the Battle of Kadinjača in 1941. I had seen the movie about this battle, *The Užice Republic*, at least ten times. As well the German occupiers and Yugoslav Partisans, the film also featured Chetniks. Now, in this war, I thought, there are no Germans, just Chetniks. Actually, given their tanks and weapons, the Chetniks are now what the Germans were then. And who are we then? We must be Partisans.

Looking towards the lights I nodded off briefly. For a moment it seemed as if I were sitting on the plateau illuminated by flood-lights, holding a cigarette. I lit the cigarette and pulled on it with enormous satisfaction. All of a sudden music started somewhere. I heard applause. And then I woke up. It was a pleasant dream but way too short.

Man, it had been such a long time since I'd had a cigarette! I was desperate for one, just one! I'd noticed some of my comrades taking a pinch of tobacco directly from their pockets and rolling cigarettes almost in secret. Nobody offered, and I was too ashamed to ask.

After midnight our shift commander came back and ordered me and another guy to take the automatic rifles and stand guard some hundred metres away from the assembly point. Our task was to wake the others up if we heard anything unusual. We couldn't see anything but trees. We stared into the pitch-black night knowing that the Serb village was further down the road and Serb forces somewhere on the other side of the mountain.

I didn't know my companion's name, but I noticed he was a bit of an odd one. First of all he was wearing a light shirt, and the cold didn't seem to bother him. For footwear he wore rubber boots cut off below the ankles so they had no support. I could see he didn't have any socks on. I was fully dressed and still shivering. At first I felt sorry for him, thinking how destitute he must have been, but he never complained, not once. He held his rifle so close to him that it seemed he couldn't wait to use it. The events of the next day convinced me that he was even stranger than I could possibly have imagined – of which more later.

At some point before dawn we heard strange animal noises coming from the forest. Both of us were afraid and aimed our rifles towards the trees.

'Oh God, I hope it's not a bear,' I said, while praying for a bear rather than a Chetnik. When it was clear the sounds were coming closer I threw a heavy rock into the trees, and it rolled down the slope towards the noise, which stopped for a moment then started up again, this time even closer to us. I jumped up and yelped in fright, 'You stay here. I'll wake the rest of them up', and ran to the shelter and roused everybody. We all shot back as fast as we could, thinking that a bear or a Chetnik might have already killed the man who had stayed behind in the dark. For a moment I couldn't believe my eyes. What I saw was an enormous black beast and the weird guy standing next to each other as if they were friends. The rest of the men burst out laughing. The beast was a large black ox.

'See what it's come to,' somebody lamented. 'Cattle are roaming the forest like wild animals. Who knows where this ox came from?'

'Must be from Podžeplje or from Krivače. People got out of there as fast as they could and left everything behind,' somebody answered.

'Ah, what a feast we're going to have tomorrow,' they all agreed. 'Should we slaughter it here or take it to Luka?'

I refused my share of the meat. I have no idea how it was distributed in the end, but, given that I didn't see the ox the next morning, somebody must have taken it to Luka – somebody who thought that was more important than fulfilling his guard duty.

In the morning a new group joined us – five or six men with a few hunting rifles. They had arrived from Žepa where, they said, there was a real war going on with the Chetniks attacking from all sides. The country was on fire and people were fleeing in large groups towards Luka with the intention of reaching Srebrenica. 'Žepa is about to fall. Everybody knows it, but the fighters won't give up. The Chetnik infantry couldn't get through; they must have suffered a lot of casualties, too,' said one, while another added, 'We were sent here because the Žepa fighters are worried about an attack from the direction of Šarena Bukva. Something needs to change – instead of passively waiting we should be sending reconnaissance patrols deeper into Serb-controlled territory. We can learn if an attack is being planned, and then we can react in time.'

When he asked for volunteers to go on a patrol to Stublić I whispered to the guy next to me 'Where's Stublić?'

'About three kilometres down the road, halfway to Podravanje. The Chetniks sometimes patrol there. That means our patrol is likely to meet their patrol. I don't think I want to go,' he said.

The newcomer asked again, 'Any volunteers? Or should the commander decide?'

I was the first to volunteer. I surprised myself by raising my hand. It was as if somebody else had spoken on my behalf. Almost immediately I regretted it.

The group turned to me.

'OK. Nuhanović, right? Here's your weapon,' the shift commander said handing me a shotgun, 'and here're the two spare shells.'

I took the shells. Next, my companion from the previous night spoke up. 'I'll go, too.'

Great, I thought to myself. He's the last person in the world I want with me right now. All morning he'd been giving me dirty looks, evidently unable to forgive me for abandoning him the way I had. And he was right; I had behaved like a coward.

The next to volunteer was the oldest among us, the only man who looked over sixty, but his white hair belied a sharp mind and lively manner. When he got his firearm – he insisted that he be given an automatic rifle or he wouldn't go – he approached the oddball and me. 'I'll command the patrol,' he said. We didn't argue, first because of his age and second because he had a magazine containing thirty rounds.

We set off straight away. The weird guy led the way, and the older man and I followed him. I had no idea where Stublić was and thought we'd reach it in half an hour or so, but after thirty minutes all I could see in front of us were trees. At one point we crossed the road and continued through the forest again. It was difficult terrain with steep and uneven sections. It was uphill then downhill then uphill again. I was sweating. My two companions knew the area but said little about where we were going. I was anxious about running into Chetniks. The weirdo was clearly taking his part seriously. He showed no sign of fear. He would stop behind a tree and, without turning his head, signal that we should stop, too. He would look around and then signal for us to follow him. The older man was evidently tired. He ordered us to take a break several times, but our leader wouldn't have it. 'We move on. Follow me,' he would say. I was starting to think the guy was crazy, not just strange.

'Hey,' I called after him. 'Hey. Stop. Let's go back. Where is Stublić anyway? We've gone too far. We're just getting deeper into Serb territory.'

He rounded on me, and the next moment I was looking down the barrel of a shotgun. He jabbed the barrel into my neck, staring at me like a madman. 'One more word and you're dead,' he said.

'Wait, what are you doing? Are you two crazy?' the older man finally spoke up.

I was sure he was going to kill me. His shirt was half unbuttoned, and his flies were open.

'You're a traitor! You're a traitor!' he howled, jabbing me again with the barrel. This was much more than a sick joke.

'All right, let's move on,' I said, trying as best I could to defuse the situation.

He lowered the shotgun slowly and took a few steps back. 'Follow me and don't say another word,' he said.

I kept glancing at the older man, but he wouldn't look at me.

Ten minutes later we saw a collection of huts ahead of us. The odd guy tensed, began flitting from tree to tree. He signalled for us to do the same.

I looked all around me, at the rocks, at the forest, expecting to be fired on at any minute.

'Hey, maybe this is all mined,' I whispered, as they began to search the huts.

Nobody had been here for quite some time, that much was obvious. The huts were full of junk, and my companions started rummaging through it. The oddball took a metal chair without a seat and put it over his shoulder. Next he took an old hiking boot. 'It's good,' he said, looking at the older man for approval.

Unbelievable, I thought. These people are scavengers.

The old man found a concrete pipe that was thirty centimetres in diameter and about a metre long. 'We're going to need this,' he said, as he tried to pick it up. It was too heavy for him. He looked at me. 'Hey, you,' he said. 'Take this. We'll need it.'

Maybe we would need it at the barricades. Maybe we could fill it with explosives and make some sort of bomb out of it – that's what I thought anyway. I took the pipe and put it on my shoulder. It weighed at least twenty kilograms. With the shotgun in my other hand I wondered how quickly I could drop the pipe to defend myself if we were attacked.

The two of them kept looking for several more minutes before the weird one finally signalled to us to set off. The two of them chatted merrily on the way back. I could hardly catch my breath. I was already exhausted from the lack of sleep the night before, and the terrain was difficult enough without carrying the heavy pipe. We arrived at the lookout an hour later.

The others were lounging about on the grass. 'What's going on down there? What did you see? What's with the pipe?' they asked in unison.

The white-haired man sat down on the grass and put the rifle between his knees. 'Well, it was high time I got a drain for my latrine,' he said.

I threw the pipe to the ground. It landed with a thud. The others were laughing their heads off. They didn't know I'd had a shotgun at my throat not so long ago. You'll never see me up here again, I said to myself. I had lugged that concrete pipe through the woods, terrified I might be shot by Chetniks, so that an old idiot could finally have a drain for his toilet.

I sat on a tree stump waiting for the next shift to arrive so that I could leave that place for ever. The man was trying on the single hiking boot he had scavenged. He put it on without a sock.

ESCAPE THROUGH
THE GORGE

The next morning I left for Luka as soon as I could. It was downhill all the way, so it didn't take me long. There wasn't a soul in sight; I could hear only the cows and chickens. An old woman emerged from a cowshed. She froze when she saw me.

'Don't be afraid,' I said. 'It's me, Hasan. Ibro Nuhanović's son.'

'Eh, my lad,' the old woman said. 'How can I tell? For all I know you could be a Chetnik.'

'Do I really look like one? But where is everyone?'

'They're up there in the caves. I was with them as well. Yesterday the bombing didn't stop, but this morning I had to come back to feed my cow and give her some water.'

'How do I get to there?' I set off in the direction she described. The caves couldn't be seen from the village. You had to cross the field beyond the village and climb a steep rocky slope to spot them. Their entrances were extraordinary; huge circles cut into the rock face. Cold air hit me as I approached the first cave and with it the strong smell of damp. It was much cooler inside than out. As my eyes adjusted to the darkness I was able to make out the faces of my family.

My mother came towards me immediately. 'Hasko! Thank God!' she said. 'We didn't know if you were OK! It was really dangerous in the village yesterday. Planes . . . the whole day. But we were safe here. Are you hungry? Have you eaten anything?'

I said I'd eaten only what she had given me when I left and, yes, I was hungry. She gave me a piece of cornbread wrapped in cloth.

My father and brother were sitting in a corner, together with Uncle

Asim, who had his chessboard in front of him with the chess pieces in position.

'So this is what we have come to,' I said. 'If, God forbid, a bomb were to fall on the rock above the cave this would be your grave. You can't stay in here.'

'There're plenty of people in these caves,' my father said, 'including a group that came from Žepa. They say it's only a matter of days until the Chetniks enter Žepa. These people don't intend to stay here. They are looking for a boat to take them to Srebrenica.'

I took him aside and whispered, 'We should also pack up and leave. What do you think?'

I was afraid that Asim and his people would resent us for leaving without them, but the time had come once again for each family to think about its own priorities. There were people who put their heads together to find a common solution for their families. But, in keeping with the unwritten rule of wartime, nobody held a grudge against the other when it came to saving one's own. Each family had the right to choose its own fate.

'Let's see what's happening in the other caves and if anyone has found a ferryman yet. How much money have we got?' I asked.

'About five hundred,' he said.

'I'll ask around, see what other people think, but I don't think we've got much choice. If we are going to leave, we'd better start packing.'

My mother and Braco were both enthusiastic about the idea and agreed at once. Braco seemed permanently scared and anxious. After three months in Luka he finally reacted positively to a suggestion – to leave the place. Clearly he hoped things would be better in Srebrenica. We all did. That is, assuming we actually reached Srebrenica alive. Braco must have had this possibility in mind because I did. Not that it was ever mentioned out loud. Nobody wanted to add to anyone else's fears.

In one of the caves my father and I met a man called Osman. We learned from him that there would be two boats waiting at midnight. He didn't know how many people would come, but he was pretty sure we would be able to find room on one of them. The fee was per family, depending on the number of people, but even a single traveller had to pay fifty Deutschmarks.

Osman had arrived from Žepa with his mother, who was ill. He was a big man, and his mother was huge. She was so out of shape that she couldn't stand. They had made it to Luka with his mother on horseback and him leading the horse with a rope.

At dusk we went back to the village to pack and say goodbye to Asim and his family. I wouldn't see them again until after the war was over. It was their decision to stay, but I felt guilty for fleeing all the same. It looked as if we, the refugees, were abandoning the village and their hospitality for our own safety, as if we didn't care what might happen to them. But they had enough food for several months; we, on the other hand, were running dangerously short of supplies.

We packed in an hour, taking what remaining food we had and anything we could carry on our backs. Braco and I tried to make it as easy as possible for our parents. We set off down the steep slope. The night was beautiful, and there was a full moon. The moonlight meant that the Chetniks could see us, but on the plus side we could see where we were placing our feet. Two hours later we took a break behind a ledge covered in thick undergrowth which, unlike the surrounding bare rocks, gave you the secure feeling of being out of sight of those on the other side of the valley. We were totally exhausted – and the worst was still ahead of us. In the meantime, other groups were arriving. Some of them began the last leg of the descent without taking a break.

It was nearly eleven o'clock. 'We have to move,' I said. 'We have just over an hour to get to the boats. They won't wait for us – they don't even know we're coming.'

My mother cautiously approached the edge of the gorge. She glanced from the abyss to the three of us. From her expression I could tell she didn't believe it would be possible to go any further. I was sure she thought that this was more difficult than anything we'd been through so far. She was fighting back tears, not wanting to complicate an already difficult situation.

A few refugees passed us. They said they were from Žepa. 'What are you waiting for? The boat's leaving at midnight,' they added before disappearing from sight behind a rock below. Just a moment later we heard them again. This time they were almost crying. 'Sweet mother of God, we're going to die here! Help us, dear God!'

'Quiet! Quiet!' said another voice. 'The Chetniks will hear!'

Then Osman appeared through the dark. He was leading his horse by the reins, and his mother was sitting on its back. The poor woman was whimpering as Osman stopped and attempted to ease her down.

'The woman has got to weigh at least a hundred and fifty kilos,' I said to my father.

'Hush,' he hissed.

Osman managed to get his mother off the horse, and she sat on the ground. As he tried to explain the situation it was clear he was deeply afraid – a big man like him! He seemed to think the Chetniks had already broken through our lines and were marching towards us. He was desperate to get to the boats. To each of us on that cliff face that night Srebrenica seemed almost unreachable, and yet we all knew we had to reach it.

A surreal conversation between Osman and his mother was taking place. 'Mother, listen,' Osman said, 'the horse can't make it down the rocks. You can see how steep it is. So, well, I've taken you this far – and you know I would never abandon you – but I now have to get moving. If you can't make it any further you don't have to. You don't have to come.'

'Osman, what are you saying? Osman, don't leave me here,' his mother pleaded through tears.

At that moment a shell struck close by. The explosion was incredibly loud. Suddenly we all felt as though the Chetniks were at our heels.

Osman sprang to his feet. He looked ready to run down the cliff, a suicidal act unless he were to transform himself into a wild goat. There was a large pistol tucked into his belt. He put his backpack on, and the horse kicked and jerked aside, tearing the reins from his hands. 'I'm leaving,' he said. 'I have to go. What else can I do?'

His mother wept and begged him not to leave her. Osman took some money from his pocket and stuffed it into his mother's hands. 'Here's a hundred marks,' he said. 'I'll put you back on the horse. The horse knows its way to Luka. You'll be able to get back there and stay with the rest of them. Then whatever happens to them . . . will happen to you as well.'

We couldn't believe our ears. What was the war doing to people? We were unsure how wide the footholds down the cliff would be, so we left some of our belongings with Osman and his mother in the hope of being able to return and collect them. Braco and I carried our sacks of food on our backs towards the edge of the cliff. Our mother walked in front of us carrying her handbag and another small bag. Further ahead my father was peering into the dark for a path or something like one among all the rocks. I followed my parents down the side of the cliff. I tried to lean against the rock face for support, but the sack was getting in the way. I couldn't risk letting our food slip into the void below. I stumbled on something that felt like a trail. It was so narrow that in some places there wasn't enough space for a whole foot, and I had to choose between walking on my toes or my heels. Braco was right behind me. Our parents, just a few steps ahead, were crossing this part of the trail on all fours since they weren't carrying anything heavy. 'Don't look down! Don't look down!' my father repeated. Given his phobia of heights, he was probably saying it more to himself than to us.

At one point I couldn't find any support for my heel, and I had to stop. I was stuck, practically dangling from a 200-metre-high cliff. I could see the river at the bottom glittering in the moonlight. There was no way forward and no way back. I took a deep breath and stretched my leg as far as I could until my foot found hard ground. I took a step. I was covered in sweat. My jeans, stuck to my legs, made it even harder to walk. I took the sack from Braco with my left hand and handed it to my father with my right. Braco headed back for the rest of our belongings with his back against the rock wall. I, too, left my sack and followed Braco, who was now well ahead of me. This time I moved sideways with my face to the rock, feeling for the path with my right foot. I wanted to avoid looking down into the abyss. At one point I stepped on something soft. I thought it was a snake and was so scared I almost pushed myself off the cliff. Once I'd pulled myself together I realized it was Osman I had stood on – or, to be more precise, Osman's fat posterior. Blindly dragging himself backwards, he was forcing me off the trail.

'Hey, man! Stop!' I cried. 'What are you doing?' But Osman seemed not to hear me. Why he had elected to shuffle backwards on all fours, I don't know, but on a barely perceptible trail I could either wait for him to knock me over like a bowling pin or step over him. My position was getting more precarious by the second, and I grabbed Osman's shirt in desperation. This stopped him for a moment, which gave me a chance to step over him. As I was readying myself I suddenly saw the reason he was shuffling backwards: Osman was dragging his mother! But I had no choice – I was hovering over the abyss – I stepped on Osman's poor mother. She groaned under my weight while I stumbled on her dress and almost fell over her. Her thighs and buttocks must have been cut badly after being dragged along the rocks; the old woman was sobbing. I managed to regain my balance, found another foothold and caught up with Braco. We threw the rest of our belongings over our shoulders and set off again. Osman and his mother were still stuck on their arses.

At that moment a scream pierced the dark. I recognized my mother's voice. I was sure that Osman had pushed her the same way he had pushed me. In my mind I could see her falling into the depths.

My only real weapon, the old bayonet from Stoborani, was still hanging on my belt, and I pulled it from its sheath and swung it through the air. 'I'll kill you!' I shouted at Osman through sobs. 'You killed my mother!' Osman's frightened eyes flashed in the dark – he had stopped dragging his mother and let go of her ankles. With the bayonet in my hand I was ready to step on the poor woman again to attack Osman on that narrow rocky trail two hundred metres above the Drina. Osman froze. He didn't even try to reach for his handgun. I was about to lunge at him.

And then my mother's voice, 'Hasko! Hasko! I'm down here!'

It was as if a bucket of cold water had been poured over my head. 'Where are you? Where are you?' I cried out.

'Hasko, she's down there. I can see her,' my father sobbed.

Leaning over the edge a little I could see, just below us, the outline of a pine tree, the sort you sometimes see growing out of a rock face. My mother had got caught in its branches as she plunged towards an otherwise certain death.

'Get out of my way,' I said to Osman, and stepped over him and his mother. Braco, still not fully understanding what was happening, followed.

'She's down there. See? She'll fall out of the tree!' my father said with panic in his voice. Then he shouted to my mother, 'Hold on, we're coming to get you!'

The three of us gripped each other's arms and formed a human chain. I abseiled down to my mother, grabbed her hand and, with a superhuman effort, we hauled her up to safety. None of us could quite believe we'd been able to do it.

'I dropped my handbag. There were two bottles of oil in it,' was the first thing she said.

'Let it go!' the rest of us cried, almost laughing.

'Are you hurt?' Braco asked.

'Osman and his mother may be there, so we should get a move on!' I snapped. And we did. I never saw Osman or his mother again. To this day I don't know what happened to them.

To our great relief the trail became less steep and wider as it descended. But now our struggle was with time. The ferrymen were not expecting us; the boats would not wait. But, as my father had experienced before, there was a distinct chance they might get greedy and risk hanging around for more customers. If that were the case they wouldn't make it across before dawn. The nights were short.

The last leg of the descent was the easiest. We made out the shingle ahead, and there the boats were still being loaded. The sight of the waiting boats in the moonlight would have been more of a picture if a war wasn't raging. Sweating from effort and fear, we were totally dehydrated. I asked around for some water and thought about drinking from the river.

A man from Žepa warned, 'You'd better not.'

'Why? The water's not safe to drink?' I asked.

'It's contaminated.'

'What do you mean?' I asked.

'The bodies from Višegrad.'

I remembered the story told by the man who had come to Luka in July. 'You mean those who were slaughtered?' I asked.

'Yes. With so many bodies floating down the river we haven't managed to fish them all out.'

I thought I would only be able to quench my thirst once we had passed through the gorge, which meant I would have to wait another five or six hours – that is, if we ever arrived at all.

'We're leaving now. We're not waiting for any more,' announced the boatmen.

The boat, which was no longer than four metres, was nearly full when we arrived. My father paid the boatman, and we loaded our stuff and found whatever room we could. The boatman pulled the starter chord and, to my great surprise, the sound of the engine went roaring through the night.

'What is this? I thought we were going to row,' I cried above the noise. Above us you could see just a tiny strip of sky between the walls of the gorge. Any Chetniks on the opposite rock face could surely hear the engine. The boatman was impassive, holding the rudder calmly as if he were taking tourists down the river. The expressions of the passengers in the moonlight betrayed nervousness. Everyone seemed to be making themselves as small as possible, as if that would save them if the Chetniks opened fire. I waited for a few minutes before edging my way over to the boatman.

'Do you have to use the engine?' I asked. He said nothing, pretending not to hear me. I repeated the question, adding, 'Aren't you afraid the Chetniks will hear us?'

'What do you want?' the boatman asked.

'Don't think I'm trying to teach you your job, but this can't be right. They can hear the engine in Belgrade. They're going to kill us all.'

'Wait a bit. I'm going to turn the engine down when we come around the river bend. I know where they are, and I know where they aren't. I have to use the engine, you know. How long do you think it would take us to get there by rowing?'

I went back to my part of the boat praying the man really knew what he was doing. But he did turn the engine down as we came around the bend. The sudden silence was itself terrifying.

Then a new sound broke the silence, the *splash, splosh, splash, splosh* of the oars, which was accompanied by the deafening squeaking of dry and rusty oar locks. The passengers were silent, numb with fear – that is, until one woman noticed that her clothes were wet, which caused quite a commotion.

'What's happening? Is water getting into the boat?' Everyone began speaking at the same time.

The boatman tossed a plastic bucket at us. 'Here, bail the water out,' he said.

'You didn't tell us your boat had a hole in it!' cried the man from Žepa I had met on the shingle. 'I can't swim! I can't swim!' In a matter of minutes the boat was full of water. In all the confusion nobody thought of taking the bucket to start emptying it out. My family and I, sitting in the bottom of the boat, were soon soaked.

'What the hell? What is this? Are we sinking?' wailed the man from Žepa. He stood up. I guess he wanted to be as far from the surface of the water as possible. This rocked the boat enough for him to lose his balance. He fell against the gunwale, but his head dipped into the water. He rose and shook his wet head. The shock had quietened him down. He kneeled and searched through his pockets for something.

In the meantime, a similar cry had gone up from others who couldn't swim. In panic they, too, stood up to get away from the water. The boat was rocking dangerously, and children were crying. The Chetniks would hear this racket no matter the height of the gorge. The noise scared a whole flock of birds out of their nests among the rocks. As they flew over the boat I saw that the man from Žepa had risen to his feet again and was holding something in his waving hand.

'I'm going to blow myself up! I will, I swear by Allah! I am not going into the water! No way! Not alive!' He was holding a hand grenade. The boatman stopped rowing and sat in silence, unsure what to do.

I got unsteadily to my feet and approached the man. 'What are you doing? What are you doing? Calm down. We're not going to sink. Just sit down!' I yelled at him. I kept an eye on his hands the whole time. I was ready to jump into the river if he pulled the pin and save myself from the blast and the shrapnel. But the man from Žepa did calm down, and as soon as he was sitting down again I grabbed the bucket and started tossing out the water.

'See? We're not going to sink,' I repeated.

After a time somebody took over from me. We continued bailing for the next few hours. Everybody calmed down. The only sounds breaking the silence of the night were the splashing and the terrible creaking of the oars.

I was exhausted, thirsty and drowsy. I might have drifted off to sleep at some point. Ears pricked up – the creaking and the splashing had doubled. There was another boat ahead of us. I became alert again and ready to dive into the water at the first sign of a Chetnik machine gun. The boatman was on his feet, pointing an automatic rifle in the direction of the approaching craft. The sound of both sets of oars stopped.

'Who's there?' the boatman whispered into the darkness, but there was no reply. The boats floated on. The boatman repeated the challenge. Again there was no answer.

Then a voice from the other boat broke the tension. 'It's me! Meho!'

'Are you insane?' our boatman asked him. 'Why didn't you answer me immediately? I was about to shoot you!'

The two boatmen linked hands and the boats slowly approached each other bow to bow. The manoeuvre was carried out competently – the two guys obviously knew what they were doing. It looked like a casual meeting of two guides offering tours up and down the river.

'What's going on downstream?' our boatman asked the other.

'Everything's OK down there, but you've only got half an hour before dawn and the guns from Mount Tara. I just left a group there, and now I'm going up to transport another. I'll risk the daylight. When do you plan to go again?'

The two Drina boatmen chatted in the dark while we were still recovering from this latest shock. They said their goodbyes, and off we went again. Shortly after, an amazing sight appeared down river. Electric lights were sparkling across the water. We hadn't seen a glowing light bulb since the middle of May. We looked from the clear starry sky above to the lights ahead and the peaks of Serbia's Mount Tara range on our right. The steep cliffs were behind us.

A village appeared on our left. I could hardly wait to get ashore. As soon as we did we asked for water and then, exhausted as we were, we all fell asleep on the shingle.

When next I opened my eyes I saw my father's face in front of me. He seemed to be yelling, but I couldn't hear a word of what he was saying. My ears were filled with a loud, disorientating ringing. The sun had not yet risen above the mountains. I lifted my head and saw thin curls of smoke snaking up from the Serbian side of the river. When my senses finally kicked in I heard my father shouting, 'Let's get out of here! Let's get out of here!'

Shells of all calibres were falling around us. My mother and brother were already running with some of our things. I grabbed the heaviest of our sacks and took off after them. After a hundred metres or so I put the sack down and ran back to fetch the rest of our possessions. A barrage of mortar shells forced me to take cover behind a house in the village. There a man with a wheelbarrow full of meat was also hiding. I asked him about the meat. He said a shell had killed his cow. He was selling the meat to his fellow villagers. I couldn't believe that people were still living in that village.

It was a miracle that we escaped unharmed. We collapsed, shattered, as soon as we found ourselves on a nearby hill out of range of the shells. The valley behind us was smoking like a witch's cauldron.

That night we listened to a Serbian news programme on the radio. Milošević had declared once again that Serbia was in no way participating in the war.

Yeah, right.

THE JOURNEY TO
SREBRENICA

We soon found ourselves in a village that was hidden from the river – and, amazingly, it wasn't being shelled. My father ran into a former colleague who invited us to spend the night at his house. Given the wartime exigencies, this invitation was much more than we could have expected. But that wasn't all. Our host said he would walk with us almost all the way to Srebrenica and even offered his horse to carry our belongings – there was no way we could have done the journey otherwise. We were relieved to have survived the ordeal on the river, and the rest of the journey didn't seem like it would be as dangerous.

He told us what had been happening in the area since the beginning of the war. The town of Srebrenica had been held by the Chetniks until the middle of May. They had burned down a lot buildings, almost an entire street of houses; dozens of people had been burned alive in their homes. After a Chetnik warlord by the name of Zekić was killed the Serb population of Srebrenica left overnight. The Bosniak refugees, who had until then been trying to survive in the surrounding forests, came down from the hills and moved into the abandoned houses. All the Bosniak villages along the Drina had been targeted by artillery from Serbia since the beginning of the fighting. There were several Serb villages on the road between here and Srebrenica itself, so these Bosniak villages were practically cut off from the town. The local Bosniaks had organized themselves and counter-attacked – the aim being to form a link with Srebrenica. In doing so they burned and destroyed a number of Serb villages and hamlets. That was the first time I'd heard that Serb villages were also being burned. From April to the end of August I'd only seen or heard about the destruction of Bosniak villages, but in the Srebrenica area, under the command of Naser Orić, the Bosniaks had switched from defence to attack.

Our host told us that back in April, around ten kilometres downstream, the Chetniks had captured and executed a few dozen Bosniaks. There were children and women among them. The Chetniks continued to kill, burn and loot, clearly believing that they could get away with it. But the Bosniaks fought back. In the three years I spent in eastern Bosnia as a refugee, not once did I hear of Bosniaks executing captives or Serb civilians or committing massacres. Be that as it may, the thought of burning down Serb villages still frightened and sickened me. Although it had long been clear that in Vlasenica, Zvornik, Srebrenica, Bratunac and Višegrad the worst atrocities were being committed *against* Muslims and that hundreds of Muslim villages were being burned to the ground, I couldn't help but listen to the little voice inside my head asking, 'When will it stop? When they burn all our houses and we burn all of theirs?' But there was another voice that said, 'How can you, who has never fired a weapon in your life, judge those who are fighting to defend you from extermination? If it were not for these brave people you'd still be sitting on top of a mountain in Žepa waiting for the Chetniks to come and get you.'

My feelings were less ambivalent when, the next day, we passed through our first deserted Serb village. Our host, now our guide, didn't seem too worried, but the four of us exchanged significant looks. Some of the houses were scorched, some untouched. The empty houses, with their open windows gawping at us, gave me a haunted feeling I couldn't shift. I expected to see a face in one of those ghostly apertures. Maybe the inhabitants had returned . . . Maybe they were watching us at that very moment . . . Maybe they were waiting to ambush us . . .

'Where are the Serbs who used to live here?' I asked our guide. He was leading the horse loaded with the bulk of our stuff.

'They fled. Are you frightened? Hey, man, don't be afraid. Imagine if you were to see some real action! Don't you worry. A Chetnik won't go anywhere unless the coast is clear. They're not coming back. They thought they could slaughter us with impunity, but they fled like rats when we put up a fight.'

'And where are our fighters now?' I asked.

'There's no front line here. Everybody's guarding his own village. There haven't been any attacks here for quite some time, except an occasional shoot-out when we run into them or they run into us. They don't attack us, and we don't attack them.'

'So we could run into them now?' I asked.

He stopped and turned to face me. 'Of course we could. I told you this would not be 100 per cent safe. Do you think it'll be any better in Srebrenica? It won't. The place is shelled every day!'

We came to a clearing. We were told to run before entering the forest. Afterwards we set off down a muddy forest trail. The vegetation around Srebrenica is completely different from that in the mountains. Deciduous trees and undergrowth prevail. I've always preferred conifers and am generally happier in the mountains than on the plains. I felt less safe here – the whole area seemed to offer less shelter. The trees did not grow as densely. Somehow, everything looked hostile and sinister to me. I'm not sure how to describe it, but I definitely got the sense that I did not belong here. I'd felt more at home up in the mountains, even as we were fleeing and hiding and afraid all the time.

Even the Chetniks here seemed much worse to me. In a weird way, it was as if those Chetniks in the mountains were somehow our Chetniks while those here were someone else's. All my life I'd heard stories from my father and my uncles and aunts about 'our Chetniks'. Knowing the story of the Chetniks who shot and injured Grandpa Hasan in 1942, knowing their names, I could even imagine their faces. I was kind of used to being afraid of them, secretly, even before the conflict. But the Chetniks down here were a complete mystery to me and, although I'd never encountered them before, I imagined them to be somehow even more bloodthirsty. Unfortunately, it later turned out that my gut feeling was not wrong.

Descending through the woods we arrived in Zeleni Jadar, the Srebrenica industrial zone where my father had worked during the 1970s. Our guide said that we were to continue to the next village without pausing. It didn't take long. A few Bosniak houses appeared on the next hill. Even here there was someone who knew and respected my father. We were offered a place to stay for the night, and our guide set off for home.

I couldn't wait to find a spot where I could get a view of Srebrenica and joined the road leading to the town. Setting foot on asphalt for the first time in four months felt like a return to civilization. I found a viewing spot on a bend in the road, and the sight of the town in the distance made my heart beat faster. In Srebrenica there would be someone who could take us to Tuzla. This was still very much my plan. It meant passing through the occupied municipalities of Vlasenica and Zvornik, but I was familiar with the area or with the more populated parts at least. My father knew of the plan – I'd mentioned it often enough – but he never commented on it. He must have thought it not only risky but unfeasible. But, as I saw it, the four of us had just completed the first leg of our journey to safety.

Walking along that paved road I met a man travelling from Srebrenica. I decided to try my luck and ask him about friends and family whom I believed might be refugees in the town – assuming they had escaped the slaughter in their villages. I couldn't believe my ears when he told me he knew my old room-mates Ćamil and Fahro and that they were both living on Petriča Street in Srebrenica. I'd had no news of them since I'd left Sarajevo.

My family were planning to go to Srebrenica the next day, but I couldn't resist running down the hill that very moment, not stopping to catch my breath until I reached the edge of town. A tractor passed by, and I followed it with my eyes – I hadn't seen anything on four wheels for months! I thanked God we had escaped the forests. I was convinced, as many others were, that we would be safe here.

I found the house where Fahro and his family were living; Ćamil and his family were staying just across the road. I was glad that the two old friends from university were neighbours even as refugees. I introduced myself to Fahro's mother who told me that they were both on lookout duty. They were keeping watch ten kilometres away and were due to return the following day. I went back to my family disappointed.

The next day we arrived in Srebrenica carrying all our belongings.

We wandered through the streets until my father found out who was in charge of refugee housing. There was an official of the town's wartime administration responsible for allocating empty houses to recently arrived refugees. Offered the choice between an empty Serb house and an empty Bosniak house, we opted for the latter. More than 90 per cent of the Bosniak population of Srebrenica had fled as early as April 1992, mainly to Tuzla. Srebrenica was now populated with refugees from the surrounding villages, which were either occupied or had been razed. We were given temporary accommodation for two days after which we settled in another house. At the time we thought that this would also prove temporary, but we were to stay there for the next three years. The house was on a street called Crvena Rijeka: Red River.

Before the war the street had been the prettiest in town. The hundred or so people who had lived here used to rent rooms to the numerous tourists who came there from as far away as Germany to visit the healing waters of the Guber Spa just a few kilometres away. It must have been a pleasant half-hour pilgrimage up the hill, past the small medieval fortress of the Old Town. The thousand people who lived on this street now were all refugees from eastern Bosnia. When there was no bombing or shelling the street was swarming with people, and it was among them that you could hear all the latest news even if you were only going out for a brief walk.

The house had belonged to the Bašić family. My father had known the owners, Veljko and Razija, a mixed Serb–Bosniak couple. The front door had been smashed. We were told that almost all the deserted houses had been looted and ransacked. This was done first by Arkan's troops, whose preference, besides killing, was for looting all kinds of household appliances. The houses were then looted again by hungry Bosniak refugees. We were therefore pleasantly surprised not to find the furniture destroyed. The only things missing seemed to be the television and VCR, which wouldn't have been of much use without electricity anyway. The house was tastefully furnished, and we agreed that this was the first nice thing that had happened to us since the war had broken out.

There was a framed black-and-white photograph of Veljko Bašić on the wall in the hallway. As was my habit I immediately thought of his Hollywood double: Clark Gable. Maybe it was the moustache. The picture remained in its place the whole time we stayed there.

'I got into a fight with him once,' my father said when he saw the photograph. 'He had a short fuse, but he was a good man.'

From what I'd heard, my father was no different. I'd been told of his fights with some colleagues during the 1970s. People said that my father used to have a short fuse, too, but that his anger didn't last long. The way of making things right back then was with booze and food. Before the war my father had never talked about this, at least not to me. It was only during the war that he started treating me as an adult and telling me things he couldn't or hadn't wanted to tell me before.

The first thing I did after we moved into Veljko's house was visit Ćamil and Fahro. They were as glad to see me as I was to see them. For a moment I felt as if time had stopped and we were back in our student accommodation as fourth-year students of mechanical engineering, although we were all thinner than the last time we'd seen each other. But the period of intense weight loss had only just started – in a few months I would lose more than twenty kilos and ultimately weigh only sixty-five, which is not much for someone one metre eighty-nine tall.

Ćamil told me that next week they were scheduled to go on duty again. I asked if I would be obliged to go.

'No, there is no conscription here, you know. And anyway you wouldn't be in our unit. There are other units who need men, but you'd need a weapon to join – there just aren't enough to go around. Since you don't have one you wouldn't be much use.'

'What happens on watch?' I asked.

'The last time we were there it wasn't so bad. There was no shooting. But the time before I barely escaped with my life. I was kind of injured,' Ćamil said.

I could hardly believe my ears! Ćamil! My friend Ćamil, the always meticulous Ćamil, the excellent student Ćamil, had turned into a warrior! He was transformed. He seemed more self-confident and had matured somehow. As ever when talking to someone who actually went out to fight I felt worthless by comparison.

'And how do you manage for food?' I asked. 'We're almost out.'

'You come with us, and you'll bring food back,' Fahro said.

'Come where?'

'To the barns in the countryside,' he said.

I was confused. 'But that's Serb-occupied territory now!'

They both smiled knowingly.

'We have to get food from somewhere!' Fahro explained. 'We set off together in a column, hundreds of us. A group with rifles at the head, then the unarmed civilians in the middle, then another armed group bringing up the rear. If we run into a minefield our guys clear the way, create a sort of corridor to pass through. And all of this is done at night. We know where the barns are and which are full. The villages are all deserted. Problem is the corn itself is meant for cattle. It's a hybrid corn – you know what that is?'

'No,' I said.

'It's not regular corn, not like the cornmeal we used to make cornbread in peacetime. It's cattle feed, but there's plenty of it, and we can't be picky these days.'

'Anything you can get your hands on is good enough,' I said. 'I'm well aware of that. But I thought there was nothing left. I thought everything had been burned down.'

'Not everything. The houses were, but the barns are still standing. Maybe the Chetniks got tired or didn't feel like it. How would I know? One thing's for sure, as soon as the Chetniks figure out where we're getting food they're gonna burn the barns down, too. But until they do we have to keep going back.'

I didn't say anything, but I think it was pretty clear that I didn't like the idea.

I bumped into Fahro a few days later while I was standing in front of the department store in the centre of town. He was in a long line of people carrying huge bags and some improvised rucksacks, which were clearly very heavy. He paused to rest, telling me that he had brought about forty kilos of corn with him. He was all muddy, bent double under his load, and his trainers were almost worn out.

'A group at the rear was killed on the way back. The Chetniks opened fire on them in an ambush as they were passing through a minefield, just as I'd got through it myself. I don't even know how I managed to run uphill with a forty-kilo load on my back,' he told me.

'What happened to those people?' I asked.

'They were left behind. Maybe some of them were only injured, who knows. But nobody could go back to get them; we barely got out alive ourselves. That's the way it is, my friend.'

I watched him walk off down the street; he was a short guy, no more than one metre seventy, and the sack seemed bigger than he was. Those improvised rucksacks were made out of common sacks with belts sewn on as straps. The stronger the belts, the more you could carry. I was told that people walked a few hours in the dark under the Chetniks' noses to get to the barns. In the early days they shucked the corn right there, discarding the useless husks to fill their sacks with more cobs. With time, shucking on site grew more dangerous while food grew scarcer, so people stopped bothering and brought the whole cobs home with them. During that autumn and winter people ended up grinding the actual cobs to eat, but constipation became a common affliction, and some people even died from it. Doctors apparently used the only available method to ease the problem – inserting a rubber hose into a patient's anus and letting water flow into their bowels to help loosen their stool. From what I'd heard, those beyond help died in terrible agony.

Anyway, at ten Deutschmarks a kilogram, the forty-kilogram sack of corn my friend Fahro carried on his back that day was worth four hundred marks at the time. That was more money than my family had at the time. We couldn't have afforded that sack. Unless you had the money, the choice was simple: either risk your life to feed your family, as Fahro did, or starve.

WHAT TO EAT

On the day we ran out of food my father decided to sell his pistol. He was told he could get a lot of grain for it, so salvation from hunger was still possible. A buyer was found who would give us eighty kilograms of wheat, twenty kilograms of corn and twenty kilograms of potatoes for the gun. He even said he would deliver it all on a horse. He must have really wanted that pistol.

When the buyer delivered the goods as promised we unloaded the horse and took all the food upstairs. I developed a habit of going up and thrusting my hands deep into the sack, taking handfuls of wheat and letting the grain run through my fingers. I enjoyed it enormously and kept saying under my breath, 'Life. Life.'

In normal times wheat is cleaned before you take it to the mill. In wartime, however, that was a luxury we couldn't afford. The miller took 5 per cent of your wheat for his services if you didn't have money to pay him, which we didn't. In fact, wheat became a kind of currency. Everything you could buy for German currency you could also pay for in wheat, milk, eggs, cheese, tinned food, cooking oil and sugar. And, yes, those items could be bought. The food sold at the market must have been looted from shops, warehouses and deserted homes, and people were charging well over the odds for it. The price of salt sky-rocketed. At the time it was already one hundred Deutschmarks a kilogram; a few months later it would cost several hundred marks. An egg, by comparison, cost ten.

With what little wheat we could afford to barter we got some beans and a small amount of salt. We used to have two meals a day, at nine in the morning and half past three in the afternoon. It was always the same. We ate a slice of wholewheat bread or cornbread and some thin bean soup, which was barely salted.

I knew of a family that had got hold of slabs of rock salt that they processed by cooking, drying and pulverizing and then sold as cooking salt, even though it was, in fact, the salt used on the roads in winter. It added saltiness to the food, but it contained no iodine, which is essential for both human and animal life. People couldn't afford salt for themselves let alone for their animals. There were rumours that the cattle had gone wild and grown abnormally long hair. Apparently meat from such animals was tough and full of gristle and didn't taste the way it should. Not that anyone cared – it was food. But the most important item in our diet was bread. And it was getting scarce. A few months after the handgun had been sold we started panicking again.

Food or, rather, the lack of it was not our only survival issue. Srebrenica and its suburbs were under constant shelling from the Chetnik mortars and artillery batteries positioned on the surrounding hills. Not a day passed without shelling. It went on day and night, and you never knew when it would start or finish. Sometimes the shelling began after midnight, just as we were falling asleep. After a while I stopped jumping out of bed and running to the basement; I just rolled off to sleep on the relative safety of the floor.

My parents had some acquaintances in the Srebrenica suburb of Soloćuša, on the way to Potočari, and these acquaintances had chickens. I had been there once with my parents hoping to return with a few eggs. They told us that since the war had begun at least ten people had either been killed or injured in their neighbourhood. Shells were coming from somewhere around Bratunac and from a quarry in Serbia. The quarry could be seen with the naked eye in the distance. Long-range artillery batteries shelled the mosque in Soloćuša. This was one of the five mosques in Srebrenica, and its tall minaret could be seen from everywhere. It seems the artillery fire wasn't targeting the minaret as much as using it as a range finder, and it had not been hit even once. But the houses in the densely populated area around it were hit daily. Desperate with fear for their homes and for the lives of their children, the people went to see the imam and asked his permission to knock the minaret down. The imam couldn't believe what they were requesting, but the people insisted. 'We'll build the minaret again, God willing, once the war is over,' they told him. Their prospects were dire. They would have fled if they could, but they had nowhere to go.

In the end the minaret was not knocked down – I'm not sure whether this was because the imam wouldn't allow it or for some other reason. It would remain untouched by shells, too. Both the mosque and the minaret defied the Chetniks' shelling for the duration of the war. That is, until July 1995 when the Chetniks entered the town and set fire to it.

AEROPLANES - AGAIN

NATO had issued a warning that it would enforce a ban on flights over BiH, meaning that, at least in theory, it would engage with Serb MiGs violating the no-fly zone. The Serbs had seemingly found a way around this, however. We'd been told that Srebrenica had been bombed from the air on several occasions by 'agricultural aircraft'. These were planes with piston engines, unlike the jets that had attacked us on the mountain. In comparison with that experience, agricultural aircraft sounded almost harmless. The first time they arrived I'd almost forgotten that they were carrying bombs. They flew slowly, quite low, and made a strange *nnneeaoowww* sound. It was only when they began to strafe us with machine guns that I stopped staring dumbly up at them and ran for shelter under a terrace. A huge explosion followed.

A man who'd also run for cover under the terrace said, 'They're dropping boilers from the sky!'

'What do you mean?' I asked.

'They fill water boilers with explosives and shells and attach them to the planes. They have steel plates welded to their bellies so that shooting at them is pointless. They are flying higher this time, too.'

As he was explaining this to me we heard the sound of gunfire. Somebody did try to do some harm to the planes, but they'd only wasted their ammunition.

The plane was gone.

'Where do they fly from?' I asked while we were waiting for the next attack.

'There's a runway near Bratunac. The planes were once used for crop spraying.' the man said.

Until February or maybe March 1993 the Serbs used these aircraft to bomb Srebrenica and its surroundings; not every day but often enough to keep us all on edge. Almost as a rule, they would come after a battle had been lost – their defensive lines had been broken or they'd suffered serious casualties. They would retaliate against civilians by bombing and shelling the town.

It was around this time that one of our fighters rushed into town from the lookout on the mountain. He had run ten kilometres to bring news of what had happened there that morning. An aircraft had taken off from Bratunac while our fighters were climbing up the mountain. They were already quite high up when they saw it – having just taken off they were practically at eye level – so they opened fire and, to their astonishment, the plane started belching smoke and crashed into the ground!

Our fighters had shot down a plane! Bravo! The town was celebrating.

From then on the Chetnik planes flew at higher altitudes but were no less lethal, which was what counted.

However, the downed plane was not the only news from that time. In September, while sitting in the box office of the town's cultural centre, I heard a noise that I'd had the misfortune to become acquainted with in the mountains. Hear an incoming MiG once and you'll never forget it. Once you hear it, of course, it's already been and gone.

The box office acted as a reception point for newly arrived refugees. Registering them was now my wartime duty, which the town's administration had assigned to me. The imminent fall of Žepa had created a wave of displaced people who lined up on the street in front of my window of the cultural centre. Just as I was entering the name of another arrival, smiling and relieved to have made it to Srebrenica, the sky erupted. The smile froze on the face of the new arrival; he was still frozen to the spot as I took off to the basement, which was soon packed. This basement was thought to be the safest place in town because the building was constructed of reinforced concrete with marble tiles on the ground floor.

People would hide in their own basements during the shelling, but an air-raid was different. It caused enormous fear and great commotion. The ground shook, children cried and the explosions were felt and heard even in the basement where we were sheltering. The pilots showed no intention of leaving. They had a quota to meet. I warned people to stay away from the few intact windows. I also told them to keep their mouths open as the explosions could rupture their eardrums. I have no idea where this notion came from – I guess I must have read it somewhere.

I was horrified to find my brother among the crowd down there. I took him to one side and shouted, 'What are you doing here? You should be at home!'

I'd never heard anything like it before. More powerful than a thunderclap. Never before or since have I been that close to an explosion as the missile hit the roof of the centre. The next was even louder – it was a 250-kilogram 'krmača' that landed in front of the cultural centre. I'm pretty sure not a single window-pane in central Srebrenica survived the bombing that day.

When the planes were gone my brother and I ran out of the shelter and up the hill, fearing what might have happened to our parents. Fortunately, none of the houses on our street was damaged. The street, normally crowded with people, mainly refugees, remained deserted for more than two hours. It looked as if everyone had decided never to leave their basements again. I stood in the middle of the empty road contemplating the sky, cursing its clearness, wishing for clouds to protect us from the planes. Two of our neighbours came out and joined me.

All of a sudden we heard the sound of turbo-folk. The low frequency rumble reached us through a battery of subwoofers growing louder as the source of the music drew closer. A black Mercedes pulled up, its windows down. All three passengers and the driver had their arms hanging out of the windows.

'Naser Orić!' my neighbour exclaimed.

The driver was a handsome young man. His arms, one leaning out the window and one on the steering wheel, were enormous. He had a freshly shaven face and a fashionable haircut.

'What are you guys doing here?' he enquired.

'Nothing. Waiting for people to come out of their basements.'

The music was still blaring, echoing through the street. *Oonse – oonse – oonse.*

'Right. They should be told to come out. We're driving around with the music on loud to show everyone that planes are no big deal. Tell the people that there's no reason for them to skulk in their basements. The planes are gone. They'll be back. So what? Let them bomb us, the Chetnik cowards. We'll get them back tenfold for this.' Thus spoke Naser. The three of us were not sure if we'd been issued with an order, but we stood almost at attention, just in case.

The black Mercedes raced off down the street and took the next turn that led back to downtown Srebrenica. 'Yee haw!' cried the voice of one of Naser's pals in true cowboy fashion.

The three of us exchanged glances. That was the first time I'd seen Naser Orić, and I was left awed by him, his friends, the fearlessness, the black Mercedes and the blaring subwoofers. Naser was doing what needed to be done to boost the morale of suffering and terrified people. This was neither the first nor the last time that he, in his own colourful way, would encourage people not to become disheartened under siege at a time when more or less everyone else was ready to accept their fate without a fight.

'Wow,' I said when the car disappeared around the corner. 'What a guy!'

'What a guy indeed! He's like Rambo. You know, one day when Arkan's forces were here killing and looting Naser ambushed them on the road to Potočari! A lot of Arkan's men were killed that day but not a single one of ours. From then on there were no more attacks along the road from Bratunac. I've even heard that the Chetniks tried to bring a truck full of soldiers to Potočari without telling them where they were going. When the soldiers realized where they were headed they jumped out of the truck!'

'Did Arkan's men kill anyone here?' I asked our neighbour.

'At least fifty – mainly elderly. I guess they didn't want to flee with the rest of them. Arkan's men set several houses on fire down by the City Mosque with people still inside. You know, you've seen those torched buildings. Up there in the city,' he continued, waving towards the walled city, the collapsed walls of a medieval fortress on the highest hill in Srebrenica, 'Ake is the main man. Akif Ustić. He's got his own unit. He should have been the commander of Srebrenica proper, but he renounced it in favour of Naser.'

'Who's in charge up there in the hills?' I asked.

'That'll be Zulfo.' The same man I'd heard about in Luka.

A neighbour from across the street – a short blond man – came out of his house. They called him Medo. He was the postman.

'They're talking on the radio about Srebrenica being bombed. They say the planes came from Banja Luka,' he said. We asked him if we could listen to the news. With no electricity it would be a real treat. Medo invited us in.

His living room was packed. At least ten other men were sitting listening in silence. Somebody was hand-spinning a wheel between his legs. I recognized the wooden device from my childhood. Women in Stoborani used to spin wool on something similar. The wheel was hooked up to a small battery which, in turn, was hooked up to a cassette player that had a radio built into it. To my great surprise, as the wheel was turned, BiH Radio came out of the speakers.

I had not been in the room for long when the guy spinning the wheel in the corner of the room shouted to me, 'Hey, you, if you want to listen to the news you'll have to spin the wheel.'

I sat in his place on the floor and took over.

'The BiH army inflicted heavy losses on the Serbo-Chetnik aggressor in the Trnovo area. A large quantity of weapons and technical resources was captured . . .' the voice said, fading away and then stopping.

'Spin, young man. Why don't you spin?' the men cried in unison. I began to spin faster.

According to sources in the free territory, the general situation in eastern Bosnia is extremely grave. The area is routinely shelled and bombed from the air, and its inhabitants have little food to eat. Mrs Sadako Ogata, United Nations High Commissioner for Refugees, stated at a press conference held in Geneva yesterday that the UN is making every effort to obtain the authorization from the Serb administration in Zvornik and Bratunac for the passage of food convoys to Srebrenica.

'Sadako, what a well-chosen name,' somebody said jokingly.
'Sounds like *sadaka* – charity!'

'We'll all starve before charity arrives,' another said.

'Yeah, man, didn't you listen? The Chetniks won't let food in. They want to starve us in case we survive the shelling.'

'They know what they're doing. Right now, women are on the street begging for handfuls of flour to feed their children. If the food doesn't come, we'll have no other choice but to take food from the Serbs.'

I spun the wheel until the news ended. For months, night after night, we would gather in this room and listen to the news with hope and trepidation. Each time we thought that the end of the war was near another gory day would dawn.

HEDIJA

I ran into my cousin Hedija one day during that period. That was the first time I had seen her since the 4 June attack on Mršić Hill. She had managed to hide in an underground shelter she and her husband had dug for themselves and their two small children in the woods away from the other families.

'We waited in that shelter until the shooting died down and then fled to the mountains.'

'How did you reach the free territory then? By boat through the gorge?'

'No. We crossed the Jadar, climbed up Sućeska and came down to Srebrenica. But we weren't here for long. We tried to reach Tuzla.'

'Really? When was that?'

'In August. We joined a group of six thousand people that planned to set off towards Zvornik escorted by eighty of our fighters. But we were betrayed, I think – either that or it was really badly planned.'

'What do you mean?'

'You know, I loved my granny's stories when I was a child, and in one of them there was a wise man who used to rhyme: "When a door is opened in Baghdad, under Udrč will flow a sea of blood".'

'What the . . . ?' I interrupted.

'I know,' she said. 'Maybe I remembered it because I had no idea what it meant. But, you see, when the group passed Cerska we began climbing a mountain towards Kamenica. I asked what the mountain was called, and they told me it was called Udrč. When I recognized the name the blood froze in my veins. I was carrying baby Fikret on my back and a bag full of clothes in my hands. Ema was walking on her own. I was dizzy. I hadn't had a drink of water since the previous day. I had to save it for the children because somebody had stolen the bottle of water I had for them.

'Well, we passed by the villages near Zvornik quite quickly. They were all burned down. But, near Snagovo, where we were supposed to join the road to Tuzla, we fell into an ambush. There was a Chetnik with a machine gun lying in the grass in front of us. I immediately grabbed Ema and threw myself into the bushes. They opened fire from all sides – you wouldn't believe the noise! I covered the children's bodies with mine and their heads with my arms. I tried to keep us as close to the ground as possible. I could see bullets scything the grass around us, and a bullet even grazed Ema's chin. I tried to crawl back, towards the trees, but there was no way! Women were falling around us, hit by bursts of gunfire. People were screaming, moaning, staggering. Instead of fighting back some of our fighters were tearing off their camouflage! But there was a woman among them, a soldier who refused to take off her uniform. I used to know her before the war. She was shouting in our direction, but I couldn't hear what she was saying. I was dizzy. All I could manage to do was raise my arm a bit – the woman understood I was about to faint and came running towards us. I have never seen a more courageous woman than her. She helped me gather myself. I started running right behind her with Fikret on my back, grabbing Ema in my arms, leaving the bag with our clothing behind. It was only then that Ema started crying – she said that we would have nothing to wear!

'So Tuzla was forgotten, and everyone went running towards Mount Udrč again. If you made it across that open field and reached the forest maybe you'd have a chance. The forest was being shelled as well, but we had no option. The brave woman took my hand, and we started running. The field was covered with dead and injured, but nobody paid any attention to them. I have no idea how we managed to get across the field under machine-gun fire, but we did. Once we were in the forest more chaos broke out. Our fighters came running from who knows where, but the people thought they were Chetniks. Children were screaming, women were weeping, shells were falling all around us . . . The fighters went running through the terrified crowd, shouting, "No, no, don't be afraid. It's us. We're Muslims,

Muslims!" But nobody believed them and the wailing and weeping continued. To prove they were Muslims the fighters started reciting parts of the Quran, but that didn't help either. That's how it was! Eventually we regrouped and went back to Srebrenica the way we had come. All that way on foot, twice, with two children,' Hedija said, closing the story of one of her personal struggles.

After hearing Hedija's story I wasn't so convinced about my master plan any more. It seemed that we were stuck in Srebrenica.

Six months later Hedija and her children would manage to get on the UNHCR trucks. They would make it to Kladanj then Tuzla and, finally, Vienna. That is where Hedija, the youngest daughter of my Uncle Avdija, has been living since 1993.

The last time I saw her was at Vienna airport after the war. I was between flights, and she came to meet me. Fikret was twenty-two then. In the meantime Hedija had had another child, a daughter named Melisa, and divorced her husband. Her older daughter Ema had married and had two children of her own. Hedija was a grandmother!

THE STRUGGLE FOR SURVIVAL

That autumn was both bloody and hungry. Each day was harder than the one before. No one, except for a few individuals, had any food left. New refugees kept flowing in. One day three of them appeared at our house, accompanied by an official responsible for our street. They were a family from Višegrad, a twenty-year-old woman and her parents. The parents looked old and ill. They were all tired, dirty and hungry. Part of the house was allocated to them, and they took the three upper rooms while we stayed on the ground floor with one room and the kitchen.

We heard a clamour from outside. All along the street people were engaged in preparations for what everyone called an 'action'. They carried bags and sacks to which belts had been sewn to allow people to carry as much as possible. Somebody knocked at our door, and I went to answer. A neighbour was standing on the doorstep.

'Have you got a rifle?' he asked.

'What do you mean?' I replied, confused.

'What do you mean what do I mean?' he said. 'A rifle! Have you got a rifle? Don't worry. I'm not the police. If you have a rifle I need it for two days. I'm going on the action. We're going to Tegare.'

I had no idea where that was.

'I haven't got a rifle. We used to have a pistol, but we bartered it for wheat,' I said.

'If you did have a rifle I could get you a sack of flour for it in two days,' he said, clearly not believing me. 'Are you coming with us?'

'No. I don't know . . . maybe,' I said since I hadn't really understood what he was asking.

He shrugged and walked off.

Preparations for the action – which, by the way, was supposed to be a military secret, although every child in Srebrenica knew about it – went on through the night. Tegare was a village somewhere behind the mountain, on the Drina. Simply put, the action was a mass hunt for food in nearby Serb villages.

The next day the town seemed deserted. I was told that several thousand people had gone, the great majority of them unarmed, but, being empty-handed, that meant they would be able to bring back more food.

To reach Tegare they had to walk more than twenty kilometres up over the mountain and then down to the river. Before the war both Serbs and Muslims had lived in the village, but the Muslims had been either deported or killed. Their houses had been torched at the beginning of the hostilities.

I'd been told that an action would always happen at dawn. Running towards the Serb houses, hundreds or thousands of hungry people would create pandemonium, shooting, shouting, running about and colliding with each other. I imagined the Serbs, still in their beds, must have been terrified by these stampedes of the hungry. These battles would often end quite quickly, but sometimes they lasted for hours. I heard veterans of these actions saying things like 'We drove the Chetniks to the river.'

Artillery batteries would open fire from Serbia, and the Bosniaks who had already reached the houses had a chance to take cover. The last of the convoy to arrive were often cut down by machine-gun fire or dismembered by shells.

Imagine the scene. A human being breaks into a house to fill a sack with packs of meat from a freezer while, outside, flesh is flying through the air and blood is gushing from severed limbs.

People would hunt mainly for sacks of flour. Look for sacks, sacks of flour, grab them and get out of there – scram! Some managed to find cigarettes along the way, schnapps even. Some would break into stables and herd the cows out. They wanted milk for their children, I guess. And, again, try to imagine someone urging a cow to run across a corpse-strewn field while artillery shells fall like rain and body parts fly all around. I once heard somebody describing the apocalyptic scene in these terms – and to many it seemed like the apocalypse had actually arrived.

Following the actions, groups of people both large and small would trickle back to Srebrenica carrying all manner of things. Some of them would even be singing. Once I saw a man carrying a machine gun. He fired a long burst into the air, and it echoed through the whole town. It was in celebration of victory. Victory?

I watched as the groups passed through the centre of town. Some were eating as they walked; others hurried home silently with their heavy packs, their loot. Over the following days they would talk about the ones who hadn't come back, those who had been left lying there either dead or injured. No one went back for them. Tears, sorrow, misery. Full stomachs. Eat what you've got and then head off into action again.

My family had never taken part, not once. We didn't dare, we couldn't, we didn't want to. So while the foolhardy ones, the seasoned ones and those whose desperation had made them bold now had food to put on their tables, we sat at our empty table with our empty stomachs expecting the inevitable. For what invariably followed were hundreds of artillery shells for every Serb killed and then an air-raid.

After the brief euphoria of victory panic would spread throughout the town. We had the frightening feeling that each response to an action was fiercer and bloodier than the one before. With more and more people being killed by shells in the streets and in the surrounding villages and hills, you almost didn't dare to stick your nose out of the door. But you had to, of course. You had to look for food. I used to walk through the whole town in search of something to eat or walk to nearby Muslim villages, often arriving at the defensive lines on the borders of Srebrenica's free territory. I sometimes went with my father and sometimes without him, but we never let my mother and brother come with us.

My father often seemed on the brink of madness – I imagine because the family was in such desperate circumstances and he thought it was his fault. There were days when he walked more than fifty kilometres hoping to find his pre-war acquaintances or friends, anyone who would be ready to give him some food or sell it for a regular price. His insistence on going on these solo expeditions caused many a heated argument between the two of us. On a few occasions he grabbed me by the collar. He would then break away, don his backpack and leave without a word. Every time it happened we thought he wouldn't come back alive.

Rather than participate in the actions on Serb villages he explored the territories 'under our control', those that had already been 'freed' or not yet taken by the Chetniks. He once went as far as Konjević Polje. Given how many people had been killed or gone missing trying to get there, this was truly amazing. He returned home after three days, threw his backpack on the floor, sat down, pulled out a tobacco pouch, rolled a cigarette and lit it. We waited for him to catch his breath.

'I found a guy from Birač,' he said, meaning a colleague from the firm where he had been director before the war. 'He gave me a bit of tobacco.' My father looked worn out, but his eyes sparkled with pleasure every time he took a drag. 'There're about ten kilograms of corn in my backpack. I paid a hundred marks for it,' he said taking his socks off.

The socks were worn to shreds, and my father's feet were covered in blisters, some of which were bleeding. The ten kilograms of corn he'd brought was the only food we had in the house.

My mother got it out. 'Half of it is rotten,' she said.

'We'll have it ground as it is,' my father replied, looking at her.

He told us about Konjević Polje. Apparently there was more food there, mainly because there were fewer refugees than in Srebrenica. People lived in their own houses and had their own supplies. But the place was being shelled from four directions.

'They are completely surrounded, just like we are here,' he said. 'They say that a few hundred people have managed to reach Tuzla –'

'So it *is* possible!' I interrupted him, thinking of my long-standing plan.

He gave me an exasperated look. His eyes were full of pain and reproach. 'Hasko,' he said, 'a few people have succeeded, but many have been killed on the way. I've been told about groups of refugees who were slaughtered, including women and children. Those who manage to escape freeze to death hiding in the woods. It is too risky. It's not possible.'

Once again my 'let's do it come what may' initiative came to nothing. We were each too afraid that something might happen to one of us. We, along with thousands of other refugees in Srebrenica, were determined to wait for someone to save us. It seemed that many of us had become reconciled to our fate and were not expecting to survive this whole ordeal. But everyone did their best to survive the day. Day after day. And so the days passed.

At the end of October my father informed us that he'd decided to go to Stoborani. His decision completely bewildered me. It was madness; more than fifty kilometres of extremely dangerous and difficult terrain to get to a village that was full of Chetniks! But my father was adamant. He had decided to go there to harvest the potatoes we had planted around Aunt Mila's house in the spring. My father believed with absolute certainty that the Chetniks would not have bothered to dig them up – they had enough food, he argued. So he had made an arrangement with a man who owned a horse to take him to Stoborani and bring the potatoes to Srebrenica and divide the spoils 50:50.

Once again we were convinced that we were saying our last goodbyes. Once again we didn't hear from him for days. Then someone told us that that morning a group coming from Žepa had been ambushed near the village of Podravanje and everyone had been killed. I didn't dare imagine that he had been among them. Something ached in my chest. I spent the whole day in front of the house looking down the street. And then, in the early evening, two men and a horse appeared at the end of the road. My father was limping; his feet were badly blistered.

We learned later that they had passed through the site of the ambush. My father and his companion were allowed to proceed unharmed. It was a miracle. Rather than give themselves away the Chetniks must have decided to wait for a bigger group to pass by. After hearing about the ambush my father claimed he had had a strange feeling about the place.

They spent a night on the mountain. When they approached Stoborani they realized that no Chetniks were there and that the potato field was covered in ice and snow. Aunt Mila's house had been razed, and they couldn't find anything in the ruins to break the ice with. Using only their hands, and hurrying because the Chetniks could appear at any moment, the two of them didn't stop until two sacks were filled with potatoes. There you go. The two men walked for several days, a hundred kilometres, through minefields and Chetnik ambushes, for a twenty-kilogram sack of potatoes.

'But that's not all,' my father said. 'I managed to bring a car up the mountain.'

The three of us looked at him, dumbstruck.

'What car? How did you manage that?' my mother asked.

'Our car! Somewhere around Žepa I met Zoran,' my father said. 'You know how he is, always ready to help.'

Zoran's real name was Ramiz Čardaković, but nobody had ever called him anything but Zoran. He had a lot of interesting stories about how he got this nickname, not least because Zoran is recognizably a Serb name.

'We found the car exactly where I'd left it back in May, still covered by the branches I'd hidden it under. When I cleared them away I could see that it was largely undamaged – although a piece of shrapnel had pierced it near the fuel tank. As I was inspecting it we heard a noise from the village. It must have been a Chetnik patrol. That scared me to death, and I wanted to get out of there, but Zoran wouldn't let me. He said it would be a shame not to rescue the car, and we got in. The car was out of fuel. My hands were trembling so much I couldn't put the thing in neutral. So Zoran sat in the driver's seat while I pushed and then watched as it rolled down the hill. The car bounced over the uneven ground, but Zoran skilfully steered it around the potholes – I was running behind him all the way to the valley. He got out of the car laughing. I was still shaking with fear. What a man! He's as mad as a hatter. Anyway, we ran into a guy from Žepa with two huge oxen. His oxen pulled the car up to Zlovrh Peak. The next morning I managed to freewheel it down to Vukoljin Stan, and that's where I left it.'

Unbelievable, simply unbelievable. My father had not only managed to dig up the potatoes from right under the Chetniks' noses but drag a car up a mountain!

'OK,' I said, 'but who needs a broken car with no fuel?'

'Maybe we can sell it. Who knows?' my father replied. I assumed that would be impossible, but in a few months I would be proved wrong. And not for the first time.

Meanwhile we had twenty kilograms of frostbitten potatoes, enough to feed the family for ten days or so. Then we were hungry again.

When, a few days later, my father heard that Hrustem, a man from Stoborani, was in hospital in Srebrenica he immediately went to see him. Afterwards we visited him together. Hrustem had been badly wounded in both legs. He had been in the group that had been ambushed by the Chetniks who, luckily, had let my father pass.

That day he had set out, as so many times before, in search of food. 'There were twenty of us altogether. We walked in single file – two guys with rifles in front, women at the back of the line, the rest of us in the middle. Some were leading horses. I remember thinking that something was wrong. I'd never heard such a silence before. There wasn't a sound, not a thing, not a bird. When the shooting started we didn't know what was happening! It must have been machine guns, M84s. They were behind a mound, and they just cut us down as we ran. I was hit in both legs. Somehow I managed to crawl behind a tree. I was bleeding badly, but my fear was stronger than the pain. I was clutching a knife in my hand because I'd decided to kill myself rather than fall into their hands.

'I looked around the tree. I saw at least ten bodies on the path. I wasn't sure if all of them were dead, but nobody was moving – and then I saw one woman raise her head. The Chetniks came out from behind the mound – about twenty of them, I think. Some keeping watch, the others rolling the bodies over. I saw it all clearly, for I watched carefully in case somebody decided to come my way. The woman called out; I think she was begging them for something. One of them went towards her, bent down and tore a necklace from her neck. Then they pulled out a handgun and shot her in the head. They probably took her money as well since they searched everyone's pockets. We all had money because we were on the way to buy corn. They left soon after that.

'Less than ten minutes later shelling started. The artillery must have opened fire to cover their withdrawal. I was bleeding so much that I passed out. When I came to it was pitch black. It occurred to me that they might come back in the morning, and that's why I started thinking once more of killing myself. But my knife was blunt. How could I kill myself with a blunt knife?

'The first person who passed that way in the morning was a young man all on his own. As soon as I called out he started to run away. He ran into the forest and hid. I shouted that I was a Muslim and that I was injured. When he finally approached me he was trembling. I managed to convince him not to go to Srebrenica but to go back to Žepa and call for help, to find someone to come and fetch me with a stretcher. The guy gave me a piece of bread and left. I was alone again. In the evening four men finally arrived and took me to the infirmary in Žepa.'

Hrustem and several other wounded from Žepa had been carried across the mountain on stretchers to hospital in Srebrenica. The doctors were going to try to remove the bullets from his legs as soon as he had regained some strength.

'I felt horribly sorry for the men who carried me. And ashamed. All the trouble they took for an old man.'

The autumn of 1992 was not only hungry and bloody but freezing as well. The temperature frequently dropped as low as −10 degrees Centigrade. We knew this because there was a thermometer on the façade of Veljko's house. It didn't take long for me to me to get sick spending day after day in the unheated concrete-and-marble building I had to work in. I got scared when blood began appearing in my urine and went to see a doctor. The medical clinic for civilians was in a house in my neighbourhood, next to the mosque on Crvena Rijeka Street. Dr Nijaz told me he could give me a shot of penicillin. Preparing it, he asked me if I knew how much a single shot went for these days. I had no idea.

'A hundred marks!' the good doctor exclaimed. 'Hasan, can you believe it? A hundred marks! A shot that means the difference between life and death. People die from gunshot wounds. Wounds get infected; there are maggots in the wounds, gangrene! We have to cut arms and legs off because of things that would be harmless in normal circumstances.'

I had known about this for a while. I'd heard the most awful bloodcurdling screams when passing by the hospital. Each time it happened I would speed up, but the screams could be heard from a long way away. Even basic medical equipment and supplies were lacking. Surgeons had to cut through flesh with a scalpel and then cut through bone with a handsaw. Amputations were performed without anaesthesia; amputees-to-be would sometimes be given schnapps instead, if their relatives could get hold of it. That in itself was dangerous because alcohol thins the blood.

The hospital was surrounded by row upon row of washing lines where bandages were hung out to dry. The bandages, used and reused and washed over and over again, formed a yellowish wall around the hospital. Inside the hospital everything smelled of pus. It smelled of pus, sweat and faeces. It smelled of corpses, too, for sometimes there would be dozens in the hospital morgue. The nauseating stench spread well beyond the building, and for all those who were not used to it vomiting came quite naturally. The stench of death was overwhelming.

Deep down I was determined that I would never be a patient there. I would never be injured. I'd rather be dead . . . much rather be dead. Death didn't frighten me as much as being maimed. I was sure that under the rain of shells or bullets everyone was silently praying for a mercifully quick death. We all thought we were dead anyway – we were all just waiting for the day, for the moment, when death would come to claim us. Death was like a friend who never left our side. It was our travelling companion.

Dr Nijaz gave me a shot of penicillin, and after a few days I stopped peeing blood. Whether it was the penicillin or the bitter teas Mother made with herbs a neighbour had given her, I'm not sure. My kidneys and bladder still hurt, but hunger made me forget about that.

In the meantime, the price of one shot of penicillin had risen to 150 Deutschmarks.

PODRAVANJE

There were rumours that our fighters were planning an attack on Podravanje, a Serb village on the road connecting Serbia to the BiH territory under Serb control and, significantly, situated between Srebrenica and Žepa. During that summer and autumn a lot of Bosniaks, mainly unarmed civilians, had been killed around Podravanje trying to reach Srebrenica from Žepa and vice versa. Needless to say, the word around town was that there was plenty of food there, and so, just as before, the starving population didn't need to be told twice to get prepared with sacks and backpacks. Enquiries were made about packhorses, trollies, weapons.

The four of us stayed at home, but many people on our street decided to go. As I watched them leave I couldn't help thinking about what had happened last time. Who among them would come back?

At dawn we heard the distant sounds of battle. According to protocol, the Serbs began shelling Srebrenica and the surrounding villages in retaliation.

I ran to the marketplace hoping to hear some news. Several hundred people were in the marketplace. Some soldiers had already returned.

'Podravanje fell!' somebody shouted. Cheers went up from all sides. Rounds were fired into the air. One man was holding a bottle in one hand and a rifle in another. He took a swig from the bottle and then the guy next to him grabbed it and did the same. Others appeared down the street carrying sacks of food: potatoes, flour, cooking oil, fresh meat, cured meat, livestock. This was as much as I could see in all the confusion.

And then I saw something utterly unexpected – two tanks were coming towards us! For a moment I thought the Chetniks were entering Srebrenica, but it was our fighters sitting on the tanks. They had captured them! This had never happened before. Man, this is something else, I thought. The iron monsters trundled noisily down the street. I'd never seen a tank up close before. At least ten fighters sat on one of them. Proud, relaxed, dishevelled. Some were even drunk. As they turned the corner towards the hotel we all ran behind them. Everybody wanted to see this marvel.

We found both tanks parked in front of the hotel. There was a lot of noise – screaming, squeals of joy, shooting in the air. I was afraid of stray bullets, but I couldn't resist getting a closer look at these beasts, now tamed. Tamed by our fighters, here, among us.

Two men spilled out of the group in heated dispute. The crowd moved apart to make room for them. One of the fighters had his arm bandaged and supported by a sling. He seemed a strong guy, dark, with cropped hair.

'I'm taking it to my village,' he said.

'No way. It has to be taken to the front line,' the other yelled at him.

'No,' the first one insisted. 'I captured it, and I won't let anyone else touch it.' He reached down with his free hand and grabbed the handgun at his waist. He seemed ready to use it. But then the crowd separated again, forming a corridor for someone to pass through – someone even tougher than these two: Naser Orić. Everybody fell silent. The two men watched Naser marching towards them. He looked displeased.

'What's happening here?' he asked sharply.

'I captured this tank,' the first fighter said.

'Not true. My unit surrounded the tank. We captured it before these guys even arrived.'

'The tanks don't go anywhere,' Naser said loud enough for everybody could hear. 'They don't belong to you or to you. They don't belong to me or to anyone in particular. They are *ours*. They will go where they are needed. Is that clear?' The question was directed to everyone present. Naser was looking around the crowd. No one said a word. The two fighters gave affirmative nods.

As the crowd began slowly to disperse I could see that other weapons had been captured. There was an anti-aircraft cannon with three barrels and a rotating platform. Velid was sitting on it. He was said to be a capable man, very knowledgeable about weapons. He was pressing a pedal with his foot and turned it in a full circle.

'Wow! Look at that,' someone in the crowd commented. 'It moves in all directions.'

I got closer because I couldn't believe my eyes; etched into the barrel, right next to the breach, was a Nazi eagle and swastika. 'Man, I had no idea that the JNA was using German weapons from the Second World War!' I said to someone standing next to me. The weapon looked as if it had just rolled off the production line!

Plenty of food had been taken from Podravanje. People went back and forth for days afterwards. The four of us did not. We went hungry.

Up in Sućeska some people were able to get a signal on their battery-powered televisions. The only channel they could watch was a Serb one. People in Srebrenica spoke about a news interview with an old man, a Serb, who had survived the attack on Podravanje. Apparently, when asked what had been the worst thing about the attack, the old man said, 'I hid in the bushes. The Muslims attacked from everywhere. I honestly don't know how I got through it. It was only when the shooting stopped that I dared to flee. What was the worst thing? The worst thing was the special forces who attacked with their bare hands jumping in through the windows.'

The 'special forces' was the hungry army of civilians who attacked Podravanje the way they had attacked other Serb villages around Srebrenica, that is, without firearms, on the heels of the armed fighters. Whoever got there first would be able to break into the Serb houses, barns and stables and get to keep everything for themselves. Those who arrived later wouldn't get anything, so the civilians would break into houses while the battle was still on. It was a mess. I'd heard of people entering through a rear window while the Serbs were still inside shooting at those attacking from the front.

The hungry people brought back from Podravanje everything a human stomach could digest.

THE LIBRARY

On the first floor of the cultural centre, above the office where I spent my days, was the town's library. There was a hole in the roof from the air raid, and the ceiling now leaked. I was told that the library had about five thousand books, but as far as I could see no one was interested any more – we couldn't eat paper. However, an interest in books was unexpectedly rekindled after a shortage of old newspapers left people without cigarette-rolling material. Apparently there was still tobacco, but all the paper had been used up. I was told not to let anyone into the library, and I guarded the territory well.

However, I did make an exception for a doctor, whom we called Dr Benjo. I was extremely glad to see him when a group arrived from Žepa. He wanted a few of Meša Selimović's books. On my recommendation he also took Derviš Sušić's books back with him to Žepa. I'd always liked the writing of Derviš Sušić, but when I reread his books again during the war I found that everything he had written about the Second World War was far more relevant than before. A scene in one of his books that I found most interesting was a description of a German offensive against the Yugoslav Partisans, in which the Chetnik collaborators were positioned on the left flank and the Croatian Ustaše on the right to prevent any possible contact between them.

I discovered a book about pogroms against Jews in Russia and Poland in the late nineteenth century and learned that Hitler hadn't been the first to start the mass killing of European Jews. I couldn't remember learning anything about that at school. For thousands of years human beings had persecuted, murdered and starved to death their fellow humans. While my stomach was rumbling from hunger all day long, I read about Jews suffering and starving in Polish ghettos and prisons, persecuted and tortured because of their Jewish names. Even my own suffering somehow diminished in comparison. We, the Bosniaks, the Bosnian Muslims, were not the first – nor the last – people to be persecuted and murdered because of our names.

Another book on medieval Bosnia – I don't even remember the name of its author – gave me insight into things I had never heard of previously. An entire paragraph was dedicated to Srebrenica; Serbia and Bosnia had been at war three times over the town. This was in the thirteenth century, long before the Ottoman Turks arrived. Their wars must have been over the silver mines. Ah, this can't be good, I thought. Then I read that in the fifteenth century the Turks had taken the first census of Srebrenica: 80 per cent of the population had been Catholic at the time. That was all news to me.

My next discovery was a four-volume history of the Second World War. I had been a keen student of history since childhood, and I thought I knew a lot about it, but those volumes changed my notion of what *a lot* meant. That autumn we were subjected to weekly Serb bombing raids. I was reading about the Allied raids on Dresden in which tens of thousands of German civilians had been killed in a single night, engulfed by a huge conflagration created by British firebombs. I figured that those four Serb MiGs were maybe not so terrible after all.

WHERE ARE YOU FROM, MATE?

The house we lived in was only a ten-minute walk from the cultural centre, and right across the street was the marketplace, the liveliest part of town – which is why so many people ended up being killed there. Regardless of the danger, it was always busy because it was where all trade was done. Some would come only to get news and information – such as where to get the cheapest corn, in which burned-out Muslim village could you still find food, where the Chetniks were positioned, what had been on the news the night before, whether NATO was going to intervene or when the war was going to be over. The place was a scene of absolute confusion – dirt, shards of glass, horse dung, large chunks of plaster that had fallen off buildings and people in ragged clothes and shoes. Worn-out shoes were maintained by wrapping pieces of rug or sheep or cow skin around them which were then secured with string.

Winter was just around the corner, and the first few air-raids had left the town's houses without any glass in their windows, so windows were covered with blankets, pieces of cloth and anything else that came to hand. It made me think of scenes from *The Day After* and *Mad Max 2*.

Men and women from the undamaged mountain villages gathered to sell corn, potatoes and eggs. A single egg would sell for ten Deutschmarks or a kilogram of shucked corn. Tobacco! It was no wonder that almost all the tobacco sellers were armed, as tobacco had reached the price of three thousand marks a kilogram – three thousand! Everyone preferred German currency to US dollars; villagers didn't know the exchange rate for the dollar, I guess. Given that new banknotes were not entering Srebrenica, it was always the same ones being circulated, so even they were worn out and torn. At that time my family had all of three hundred marks to its name. Hoping that prices would go down we would buy a kilogram of corn at a time, but prices only went up.

Since I didn't have any money I just walked around the marketplace to look and listen. I would sometimes run into groups of mostly young armed men. Older men were wiser and often claimed exemption from duty on the grounds of 'poor health' and 'children', so the responsibility to defend the people thus fell on the shoulders of the young. Some young men, not all, embraced this with extreme pride and some with childish enthusiasm. Not all of them wore a uniform, and some wore only the odd item of uniform. The ones who had full uniforms must have taken them off dead Chetniks. They would parade through the marketplace in full combat gear, some with ammunition belts across their chests. They were showing off in front of the girls, I guess. Some of them were already seasoned fighters who had witnessed much bloodshed, much death.

Whenever I ran into such a group in the street their stock question would be 'Where are you from, mate?' I must have looked like a perfect candidate to become, say, a machine gunner – before I lost too much weight that is . . .

I would get confused, not knowing what to answer. I would finally say, 'Well, I'm a refugee.'

'OK. Where from?'

'From Vlasenica.'

'OK. So which unit are you in?'

That was the question I feared. I would rather not have answered, as I was ashamed to say that I was working, temporarily, for the town administration, the Civil Protection Service, but I'd say, 'None.'

They would exchange glances. That wasn't an acceptable answer. All of them were members of military units. At the time such military units were referred to by the names of their commanders. The ones I had heard about at that point were Hakija's Unit, Naser's Unit, Ahmo's Unit, Zulfo's Unit and Lieutenant Nedžad's Unit.

These encounters always made me feel uncomfortable. I struggled to define what I was or my family were. Were we refugees?

Stragglers? Foragers? Fugitives? All we had done for months was to look for places to stay, for food, water and firewood without being killed or freezing to death. This might take hours of effort each day. On top of my work for the administration I had no time to become a fighter, even if I had dared. And, anyway, what kind of fighter could I be without a rifle? There weren't enough weapons, not to mention ammunition, uniforms, military boots, or suitable substitutes for that matter to enlist new recruits.

On other occasions when I was asked to define my role in Srebrenica 'A moving target' would be my answer. Which was not untrue.

Since there was no conscription in that part of Bosnia for the duration of the war people took up the fight against the Chetniks in all sorts of ways. Before joining some had been avoiding any contact with weapons and armed groups. They had been looking after their families and trying to find a way to get them out before the door slammed shut on all of us.

Sometime around 1994 I met one of those men. This is his story. 'At first I refused to join the small bands that had armed themselves somehow. I watched it all from a distance, even viewing them with scorn. That was in Potočari during the first few weeks of the war. Then the Chetniks started pounding Potočari with mortars and artillery – house by house. When I was told that mine had been hit I ran home like a mad thing because I had no idea who'd been there at the time. Luckily all of my family were safe and unharmed, but the inside of the house – the living room was completely destroyed. A shell had passed through the window and smashed my brand-new wardrobe! That's when I got my gun, saying, "You Chetnik bastards, you're going to pay for that wardrobe!"'

And that's how one individual became a fighter.

Here's another story – this one I heard from people who had witnessed the crucial defence of Sućeska in May 1992. Thanks to the exceptional courage of its defenders no part of the Sućeska region was ever taken by the Chetniks until the final fall of Srebrenica in July 1995. But the first time Sućeska was attacked – with infantry, tanks and several APCs – the lines were breached. One man decided to fight until the last bullet, long after his comrades had retreated.

He threw a Molotov cocktail at an APC and set it on fire. Unaware that there was no one on the left and right flanks, he rushed forward shouting, 'Attack, attack!' The Chetniks retreated, Sućeska had been defended single-handedly. The question remains as to whether he would have done what he did had he known about the retreat of his comrades, but it is chance sometimes that makes heroes. That's how it is. People do things they never knew they were capable of.

I heard another story that is worth telling, about how a man from Voljavica joined the fight and what motivated him to become one of our bravest fighters. They called him Miš, which means Mouse. In May 1992 the Bratunac Chetniks surrounded his village and took all the men prisoner. Miš somehow managed to escape into the forest with the women and children. The prisoners were either killed on the spot or taken to the detention camps in Bratunac. Anyone who stayed in the village was burned alive in their homes, including Miš's parents, who were locked in their house with six other people. This was all before a single shot was fired at the Chetniks.

FISHING BOOTS AND LEVI'S 501

Long after the first snow thousands of people would roam the surrounding hills cutting firewood. Wood was in abundance and wasn't hard to get to, unlike in Sarajevo at the time. Men, women and children dragged tree trunks home with ropes and wire – that is, until there wasn't a single tree left standing. With the hills stripped of trees, firewood became a problem in Srebrenica as well. The closer the Chetniks got the more dangerous it became to fetch wood from further away. Then people started digging out the tree stumps.

The soles of my only pair of shoes crumbled away. They had been cracked for a long time, and it was no longer possible to patch them. No shoes meant I couldn't leave the house to collect wood, water or food.

The shelling kept us indoors. Every two or three days we would spend hours in the basement. The Bašić family kept all kinds of gear down there: piles of *Do-It-Yourself* magazine, electrical equipment, fishing rods and tackle – and a pair of fishing boots, brand new! They had been there the whole time. It seemed strange that none of us had ever noticed them before. I tried them on. They were a size too big, but with a pair of thick socks on they fit snugly. I was overjoyed. They were very long and rose above the knee. I made a slit in the upper part and rolled them down to my shins, turning them into standard Wellingtons, which we call 'miner's boots'.

The woollen trousers I had on had belonged to Goran, the son of our absent hosts, and they needed a wash. The only spares I owned were a previously unworn pair of genuine Levi's. These jeans had journeyed with me from Vlasenica through Stoborani, Luka and up the Drina. I had bought them in Sarajevo for 120 Deutschmarks, which my father had given to me as a reward with for completing a year at university. I'd been saving them for the end of the war, but there was no chance of that coming around any time soon, so why shouldn't I wear them now, just once?

I was ready for a twelve-kilometre walk to Šušnjari in a pair of brand-new *original* Levi's 501 jeans and a pair of rubber boots. According to my father we had some relatives there who might be able to spare some food. We were down to our last mark; our only valuables were a few pieces of my mother's jewellery.

I had become extremely skinny; my clothes were hanging off me. As I set off down the street I felt everybody staring. I was sure I cut a bizarre figure, gangly in my boots, legs as skinny as toothpicks in my shiny new original Levi's. But it was the boots that made everybody stare.

'Hey, you,' one man shouted. 'Do you want to trade? I'll give you ten kilograms of corn for those.' Translated into money ten kilograms of corn amounted to one hundred Deutschmarks, maybe 150 if the corn were any good. I was tempted – I had hardly had any breakfast that morning, and I'd not made it to the end of the street before the boots had given me a blister on my heel – but there was no way I could walk barefoot, so I had to decline. The number of offers I received for those boots in subsequent days made me convinced that there were people who, should I be injured, would strip the boots off my feet before checking if I was still breathing.

I was also offered ten kilograms of wheat for my Levi's. When I refused the guy doubled his offer. He had a rifle, and I had a feeling that he might use it. Years later, when I got to know him, I mentioned that encounter. He told me that I had been wrong – 'Or maybe not,' he added, with a grin.

I reached Šušnjari all in one piece and with all my clothes. Once there I tracked down our family.

'Tell your father to come,' said my father's cousin Jusuf, and a few days later I set off back for Šušnjari, this time accompanied by my father. An anti-aircraft gun behind a hill was firing so frequently that we considered abandoning our trip and heading back to Srebrenica. The Chetniks' fighting positions were right above the village. Our men had to hold the defence lines day and night. They were under near constant attack with mortars. The villagers refused to leave their homes despite numerous fatalities. They knew they wouldn't go hungry in the village. Their barns were full of corn to feed their cows, but now it fed them. They also had wheat, dried foods and pumpkins.

When the shelling became less frequent we took a muddy trail and climbed up to the village. We were warmly received by our relatives. This would have been normal once, but things had changed and 'warmly' was rarely the way anyone greeted anyone else these days. Refugees who asked for food were treated like beggars and often driven away with curses. It was one of the greatest humiliations one could experience.

This time Jusuf invited us to join his family for lunch. The meal was served in the traditional way, a practice that endured during the war because it was a good way of making food go further: a white sheet was spread on the floor and a large pan of *pita* was placed in the middle; a circle was cut out of the centre of the *pita* and a bowl of yoghurt put in its place. We all sat around it eating from the big pan, spooning the yoghurt directly from the bowl.

Jusuf gave us about twenty kilograms of corn, and he brought approximately the same amount from his brother. He put it all in a sack and then weighed it – a total of forty-four kilograms! Although it would be pretty exhausting I was more than happy to carry the forty-four kilograms of life back home. My father helped me to position the sack on my back – or, to be more precise, on my cervical vertebrae. I carried it for hours that way, all the way to Srebrenica. I could barely move my head, and this made it impossible for me to see where I was heading. I still don't know where I got the strength. I was at the end of my tether, but the expression of relief and happiness on the faces of my brother and mother was my reward. They knew the corn would last us the whole month if we were careful.

After a few weeks, with supplies again running low, my parents decided it was time to use my mother's jewellery. She had been collecting it since her wedding day, adding to it in the intervening twenty-five years. She put the tiny bundle on the table, unwrapped it and placed a gold bracelet, a gold necklace and several beautiful rings into a separate pile. The rest of it – the little that was left – was wrapped in the cloth once more and put back into my mother's handbag.

My father and I set off for another village near by. We were looking for yet another distant relative of ours and found him in front of his house. The cold expression on his face never changed. He didn't even say hello.

'What's your business here?' he asked.

My father unwrapped the little bundle, and the pieces of my mother's jewellery flashed in the sun.

Our distant relative dismissed it with the same contemptuous look he gave to us. 'This is worth almost nothing,' he said. 'My house is full of trinkets like these.'

My father's face grew pale. Words stuck in his throat.

I felt like a beggar. Tears filled my eyes, but I fought them back. Our cousin entered the house and came back out with a bowl of flour – maybe a kilogram or two.

'This is what I can give you for what you've brought. The other day a woman came to me with a lot more gold; she was satisfied with a bowl of flour. Take it or leave it – but don't come to my house ever again.'

I glared at him but said nothing. There was a dull ache in my chest. I was caught in a fog of shame, a fog of fear that we would soon starve to death, a fog of grief for the loss of human kindness.

We returned with enough flour for just a few more days.

ENGLISH

There were all sorts of wonders in the Bašić family's basement. Once I found a cookbook full of coloured photographs; I opened it to a page with a grilled fish served on a plate of baked potatoes, fresh salad, white sauce, onions and lemon wedges. As I looked at the picture I started to salivate. I imagined eating the fish and tried to remember how it might taste, and for a short while it seemed my hunger could be sated by my imagination. The next moment I was looking for scissors. I was thinking of cutting the photograph out of the book so I could . . . eat it. For a moment it seemed like a good idea, and I wasn't so far from actually doing it.

'If I ever get out of this hell alive I will never again utter the name Srebrenica. I will never again use any word beginning with S,' I said to myself. 'I'd take the North Pole over Srebrenica. I'm sure I could find more food there. Or jail, somewhere with three meals a day, no shelling, no Chetniks. If I ever get out of this hell alive I will not spend a single day longer than I have to in Bosnia.'

Then it dawned on me that I'd have to learn English. I had to learn English at all costs.

After a while my mother called me up from the basement because the fire had gone out. I had to go to fetch some embers from our neighbour. We were living a prehistoric life in Srebrenica. Before the war had it ever occurred to anyone that matches were important? But now nobody had any matches or lighter fluid for lighters. If you wanted a fire you either never let it go out or you had to go to your neighbour's house and borrow it.

Once we were given a whole carton of matchboxes by Ahmo Tihić, my cousin Sabera's husband and a commander in the local militia. My father and I had run into him and told him that we had nothing to eat. The matches could act as currency. Thinking they would be in demand, we toured several villages unsuccessfully offering them in exchange for grain. We experienced some very humiliating responses on these travels, with villagers screaming and swearing at us and slamming doors in our faces. I had never felt more sorry for myself or my family. What a dog's life it was.

Eventually we managed to trade the matches for a few kilograms of grain, albeit much less than we had hoped for.

On the days that we had flour my mother made bread. She would remove the bread from the oven at half past nine in the morning. The loaf was usually no more than twenty centimetres in diameter, and it was always divided into four pieces as precisely as possible – although not always precisely enough, and on one particular occasion I went berserk thinking that my brother had been given a bigger piece than me.

'What is this?' I yelled. 'Why is my piece smaller than his?'

Sitting there at the table my father was thunderstruck, my brother was stunned into silence and my mother burst into tears. She pushed her piece of bread away saying, 'I won't have any.'

I ran out of the room and into the bathroom. I stood in front of the mirror and looked at myself. There was nothing left of me – just skin and bone with sunken eyes. I had lost more than twenty-five kilograms, but my father had lost nearly forty. What was happening to me? Had I gone mad, demanding food from my brother, father, mother?

I went outside and stepped into a blizzard – it was so cold that I rushed in the direction of Ćamil's house. I decided I was not going to eat with my family any more. I didn't know who I was angry with, but I was very angry. On the way to Ćamil's I ran into his neighbour Emir Suljagić. I knew that Emir lived with his parents and sister. He was six or seven years younger than me – more or less my brother's age. I was used to seeing Braco's peer group as children, but Emir definitely looked like an adult; he was taller than me, and he had a more adult demeanour than other kids his age.

'I just found out that my father was killed by a shell down in Voljavica,' he told me.

I didn't know what to say. As far as I remember I eventually blurted out something like 'You have to be strong for your mother and sister. Someone has to take care of them. You are the head of the family now.' Even as I was saying it I knew the words were cheap platitudes. I wouldn't know what to do if the same thing were to happen to me. Emir disappeared into the blizzard, heading into town to learn more about his father's death. I continued towards Ćamil's.

He invited me in. His house was warm and smelled like a bakery. I could see there was something in the oven.

Ćamil's mother took a *pita* out and started slicing it.

'This is *tirit pita*,' she said. 'A special wartime recipe. You know what that is?'

'No idea,' I said.

'It's *pita* with corn stuffing.'

'Aha,' I said.

The *pita* was cut into four, for Ćamil, his brother Fikret, his father and his mother. I sat there with my empty stomach and watched them eat. They didn't invite me to join them, and I didn't expect them to. That simply wasn't done now; it was against the rules of survival that everybody had accepted.

'So, Hasko,' Ćamil said, 'what's happened to that girlfriend of yours?'

I told them how Mirza and I had parted at Sarajevo bus station back in April. 'I think about her all the time,' I said. 'I miss her. But . . . if I were to choose between seeing her this very instant or having a nice slice of *pita* I'd choose the *pita*.'

They laughed. They probably had no idea how true my words were.

'Ćamil,' I said, 'do you know any English at all?'

'None,' he replied.

'Listen, I found some English-language textbooks in the library the other day. Brand new, just sitting there on a table. I started the course on my own, and I think I'm doing pretty well.'

'What do you need English for?' Ćamil said, surprised. 'Where did you get the idea?'

'You know what, if I survive this I'm going to need it. I intend to get as far away from Bosnia as I can.'

They looked at me as though this was a crazy idea. Oh, come on, English of all things? In this time and place? Right!

There was a knock at the door. It was our friend Fahro.

'*Salam alaikum*. Oh, look who's here!' Fahro said. 'Hasko, I was thinking of you just this morning! Listen, my father went to Konjević Polje the other day and brought back some tobacco leaves. I saved you a few leaves to roll a ciggy.'

'Oh, thank you!' I was on my feet at once. 'Do you think there's enough to roll one for my father?'

He reluctantly reached into his pocket and pulled out some crushed leaves. We then took an old textbook and tore off a strip of paper and went out into the cold for a smoke. I was pulverizing the tobacco leaves when we heard a distant explosion, a muffled *boom boom boom*.

We exchanged glances.

'It's from Rogač,' Ćamil said. Rogač was a notorious Chetnik artillery position somewhere above Milići. From there they could shell the entire region.

Swish. Boom. Swish. Boom. Swish. Boom. Baroom.

Three shells flew in rapid succession and exploded just under the walls of the Old Town fortress, not far from where we were standing. The ground trembled under my feet. My tobacco fell to the ground. I suddenly realized I was on my own. Fahro and Ćamil had already bolted for cover. I ran blindly around the house looking for a place to hide. I noticed a basement door, which I struck with my fist. 'Let me in, let me in!' I was pulled in by Ćamil. Fahro and Ćamil's family were huddled in a dark corner. The shelling lasted for at least half an hour. The whole house shook from the detonations. Between the shells we could hear screams coming from the street.

'I bet they're shelling the whole town. It's been a while since they used the large-calibre artillery on us,' a voice said from the dark.

'What was the equation? Two alpha over v? Or was it v over two alpha?' Ćamil asked.

'Two alpha what?' Fahro retorted. But I had figured out that Ćamil was talking about a kinetics course that had been part of our second-year engineering curriculum. It hadn't been an easy examination, but the three of us had all passed.

'I remember the lesson,' I said. 'Slant projectile motion.'

So we started calculating the firing angle alpha and the projectile velocity v needed to hit the street directly, running as it did between two hills. We calculated that it was not possible for a piece of heavy artillery to achieve such a high-angle trajectory. Mortars could do it, but this was a 105-calibre cannon, maybe even a 155, as far as we could tell by the sound of the explosions.

I had nothing to eat that day or the next. I could feel all my strength disappearing – I felt the emptiness not only in my stomach but in my head as well. I was really ashamed of my behaviour at the dinner table. I refused all food. My mother begged me to eat. I guess I was trying to punish myself. By the end of the second day I felt so dizzy that I was sure I was going to faint. I had a glass of water and a piece of cornbread and then asked my mother to give me two kilograms of cornflour. I took it to Ćamil's house and persuaded them to give me half a kilogram of wheat flour for it. I felt I needed some proper bread or a real filo-pastry *pita*. The next day my father bartered a kilogram of cornflour for half a kilogram of meat. That was how prices were matching up at that point. And thus we had our first proper meal since leaving Luka. My mother made a meat-filled *pita* with unbelievably thin pastry in order to save the flour for another meal. Despite that we took time to admire the *pita* and inhale its wonderful aroma. Then we ate it in the blink of an eye.

It was to be our last decent meal for many months.

I stuck to my plan and, shelling or no shelling, kept up my English grammar. *To be. To do. To have. I, you, he, she, it, we, you, they.* I was sure that my own brother thought I was crazy, but then, he had always thought I was odd. I stood out from his friends. Every evening my brother would give me a significant look before turning his back and going to sleep. I would move the oil lamp closer and recite: *I was, you were, she was . . .*

A HAIRCUT

Believe it or not, despite all the horrors of our daily life, people in Srebrenica actually still cared about their looks. Most of the men had neatly trimmed hair, and the most popular cut at the time was the one Naser Orić rocked – short back and sides with a long fringe. I was disappointed when I realized it wouldn't suit my face, otherwise I might have tried it, too.

Ćamil had a hitherto undiscovered talent for haircutting. He only did it for his friends as a special favour. I would always ask him to come to my place because my sinuses were in a worsening state, and I was wary of stepping outside with wet hair. There wasn't any medicine for the injured, let alone for someone with chronic sinusitis.

Ćamil arrived with a pair of rusty scissors. 'I don't like to stay away from home for long,' he said while moving around me. 'The shelling and bombing could begin at any moment, and I think my mother would have a heart attack if she didn't know where I was when it started.'

'Don't rush now, please,' I said. 'You left it longer here, see?' *Snip, snip* went Ćamil's scissors, but then a different sound reached our ears.

'What's that?' I said, jumping off the chair and rushing out on to the veranda. Ćamil followed along with my parents and brother. We couldn't see it yet, but we could clearly hear the agricultural plane returning. Next came the sound of gunfire from the town – people were probably trying to take it down with their automatic rifles, but in vain. We saw people in the street running for shelter. Mothers were anxiously calling out the names of their children. A few moments later we saw the plane. It was flying so low that we could make out the pilot. We rushed to the basement, lay down on the floor with our mouths open and covered our ears with our hands. The bomb whistled and fell seemingly on top of our heads. The explosion almost bounced us off the floor.

A second plane was incoming. While we were waiting for the next explosion we heard the sound of the anti-aircraft gun our fighters had captured from the Chetniks that was positioned up on the hill. But, as with every other captured weapon, there was the problem of ammunition. The cannon shots slowly followed one another. You could tell that they were trying to save the rounds. The gunner lived on our street. People called him Aće – I guess Akif was his real name. He was tall and brave. His hair was long, and his slightly pointed nose appeared to have been broken. I could imagine him up on the hill with just a few pieces of ammunition giving away his position to defend the town.

The duel probably lasted no more than a minute or two, but it seemed like an eternity to us. Aće's cannon fire had done the trick and scared the second plane away before it could drop its bombs. We started shouting, 'Aće, bravo! Bravo, Aće!'

When we finally dared leave the basement we saw that all the windows in our house had been shattered, and even the door and window frames, including the door to the veranda, had been damaged by the blast. The bomb had fallen some fifty metres away, hitting the local mosque and the house next door to it, in which Dr Nijaz ran the civilian clinic. The good doctor had been standing right in the doorway when the bomb exploded. He was killed on the spot – his body cut in half. Ten metres away were two more lifeless bodies, a woman and a child. The child couldn't have been older than five or six. I remember the woman's scarf. It looked as if she had tried to reach the house while carrying the child in her arms but had been caught by the force of the explosion and smashed against a wall. The blast had melted the snow and ice on the street. There was a strong chemical stench in the air, which would linger for at least a month after the explosion.

'I'm going home,' Ćamil said.

After a few days I asked Ćamil to come over again since he'd left my hair half done. Reluctantly, he returned. He grumbled about more and more people being killed in the street. The shelling had become more frequent. Every day, several times a day. Sometimes it would just be one mortar shell, sometimes two, three. Sometimes there was a whole volley of shells.

There was a knock at the door, and my mother went to answer it. She came back very embarrassed because two children, a girl and her younger brother, had asked her for food, a piece of cornbread, anything. But she had nothing to give them.

'What could I give them when we're down to our last handful of cornflour?'

'And there are so many of them. I have no idea where they come from, but they come to our door every day,' Ćamil said as he cut my hair.

Suddenly – it was always suddenly – a mortar shell fell outside the house. There came a scream and then the sound of weeping. Ćamil was the first to run out into the hallway, and we were hot on his heels.

Ćamil looked at me as if it were my fault. 'Man, every time I cut your hair something bad happens,' he said, visibly upset.

We all ran out into the street. The little girl who had been at our door just a few moments before was holding her brother in her arms. 'Brother, wake up, wake up,' she sobbed. A man was standing by her side trying to take the boy from her arms, but she wouldn't let him.

Still wrapped in the white sheet covered with hair I stood, shocked. This is sheer horror, I thought, and then: Thank God my brother isn't here. I knew Braco was with his friends somewhere in the neighbourhood. As always in similar situations, my first thought was: Thank God it's not one of us.

The man finally succeeded in taking the little boy from his sister's arms and carried him down the street. The girl ran behind him, crying. The neighbours silently watched from their windows. I was sure that they were all thinking the same thing: *Thank God it's not one of mine* and *Yet another one missed us*.

The street would forget the boy and girl as soon as they had disappeared around the corner.

'Listen,' Ćamil said, 'I'm going home now. Please don't ask me to cut your hair again.'

BLUE HELMETS

We listened closely to the radio, hoping to hear that our turn had come to receive humanitarian aid. But every time the UNHCR convoys reached Bratunac local Serb women blocked the road banging on the truck windows, swearing and saying they would not allow the UNHCR to 'deliver food to the Muslims who kill our sons, husbands and brothers'. They seemed to have no problem with the UNHCR delivering aid to the war-affected Serb population, despite the fact that the Serbs had been killing Bosniak sons, husbands and brothers.

During 1992 food convoys were able to reach almost every part of BiH except Srebrenica and Žepa. One would think that the Serbs hated these places more than any others, but this was actually part of the plan for the 'ethnic cleansing of Bosniaks in Podrinje'. We, of course, tried to figure out why convoy after convoy had been stopped at the bridge in Zvornik and returned to the UNHCR warehouses in Belgrade. We had no idea what was happening on the fronts across the country, but we knew that around Srebrenica and Žepa our fighters had not lost a single battle since June 1992. While it was true that during the summer of 1992 several Muslim villages were attacked and burned down around Žepa, the Chetniks had hardly been able to break through the front lines in the areas of Srebrenica, Bratunac, Konjević Polje, Cerska, Nova Kasaba or Kamenica near Zvornik.

In the meantime the territory liberated by units under Naser Orić's command had apparently grown to approximately one thousand square kilometres. Our fighters had not suffered a single major defeat. By the autumn of 1992 the handful of villagers who had decided to defend their homes in the spring of that year had grown into a force of several hundred, if not even more than a thousand fighters. Needless to say, almost all their arms and ammunition had been captured from the Serbs, which was obviously too bitter a pill for the Serbs to swallow. This was an area that they had almost fully controlled at the beginning of the summer, but they had lost territory despite their weaponry, tanks and aeroplanes, despite mass expulsions of Bosniaks, concentration camps, executions, torture, torched villages and a large population of starving refugees for the Bosniaks to worry about. The Serbs were furious. Rumours were circulating in Srebrenica that the Serb army in the Drina valley was on the brink of collapse and that a plan was in place to evacuate the Serb population. The Serbs were, therefore, determined to destroy the besieged Bosniaks through starvation. Any aid in the form of food was out of question. No food convoys were allowed to reach us.

However, in mid-November another rumour went around that a food convoy would finally be allowed to pass through Bratunac. Only news of the end of war would have caused greater joy among the hungry people of Srebrenica.

The miracle of a UNHCR convoy arriving in Srebrenica was announced on the radio. As soon as I heard about it I rushed out of the house and ran down the street to meet the convoy. I found myself in front of the department store, and there I saw a scene I will never forget. Several white UN APCs were driving in front of about twenty trucks clearly marked with UNHCR insignia. Two burly UNPROFOR soldiers with moustaches were sitting on top of the first vehicle. Hundreds of men, women and children were rushing towards them from every direction, eventually blocking the street. Our fighters appeared out of nowhere and escorted the convoy through the crowd. One of the drivers threw a bag of sweets out of the window, and all the children threw themselves into the mud to claim it.

It all looked completely unreal. They had finally reached us! The Blue Helmets themselves! Our saviours! They had brought us food, maybe even safety. Maybe the shooting would stop now. Maybe the Chetniks would stop shelling us. We had endured hell, but we were going to be saved. The world was with us. My eyes filled with tears.

'They're moving on! They're moving on!' the crowd began to cry. The whole convoy was passing by like swans on a river. They proceeded towards the upper part of town.

'Where do you think they're going?' I asked a man standing next to me.

'To unload the food, I reckon, up there at the Petriča Warehouse in Klisa,' he said.

I rushed after them, running up the hill with as much energy as I had left in me. I had to get something from those trucks, it didn't matter what. Who knew what was in there? Maybe cigarettes! On the way I ran into my cousin and namesake Haso, who joined me in my campaign.

'Let's take a shortcut,' I said. 'We'll get there before anyone and ask the soldiers to give us a cigarette each.'

'How can I ask them for anything?' Haso asked.

'Just say "Give me, please, one cigarette",' I advised, using my English.

He tried to get his tongue around the phrase as we went running up the hill. We arrived in time to see a soldier throwing a packet of Marlboros to the crowd. A fight immediately broke out. People started swearing at one another, shouting, 'It's mine! I got it first!' Haso and I approached another soldier. He was standing with his rifle at the ready. He had a blue helmet and dark sunglasses.

'Hey, give me, please, one cigarette,' Haso and I said in unison.

The guy weighed us up very seriously at first, but then he smiled and put his hand into his pocket. He drew out a packet of cigarettes and offered one each to Haso and me. We lit them at once. And so we had our smokes. After all that time the effect was strange. We were stoned out of our minds.

'I'm definitely not telling my father about this,' I said.

'I can't believe it burned so fast. He seems like a nice guy; maybe he'll give us some more,' Haso said cheerfully.

But then a commotion started at the head of the convoy. The unloading had begun. More and more people were arriving – many more, perhaps thousands. People started climbing on the trucks. The UNPROFOR soldiers seemed troubled: they did not know how to control them. Then we heard gunfire: our fighters had started shooting into the air to disperse the crowd. They managed to form a cordon around the convoy. The representatives of the local authorities from the Wartime Council addressed the crowd saying that all the food was going to be unloaded and distributed fairly. Things quietened down only after the last truck had been unloaded, at which point they set off back down the hill to form a convoy and head back to Bratunac.

I noticed a group of civilians jump out of one of the trucks. They were journalists, and there were several television crews, mainly foreigners; two of them were American, the rest were from Serbia – I could tell by their accent. They were probably interpreters. They were coming right towards me. Although I stood out in my green jacket I think that maybe they found me interesting because of my glasses. One of the lenses had fallen out, and I'd just about repaired it using wood glue. The lens was smeared all over except for one tiny section that I could peep through.

The cameras turned on me, and they put a microphone in my face. They spoke to me in English, but I could understand very little. Then an interpreter with a Serbian accent asked me, 'Could you tell us how you manage here and how much longer you think you'll be able to hold out under such circumstances?'

This concern about how we're doing and whether or not we can keep going, this also comes as part of the convoy, I thought. This recording, my message, might be seen by the whole world. I had no second thoughts about what I would say; I could hardly wait to complain about our situation.

'My family and I are on the edge here. We've been starving for months. Without food we'll die of starvation within the next twenty days.'

While I was delivering my short statement the crew turned its attention to something going on behind me. I turned around and saw that Naser Orić was standing just a few metres away. He looked like a mountain of a man. Dressed in camouflage, his M-84 machine gun – which the Serb soldiers called the 'sower of death' – balanced casually against his shoulder he was standing with his legs firmly apart and a very serious expression on his face. Two fighters standing either side of him looked almost exactly the same, with ammunition belts across their chests and hand grenades on their belts. They stood in the cold as if it were their natural element. Proud. Calm. No sign of fatigue on their faces. Ready for action.

The American journalists immediately flocked to Naser and asked him the same question they had asked me. 'How much longer can you hold out like this?'

Naser responded, 'Pass this message on to the Serbs in Bratunac. We can continue like this for the next hundred years if we have to.'

As soon as he said it I realized that he had probably heard my answer. I expected him to knock me down with that machine gun of his because of what I had said to the camera. I thought my words might actually have been treasonous. I backed away a few steps and then scuttled down the hill as fast as the snow would allow me to.

The moment I was out of sight the fighters I returned to the convoy. I found an UNPROFOR soldier willing to listen to what I had to say in my broken English. I told him about our struggle to survive without food, water and electricity. I told him we were being subjected to shelling and aerial bombardments. He nodded. When I'd finished he said that the convoy had been given a two-hour deadline to unload the trucks in Srebrenica and return to Bratunac. That's when I realized that the convoy was just a small unit, a platoon maybe, of Belgian soldiers and several armoured transporters from the Ukrainian UN contingent.

The Ukrainian soldiers had somehow learned about two Ukrainian girls who had accidentally found themselves in Srebrenica in May 1992 and had been unable to get out. Since the beginning of the siege they had shared the fate of all the people in the town. Now a big Ukrainian soldier was putting the two girls into one of the APCs. They were evacuated from the hell of Srebrenica. As I watched the convoy depart I thought about how being Ukrainian sometimes makes all the difference in the world. I envied the girls.

The next day we were told that there would be two and half kilograms of food per person. The four of us got a half-kilogram pack of feta cheese to share. We immediately divided it into eight portions to make it last for two days. We also got some oil, maybe half a litre, and a few kilograms of wheat flour each. For the first time in several months we had real bread. It was a veritable feast, but it didn't last long. The world had sent each of us two-and-a-half kilograms of food. That was all the aid we got in eight months, from the beginning of the war in April until December 1992.

Soon after the convoy left I met up with some of my new friends on our street at Suso's house. Suso came from Voljavica, a village in the Bratunac Municipality. Suso's brother Sead, who'd become close to my brother, was also there with two other guys who were staying in the same house. All of them had extended families, lots of cousins and friends and pre-war neighbours who used to keep watch on the defensive lines that were extended towards their burned villages. That's how I got my information about the more remote locations within the free territory.

'So the convoy's gone,' said a voice from a darkened corner. A lamp in the middle of the room was flickering because the windows had no glass, just nylon sheets and blankets nailed to the frames. It was –10 Centigrade outside, and we kept the room warm by feeding logs into the stove. On some nights the temperature would drop to –20.

'I wonder how the Chetniks are doing up in the mountains,' another voice said. 'Are they as cold as we are?'

'Hell yeah, but they've got the military equipment to cope. They've dug trenches, ditches, bunkers, and it's all covered with tree trunks. They've got a stove in every bunker. They've got tinned food. We get sent to the front line with nothing but what we have at home. We're misery itself! It's a miracle we're still holding out.'

'In every sense,' I joined in, 'they've got an advantage over us. I mean, not only because of the weapons. Let's take these sanctions, for instance, that are supposedly being imposed on Milošević. Sanctions or no sanctions, Vojvodina alone is so big and fertile that Serbians will never go hungry, or at least not for a very long time, and by then we'll all be dead here.'

'Dead right,' everyone agreed.

Suso said, 'I watch them through my binoculars, you know, almost every day. We can see them, and they can see us. They don't shoot, and we don't shoot. I guess we all think we're better off that way. Mind you, they're within shouting distance, less than two hundred metres. The other day I called out, and one of them answered. I asked, "What's for lunch over there?" and he said, "Beans, the same as you." And then he threw a tin plate into the air. The plate landed in the minefield. He clearly didn't know that we had no beans. We didn't have anything. But then, how could he *not* know? He must have known.'

'They're cosy enough in their bunkers, all right,' another said. 'They've got food, they've got booze. They can fire five grenades at us anytime they want, ten even if it pleases them. They've got hundreds to spare. Man, there's no way we can cope with this lot, not like this.' After a short pause he added, 'Meanwhile, I'm sitting in the trench, freezing. I can't even light a fire or else they'll know where I am, and then I'm as good as dead. I usually bring a piece of cornbread with me. The other day my mother wrapped a tiny piece of cured meat for me, a really tiny piece, like half a fist, and I chewed it, and it was as hard as a rock. At the same time I know I've got five bullets in my rifle – that's it. If the Chetniks knew we had so few they'd attack us right away. Right away! They would enter Srebrenica in less than an hour. But they don't seem to know.'

'That's why Naser says we can't just sit around and wait,' a voice said from the corner, 'because this trench warfare is easy for them. They're a professional, well-equipped army. We can't fight in the trenches. We have to fight like guerrillas. Like the Partisans in the Second World War. Naser says we can only survive if we attack. You know why? Because you take as many bullets as you can afford and attack for as long as your ammunition lasts. You either win or retreat. If you take them by surprise you capture their ammunition and weapons. Then you have a short rest and attack again. You don't allow them to regroup or to know where you're going to hit next.'

'Too right,' the others concurred.

Suso opened the stove door and tossed another log into the fire.

'Yeah, that's the way,' our strategist continued, 'that's the only way. If you wait for them to attack you'll run out of ammunition before they do. Then you're finished. That's it.'

'It's late. I have to go,' I said getting up.

I hurried across the icy road. It was so cold that my breath turned froze on my nose. I found my father and brother already in bed, their heads covered with their jackets. During that winter we always went to bed fully dressed, wearing our woollen sweaters, socks, everything we'd had on during that day. The fire was crackling in the stove. Mother was still up. No explosions could be heard. I guess it was too cold even for the Chetniks.

We could hear the *azaan* from the mosque, the evening call to prayer.

'I wonder if the imam is cold up there on the minaret,' I said facetiously. 'What do you think?'

Loudspeakers were of no use since there was no electricity. The muezzins had had to return to the traditional way of reciting the call to prayer. In order to be heard they either had to climb the minaret or stand in front of the mosque.

'Mother, do you believe in God?' It was probably the first time in my life that I had asked her that question.

'Hasko,' my mother began, 'I've thought about that so many times since the war started. I watch my only two sons suffering and keep asking myself what could we have possibly done to deserve this from God. And then I think of those tyrants like Milošević or Karadžić with all the planes they have to bomb us with and all the power they have to starve us, and I think, who knows what else they would do if there were no one above them, no higher power? They would surely exterminate us. God is the only one who can save us.'

In bed I rolled myself into a ball to get warmer. Through my windows, which no longer had any glass in them, I could hear the bark cracking on the frostbitten trees.

NEW YEAR

The year 1993 was approaching, our first new year of the war. We didn't know it at the time, of course, but we would welcome in two more in Srebrenica.

On New Year's Eve my family was sitting around the table wondering what to eat once our supplies of rotten cornmeal, polenta and salt were used up. To make things worse, the Serbs had mined the water-supply system. Hundreds of people now had to queue to use the town's wells every morning.

Outside it was a true winter wonderland. Thirty centimetres of snow had fallen overnight and blanketed the roofs and houses charred by shellfire. The whiteness seemed to mask all our suffering.

I was enjoying the moment when there was a knock at the door. It was Adem, a refugee from Voljavica, who now occupied the house right across the street. He had a wife and two small daughters and, just like us, spent most of his time wandering around Srebrenica and the surrounding villages looking for food.

'Salam alaikum,' Adem said as he came in. 'Ibro, how about going to Voljavica? Almost all our guys are retreating. People have brought back quite a lot of food from there over the past few weeks.' He was referring to the most recent action, which had probably covered the widest area to date. Several groups of fighters had penetrated deep into Serb-controlled territory to cut off the Serb reinforcements from Bratunac. It had been a hazardous yet successful manoeuvre, and this time our fighters hadn't withdrawn immediately. The skirmishes behind enemy lines went on for three whole days, and there was a genuine risk that our fighters would not be able to get out and make it back to Srebrenica. One of the guys who'd participated was Hamed. I had run into Hamed before the action. It was not usual to see him dressed in a scrappy uniform and carrying a rifle. It might have been his first action, all the more important because he was, like many of his comrades-in-arms, going back home to his scorched village where many of his relatives and neighbours had been killed back in May. It was an important day for them. A few days later I bumped into him again. His hand was bandaged. He told me what had happened in Voljavica.

'When we first emerged from the trees we took the Chetniks by surprise, but they quickly recovered. We were pounded with mortar fire from Tablja on the left and artillery fire from Serbia on the right. They opened fire on us from Bratunac with whatever weapons they had available. Man, can you imagine getting attacked from three directions and having nowhere to hide? All the houses were reduced to rubble, and the only thing we could use as cover were a few concrete foundation walls half a metre high, a metre maybe in some places.

'They would fire a hundred shells or so and then send in the infantry to check if we were still alive. Only then would we start shooting, and after a short skirmish the Chetniks would go back and their artillery would take over again.

'A piece of shrapnel hit me in the hand. I was lucky. My neighbour was killed in front of my eyes. A shell took his head off. Many more were killed or injured. There's no way that the fighters down there can hold out for more than a few days. They'll have to withdraw.'

They were attempting to withdraw at the time Adem knocked on our door to ask my father if he would go to Voljavica.

'I'll get the sledge and we can head off,' Adem said. 'I guess it'll all have been looted by now, but we might find a thing or two in the Serb houses in the area. If you want to come, be ready in ten minutes.'

My father got ready to go leave.

'This time I'm coming with you,' I said. 'You never let me come on these insane missions, but this time I'm not asking. This time . . .' I went on and on while he was getting dressed. He had lost almost forty kilos, his eyes were sunk deep into their sockets, his skin had darkened with worry. His hair had gone white – it used to be salt and pepper before the war.

Since he refused to look me in the eye I stood right in front of him yelling, 'Do you hear me? I'm talking to you! You are not going without me. You leave me here every time. Why are you the only one who gets to risk his life around here?'

My mother and brother arrived just in time to separate us before we started grappling. My mother was on the verge of tears, and Braco was also welling up.

'You are not going anywhere,' my father said. 'I'll be back in two days.' And he was gone. Adem was waiting for him outside. We watched them walk down the street, dragging the sledge behind them and leaving a trail in the snow.

I went out for a walk. My first idea had been to visit Ćamil, but I realized I wouldn't be good company. The previous New Year's Eve seemed so unreal to me now. I had celebrated it in Vlasenica with all my friends. We had been at Hamo's house, which was full of food, booze, music. So I went to bed at nine as usual. Going to bed early was a way of saving energy. We also hoped we'd be less hungry if we slept more. At midnight we were woken by a fireworks display of machine-gun and rifle fire. Even hand grenades were let off. Some people just didn't care that each bullet was precious. The shooting was so heavy that at first I thought the town was under attack.

My father and Adem returned home on 2 January. There was a huge pot on the sledge they were dragging. After the two of them had unloaded my father brought it into the house.

As soon as he sat down he started rolling a cigarette. He told us he'd been given a pinch of tobacco by someone he'd met at our lookout post on the banks of the Drina.

'Ibro, what is in the pot?' my mother asked in disbelief.

'It's lard. Pig fat,' he said.

We exchanged surprised looks.

'There was nothing else left! People had taken everything else. Adem and I found this pot in a deserted Serb house. I reckon nobody wanted it. This stuff can't go off, so it's edible. Adem will take half of it, so we get about five kilos. Naska,' he addressed my mother, 'could you please find a dish big enough to put our half in?'

He told me that I was to take Adem's share across the road to him in the huge pot.

While my mother was transferring the lard from one pot to another Braco and I wondered out loud how this dense, off-white fat could help ease our hunger.

'Stop it you two!' my mother said to us. 'We've been eating polenta with no shortening for months. I haven't seen any cooking oil since November.'

She was already busy at the stove, turning out cornmeal doughnuts fried in the lard. She served the doughnuts with some herbal tea – sugarless, of course.

The whole house smelled of lard. Our stomachs began to growl and function again.

We heard our upstairs neighbours commenting on the unusual smell, but we didn't care. We had never asked them what their food situation was nor had they ever asked us. For all I knew they thought our pantry was loaded with all kinds of things to eat or that we were loaded with money. It wasn't their fault that we'd chosen not to go on the actions.

Much later, after the war, people would often ask me why I'd chosen not to take part in the actions. My answer was always the same. 'First, because I didn't want to get killed but also because I wasn't sure if I was ready to kill.' After the war people would quiz me about all sorts of things. I've been asked, for instance, why we hadn't hunted for rabbits and deer. I answered them with, 'Man, I'm no Tarzan!' My friend Salko has even done some calculations about this, saying, 'There were sixty thousand people in Srebrenica at the time. So you would have needed about a thousand rabbits a day or a thousand deer every few days. Were that many animals ever seen around Srebrenica and Žepa?'

Anyway, a few days after New Year, on Orthodox Christmas day, the people were preparing for the next action to Kravica. The snow was deep; everything was frozen over. But the mood of the people preparing to set out was buoyant. As a friend of mine from Žepa put it, 'This lot are singing as if they're going to a wedding and not to their deaths.'

The people who gathered in the streets had tried to dress warmly, all wrapped up in rags. Off went the bedsheets of Srebrenica – they were hastily altered into capes for the fighters to use as camouflage.

Those in white departed first, followed by thousands of men, women and children. The latter group was not in camouflage. Maybe all the available sheets had been used for the fighters, or maybe they thought no concealment was necessary for them.

'Eh, the Serbs will surely have a frozen roast today,' I overheard my elderly neighbour Avdija say as he prepared himself to move off with the crowd.

'Meaning what?' I said. 'I don't get it.'

'Well,' he said and gave me a funny look. 'The Serbs like it when it's cold at Christmas. Surely it would have been much better for us and for them if they'd let the food convoy pass.' He tied his shoelaces – or, to be more precise, wrapped a piece of string around his boots. He had a woollen cap on his head. When he straightened up I saw there was frost on his moustache. He raised the collar of his coat and headed off down the street without looking back.

COUSIN ALJO

My cousin Aljo was among the crowd. He was seventeen years old at the time, the same age as my brother. No one had heard from Aljo's mother since she'd gone back to Vlasenica taking her younger son Muamer with her. None of us had ever dared mention to him any of the disturbing rumours concerning their fate. We let him live in the hope that the two of them had managed to escape Vlasenica, although Aljo surely knew that the general belief was that none of the Muslims there had survived.

Aljo had arrived in Srebrenica with his uncle Ramo and his immediate family. He would sometimes come by our house, and we would share our meagre meal with him, but he could see for himself how scanty our food supplies were. A few days before the Kravica action Aljo confided in me that he felt he wasn't welcome at his uncle's house any more; he had overheard the family discussing the hardship of having one extra person to feed. One of the family members had said that Aljo should participate in the action so he could feed himself. He figured that if he managed to get hold of some provisions he'd be able to continue living with them.

My brother and I went to see him off. We thought we might never see him again.

Two days later, while fetching firewood from the back of the house, I found Aljo and my brother secretly enjoying a cigarette. I scolded my brother for smoking, but I was quickly appeased when they offered me what was left of the cigarette.

Aljo told me that he'd bartered flour he had brought back from Kravica. There was so much of it that he could even afford a bit of tobacco. From behind the mountain there was the constant background rumble of Serb artillery as he spoke. It had started two days earlier and had not stopped since. He described how he had walked through the snow for about thirty kilometres carrying almost forty kilograms of food on his back. He had walked the whole night.

'There were several hundred of us in the group plus a few armed fighters. To get to Kravica we had to cross a minefield. Mortars were shelling us the whole time, and we could hear machine-gun fire from somewhere, but you couldn't tell where exactly. I don't remember ever being so terrified. Our fighters attacked the Chetnik trenches. You know how these things go – you have to make it to the houses before everyone else otherwise you won't find anything left. And I was hungry. I hadn't had anything to eat since the previous day. So I closed my eyes, jumped from my cover and ran like crazy. I headed for a house with its roof on fire. I thought I'd better rush in before the roof collapsed. When I opened the door two of our guys were entering through the windows, one from the left and the other from the right. The three of us found ourselves in front of a table set for Christmas dinner: plates, cutlery – all we had to do was sit down and eat. There was a big roasted bird and, in the middle of the table, a cake!'

'A cake?' we repeated incredulously.

'A cake', Aljo confirmed, 'with a thick layer of whipped cream on top. We all just froze in front of it, goggle-eyed, with the roof on fire above our heads and the shelling and shooting outside. Then all of us started attacking the cake with our fingers. I was stuffing myself with the whipped cream like a madman.

'Then we spread around the house. I ran down to the basement and found a freezer full of chickens and some cheese. There were sausages hanging from the ceiling – and what sausages they were! – but flour was nowhere to be found. I shot back up the stairs and out of the house. I remembered seeing a shed outside. I ran in, but it was pitch dark, I couldn't see a thing and then – *bam!* – I ran into something metal. I bashed my head against it so hard I fell on my arse.

'When my eyes got accustomed to the dark I saw a huge cross hanging from the ceiling joist. It was swinging on a rope.'

Braco and I had a good laugh listening to Aljo's story.

'Bullets began peppering the shed,' Aljo continued. 'I had to get out of there quickly. But just then I saw sacks lined along the wall. I dipped my finger in and tasted flour. I grabbed a sack and noticed a crate of cooking oil, grabbed a few bottles of that, too, sped out of the shed and ran and ran. I have no idea how I made it across the clearing with forty kilos on my back. I was stepping on the dead lying all around. The snow was all muddy and bloody. When I finally managed to find shelter behind a knoll I threw myself to the ground. I was so hot from running that the snow melted underneath me! I caught my breath, took stock of what I'd got. Forty kilos of flour and two bottles of cooking oil – quite enough, I thought, for a month or two. Nobody can tell me now that I haven't earned my share of a meal.'

He grew silent for a while and then said, 'Then my mother and Muamer came into my mind. Who knows where they are now?'

Not knowing what to say, Braco and I lowered our eyes.

LET THE CONVOY PASS, OR WE'LL COME AND TAKE YOUR FOOD

Aljo was not the only participant in the Kravica action whom I met and spoke to about it. Each of my encounters, each of the stories I heard, contributed to the vividness of the images forming in my mind: the snow everywhere you looked, the Serb houses in the valley and scattered about the surrounding hills, the Chetnik trenches, the minefield, the machine-gun nests.

Imagine having to pass through all of these obstacles to get food while the Chetniks watch from their trenches.

The attack started at dawn. Our fighters numbered approximately five hundred. Each fighter had ten to twenty bullets. Behind them were ten thousand men, women and even children waiting for the attack to begin, their teeth chattering with cold.

From their trenches the Serb soldiers look through their binoculars and see what is coming at them, counting: one *Baliya* . . . two . . . five . . . ten *Baliya* . . .

A soldier without binoculars asks, 'What is it? What do you see?'

They tell him, 'There're thousands of them out there.'

The other soldiers turn pale, terrified. How can this be? they wonder. Aren't they all dead already, from starvation if not from all the shells we've thrown at them?

They do not know that those ten thousand are desperate souls, mainly unarmed. They do not know that the masses are after food not Serbs. The Serbs do not know because they do not want to know or because they cannot grasp it.

The Serb commander orders, 'Fire! Fire! Fire all weapons! Call Koprivno and Rogač and ask for artillery support! Call Bratunac

and ask for urgent reinforcements! Do it! What are you waiting for?'
And as he shouts the crowd comes closer, the stampede of *Baliya*
tramples everything in its path. The Serbs shoot at them, the *Baliya*
fall, but others keep springing up behind them.

My neighbour Avdija, whom I'd seen off to Kravica two days ago,
now appeared in the street, safe and in one piece. He was carrying a
sack.

'What's in there that's so heavy?' I asked.

He put the sack down when he saw me. 'Meat,' he said. 'Cured.'

I started salivating at once.

'Would you barter it for corn?' I asked.

He said nothing.

'Only half a kilo,' I tried again. 'I'd give you a kilo of cornmeal.'

'OK. Go and get it, but hurry up,' he said.

I rushed inside and grabbed a bowl of cornmeal from our supplies.
Avdija took a piece of cured meat from his sack and eyed it for a while
before cutting it in half.

'Here,' he said. 'There's half a kilo.'

I took the meat in my hands. It was more white than red.

'What is it?' I asked. 'What kind of meat?'

'Take it and go,' he said looking at me. 'Don't ask any questions.
Go home and eat it.'

When the masses broke into the village of Kravica they found a
suckling pig on a spit in front of each Serb house as is customary
on Orthodox Christmas Day. After the action only the wooden spits
remained. When the crowd retreated there was nothing edible left
in the village of Kravica.

On a Serb radio programme reporting on the event an elderly
Serb woman said, 'Children, you must let the food trucks get to the
Muslims. If you don't let them have the food they're going to kill us
all.'

It was common knowledge that the food convoys were not being
allowed into Srebrenica. The convoys cleared to pass the border
in Zvornik were often stopped in Bratunac by women, frequently
dressed in black, in what was known as a 'soft blockade'. The
convoys would then return whence they'd come. The response from
Srebrenica couldn't be clearer: *Let the food convoys pass, or we'll*

keep plundering Serb villages. Despite the clarity of this message no convoy arrived in Srebrenica during the following months. The Serb commanders' plan couldn't be clearer either: *Annihilate all the Muslims in the Drina valley area using all available means*, which meant no food convoys.

In 2006 the International Criminal Tribunal for the former Yugoslavia charged Naser Orić with burning and destroying buildings, dwellings and other property. There was no reference in the indictment to any Serb casualties in the attack on Kravica. On the 3 July 2008 the Appeals Chamber acquitted Orić on each count. The same tribunal charged several Serb officers for a range of crimes committed in Kravica, which took place two years after the action on 13 July 1995. Serb officers were found guilty of summarily executing over a thousand Bosnian Muslim men and boys detained in a warehouse by throwing hand grenades and firing rocket launchers and machine guns through the windows.

HOW TO GET
TO TUZLA

The winter was getting colder, the people hungrier, and Srebrenica was deliberating about what to do next. Encouraged by the success in Kravica, many wanted to organize more attacks as soon as possible. They could not agree on a target, however. Some insisted that Bratunac should be attacked – before Kravica this would have been unthinkable – while others countered that attacking a town was an entirely different prospect from attacking a village and that they had neither the ammunition nor the men to sustain an assault let alone hold a town should it be captured.

Fighters from the opposite side of the free territory, from the villages along the Drina, insisted on directing the next attack against the Serb artillery units that were shelling their villages. Naser, for some reason, agreed to this plan, and the decision was taken to attack the Serb positions of the Jezero plateau and in the village of Skelani. Many would say later that the decision was a grave error; it was unequivocally a turning point in the war in eastern Bosnia.

The capture of Kravica had opened up a channel to Konjević Polje, which was held by Bosniak forces but had hitherto been completely cut off from the free territory of Srebrenica. It was a miracle that our fighters had been able to hold on to it for as long as they had. The defenders faced pressure from four sides: Vlasenica, Zvornik, Bratunac and Milići. They were under constant attack from Serb tanks, artillery, aeroplanes, you name it. Making matters more difficult, refugees from dozens of eastern Bosnia's villages were concentrated there.

From Srebrenica you could safely reach Konjević Polje on foot, and from there it was possible to reach the Zvornik Municipality where our fighters controlled the village of Kamenica. This was not far from Ceparde, and a few kilometres beyond Ceparde was the territory controlled by the Second Corps of the BiH army – namely Tuzla. Tuzla! Tuzla! Tuzla soon occupied our thoughts night and day. I knew we would be safe there. The lines of Second Corps were impregnable. The area had electricity, even central heating, and the food convoys were arriving unimpeded. Getting to Tuzla had always been at the back of my mind, and after the fall of Kravica this became much more of a realistic prospect – the path was open, or almost. The challenge – the risky part of a journey often discussed around Srebrenica at the time – was how to cross the pockets of Serb-controlled territory beyond Kamenica.

One morning while I was walking around town trying to gather more information about the route I noticed that the streets were unusually lively. Hundreds of people, entire families, were heading off to Kravica. Somebody said that the road to Tuzla was completely open, but nobody could name the source of this information.

Finally, I thought, the only thing left for us to do was hike the seventy or eighty kilometres from Srebrenica to Tuzla, across ice and snow, without appropriate footwear and with little food. Nevertheless, I ran home to convince my parents to do it.

'We have to seize the opportunity before it's too late,' I said.

My parents looked at each other. It was obvious they didn't like the idea. Braco sat quietly in the corner waiting for the outcome of the conversation.

'Hasko,' my father said, 'it's better to stay where we are. We are much safer here, at least for the time being. I've just heard on the radio that the UN is in negotiations to send a large food convoy to Srebrenica. They say some British Special Forces will be escorting it.'

I couldn't wait for the news at seven. I went over to my neighbour's, who owned a radio powered by a car battery. He must have obtained the battery in one of the actions. For once, Srebrenica and not Sarajevo was on the news:

Yesterday forces of the BiH army in the free territory of Srebrenica led by commander Naser Orić won a decisive victory against the

Serbo-Chetnik aggressor, inflicting heavy losses on the enemy and capturing a large amount of his weapons.

The news continued, saying that the people of the free territory of Srebrenica were suffering from hunger and that they were appealing to the UN for help. They repeated the claim, which my father had already heard, that the UN was considering sending a special forces unit of the British army, nicknamed the Desert Rats, to Bosnia to prevent Serb forces from interfering with aid convoys *en route* to Srebrenica. The voice on the radio said that the British were permitted to use force if necessary to deliver food to the starving population.

We rejoiced at this – it was the first time we'd heard that the world was considering using force against the Serbs. We discussed the Desert Rats long into the evening. Who were they? Why Desert Rats? We figured it had something to do with the Gulf War. The whole day I kept imagining how the Desert Rats looked sitting on their tanks. I had trouble with the colour of their helmets, though; I couldn't make up my mind between green and blue. Finally, I decided that the colour didn't matter as long as they were tough and prepared to use their weapons.

THE WARRIORS

We never got the chance to see the Desert Rats. They never arrived in Srebrenica and neither did the food convoy. Even if the convoy had set out from Belgrade it must have been stopped on the cross-border bridge in Zvornik about fifty kilometres from Srebrenica.

I could clearly imagine the Serb commanders at their desks in their headquarters, checking the maps and drawing new lines, concluding that the 'Muslim forces' or 'Naser's forces' or, most likely, 'the Turks' now held the territory from Žepa on the Drina across Mount Javor to Srebrenica and then along the river valley towards Bratunac – now half-encircled – and further on via Kravica to Konjević Polje, Kamenica and Ceparde. The Serbs knew precisely how many guns the Muslims around Srebrenica had at the time. They could have simply counted what was missing from their arsenal, which I'm sure they did, but they nevertheless kept misleading both their own and the world's media by inventing stories of 'outside agents delivering weapons to the Srebrenica Muslims'. If this were true then we might have had enough men and ammunition, and the Serbs would have never been able to maintain their military position in eastern Bosnia. We'll never know for sure.

We only know what did happen and not what could have happened.

Actually, at the time I didn't reason that way; the success of our fighters used to frighten me, and I'm quite sure I wasn't the only one who felt like that. It seemed to me that the war was escalating; with every bullet fired and every dead body, be it Bosniak or Serb, we were a step further from peace. If it were up to me and those like me we would have waited for the Chetniks to knock on our doors. I'm sure I would have been able to fire a weapon – assuming I had one, of course – if my family were attacked and if the Chetniks had indeed knocked on my door and there was no chance to escape, but thankfully there were enough people among us who discovered they had the makings of a warrior in them. War is the time when warriors are needed.

A warrior was prepared to seek out and kill a Chetnik instead of waiting for a Chetnik to come to his doorstep and kill him and his family. The warriors were prepared to repel the Chetniks and not allow them to get near us. They didn't allow the Chetniks to rest or regroup. They didn't give them time to think. The warriors understood that waiting was a weakness. The Chetniks fed on our weaknesses. The warriors understood what needed to be done. Show your teeth. Treat the Chetniks the same way they treat you. Then, and only then, would they be ready to negotiate. The warriors understood that the Chetniks wouldn't consider a truce or talk peace if you asked for it nicely.

I didn't have that kind of mindset, but no doubt I would not have lasted as long as I did were it not for the warriors among us. Our warriors were mostly farmers. I had no insight into who was on the opposite side, but I was certain they were farmers, too, Serb farmers.

In the Drina valley the war was not fought between the workers. The Bosniak factory workers had fled the cities, following in the footsteps of the Bosniak middle class who had 'got out in time', as the phrase ran in those days. There were several tens of thousands of people in Srebrenica then, and almost all of them were refugees pooled from villages in the surrounding municipalities. There were no more than three hundred true urban dwellers in the town, and you could count the middle-class refugees on your fingers.

The Bosniak middle class who had not got out in time from the towns of Vlasenica and Bratunac were among the first the Serbs detained and killed in May 1992. Urban working-class Muslims at least had some sort of idea of what was going on. Those in the countryside, especially in remote villages, found themselves victims of an information blackout, waiting for instructions from the administrative classes in the towns who were being rounded up or fleeing *en masse*. From May until mid-

April buses full of Muslims from Bratunac, Srebrenica and Vlasenica were proceeding unhindered to central Bosnia. The Serbs did nothing to stop them at first, although there were incidents recorded of men being taken off buses. They may well have thought that Muslims leaving the area under their own steam was a no less effective form of ethnic cleansing.

Isolated, unsure of whether to flee or stay and wait, rural communities were left in the lurch. Then, after the roads were closed, thousands of Muslims in the villages around Srebrenica, Konjević Polje and Žepa were stuck.

There was no data on the number of Muslims who fled eastern Bosnia, so the Serb authorities could not know precisely how many remained. Only after suffering considerable losses during the summer and autumn of 1992 did they realize that they would need to send many more troops than they'd originally thought would be necessary for ethnic cleansing and the total destruction of Muslims in the area.

More significant was that the remaining Muslims, who were not supposed to have remained at all, gradually organized themselves into guerrilla units that were able to disrupt the execution of the Greater Serbia plan. The Serbs could not even be sure they would be able to hold the territory that they had gained through methods such as mass killings, detention camps, the incineration of villages and starvation. The situation at the beginning of 1993 must have looked pretty dire from the Serb perspective. By then the name Naser Orić was well known among them. Naser inspired fear and awe.

However, what the Serb generals did not realize was that the majority of the population of eastern Bosnia actually hoped for a corridor to Tuzla and that most if not all the population would be ready to leave eastern Bosnia at once. We stayed only because we had no way of getting out.

We were cornered by the banks of the Drina on the other side of which was Serbia. Who would have dared go across and surrender to a Serbian authority that was shelling and bombing us every day? Were those Chetniks different from the ones on this side of the river?

It was only our warriors who stood in the way of a Greater Serbia plan being realized. The warriors proved capable of withstanding the pressure without outside help. The government in Sarajevo and Bosnian army headquarters gave no sign of being able to do anything. Our farmers, now seasoned warriors, thought themselves unstoppable; they had yet to lose a single battle, and casualties among them were relatively low. But plenty of civilians were dying. The question we asked ourselves was how long could it last?

ZORAN AND VAHID

The attack on Jezero, a plateau high above the left bank of the Drina, and on Skelani, which was situated on the river itself, was to begin soon. I tried to show my face at the marketplace and stay in the loop, but even a ten-minute walk was becoming too exhausting for someone as hungry as I was.

Braco mainly spent his time with friends in the neighbourhood. My father would sometimes go down to the market and would often meet people from our area, acquaintances and relatives, and he would occasionally bring them home. Zoran, who had helped him rescue his car, was one of these guests. Zoran was never without tobacco, and while he was there my father would happily roll one cigarette after another. He would pitch up wearing peculiar fatigues, a mix of military camouflage and hunting gear. His unshaven face showed no fear or concern about the situation. He was full of optimism, and this would influence my father's mood in a positive way.

'My family are in Žepa,' he said. 'I just dropped by to see what's going on there.'

People from Žepa would come to Srebrenica mainly to buy grain – if they had money, of course. Everything was getting more expensive by the day. Grain had reached the price of twenty Deutschmarks a kilogram. A litre of cooking oil was one hundred marks; an egg, ten marks; a kilogram of salt three hundred marks; a packet of cigarettes 150 marks; and a kilogram of tobacco 3,500 marks. The shortage of salt was critical. Meat was still cheap compared with grain: one kilogram of grain was worth two kilograms of meat. But how could you buy meat if you didn't have grain?

Although we knew that Zoran had likely bought grain to take to Žepa we would never have considered asking him for a kilogram or two.

Zoran had heard that my father might be put forward as a candidate for the Žepa War Council. These rumours hadn't reached us, and we were very surprised to learn of them.

'Well, director' – Zoran often addressed my father by his former title – 'you are one of the few educated people around here. They should make use of your experience. I'll let you know if anything comes of it.'

After he left we had a long discussion about the news he had brought. Should this actually happen we would likely be offered some sort of accommodation there and enough food to live on. It could be our salvation. I saw tears in my father's eyes. I knew he was thinking: See, people haven't forgotten. They judge me on my merits . . . There are so many people in this region I've helped.

Around this time I ran into Vahid, a fellow ex-student from the Sarajevo Faculty of Mechanical Engineering. I spotted him at the marketplace. He stood out from the scruffy crowd, dressed as he was in an unusually complete and professional military uniform. He was neat and tidy, freshly shaven, his hair neatly trimmed. He didn't have a weapon on him – at least, none that I could see. To my great surprise he seemed upbeat, just like Zoran. He took stock of my pitiful appearance but made no comment; the last time we'd seen each other I'd weighed around ninety kilograms; now I weighed no more than sixty-five.

Seeing him there I experienced the same feeling of joy I'd felt on seeing Ćamil and Fahro for the first time, as if, at least for a moment, I'd returned to our peacetime life. I invited Vahid to visit us. We gave him some herbal tea, unsweetened, the only thing we had to offer. Vahid took a tobacco pouch out of his pocket and put it on the table. My father wasn't home, so I rolled a cigarette. After a few puffs my head started spinning. Vahid had just come back from Konjević Polje. After the war he would tell me that he had bought four kilograms of tobacco from an acquaintance for a very good price, which would explain why he didn't seem worried: he could trade the tobacco for grain or whatever else he wanted, as the price of four kilograms of tobacco was ten thousand Deutschmarks at that point. But what impressed me most was that the modest guy I'd known as a student, once my room-mate, had now been transformed into a true warrior. He was very casual about it and talked as if it were the most normal thing in the world. I had for a moment to put aside my stereotypical idea of our fighters; evidently uneducated farmers and loggers were not the only seasoned fighters after all.

'Did you manage to graduate from university?' I asked him.

'Yes, and then I found work in Han Pijesak,' Vahid said. 'When the Serbs attacked us in June I went to Žepa and joined a unit. I'm a company commander now.'

'I hear it was very difficult there last autumn,' I said.

'It was. After the June attack they tried a different way into the town, from Derventa and Radava, across the mountain. We had to form a defensive line and quickly. Fadil Turković was there, too.' (Fadil, our old acquaintance, the police commander who was to accompany us to the border.) 'We had six Strelas captured from the JNA installation on the mountain.'

'I heard about that,' I said. 'Naser asked for a couple of them when the MiGs started bombing Srebrenica. I don't know if they were sent – they've never been launched from here. The Chetniks have started flying at three or four thousand metres, so they must know we have some low-altitude missiles.'

'Yeah, they're heat-seeking missiles. No way you'll hit a plane flying that high. You put the launcher on your shoulder, turn on the sensor and aim towards the plane. We've tried it. Nothing,' Vahid explained.

'Were you on the front when they attacked?' I asked.

'I was there. It was tough. They had two tanks and one of those forestry tractors for hauling logs. The ammunition was loaded on it. There were at least 150 Chetniks. Fadil had a sniper's rifle and picked them off one at a time. We didn't have enough ammunition, so we had to be cautious. The Chetniks almost broke through our defences, and then someone remembered the Strelas. We had no anti-tank weapons, just the surface-to-air launchers, which we couldn't fire at the planes, so, we thought, let's try them on the tanks.' He had my unblinking attention. I was so proud of Vahid, my ex-room-mate, once a bit of a nerd, you might say, but now a warrior. 'Luckily we had a launcher in our trench. The tanks fired non-stop, no way you could so much as peep over the top. So this guy takes the Strela and turns it on, and it starts beeping. He stands up and quickly points it in the direction of the tanks – we, of course, hoped it would lock on to the heat of the tanks' engines. And off it went – *whoosh*.'

'And? What happened then?' I asked impatiently.

Vahid smiled. 'Well, first it scared our guys in the forward trenches, because it flew over their heads, and they didn't have the slightest idea what it was. The missile turned left then right, searching out a heat source, and then it flew, hissing, over the Chetniks' heads. They all froze, looking up, as surprised as our guys were. The missile flew over the tank. The gunner on the turret stopped firing, probably thinking he was done for. The tank stopped. The missile flew across Radava plain, over the trees, somewhere towards Han Pijesak. But it did the trick. We exploited their confusion and charged them. Fadil ran directly at the tank intending to capture it. The tank's machine-gunner cut him in half.'

'We'd heard about Fadil's death,' I said.

'He was killed instantly. But the Chetniks started to retreat pretty chaotically, and they left the tractor with the ammunition behind. They suffered heavy casualties. When we checked the documents of the dead we realized the unit had come from the other end of Bosnia. Some had come from as far as Prijedor, if I remember rightly.'

'Bastards!' I said. 'Imagine sending people from the other end of the country to attack Žepa!'

'Who knows? Maybe the Srebrenica Serbs get sent to Sarajevo. Might be some logic to it, I guess. When the dust settles no Serb can say they killed their neighbour.'

After a pause Vahid said, 'I guess you haven't heard that I'm married now?'

'No, I hadn't.' I was surprised. 'I thought you were never going to marry. Where's she from?'

'From Žepa,' Vahid said getting up. 'And now I really have to go. I have to be up early tomorrow, and what with all this snow and ice . . .'

And off he went. I wouldn't see him again until after the war.

The weather was bitterly cold throughout January. On a night when the thermometer showed –25 we were woken by the sound of cracking pipes in the ceiling. They had not been properly drained after the Chetniks mined the water-supply system, damaging it permanently. The water that remained in those pipes on the upper floor froze that night.

We all got up. That was the last thing we needed. While we looked for rags to start mopping up the water dripping down, my mother kept repeating, 'What have we done so wrong to deserve all this from God?'

THE BLOODY BATTLE CONTINUES

While everybody talked about the upcoming attack on Skelani, news started coming in about Chetnik attacks on Konjević Polje and Cerska. People were saying that it was only a matter of time before they would break through our lines of defence.

The sky was perfectly clear throughout the whole of January. The weather conditions were ideal for aerial bombing, and, sure enough, the modified agricultural planes made their return. They would bomb us for fifteen minutes or so then fly back to Bratunac. They would only bomb the urban area, never the lines of defence. Once again the town was panic-stricken. We prayed for clouds and fog, but the sky had never seemed clearer. Even today clear skies give me the creeps.

I often thought about how little one actually needed to live: some bread, some water and a tiny corner sheltered from shells and bombs. I used to think that if I could have that, nothing more than that, I would be content for the rest of my life.

What little rotten cornmeal remained in the house was consumed in meagre portions to our strict schedule of nine in the morning and three thirty in the afternoon. It had become our sacred ritual, the four of us anticipating the moment the food would be placed on the table. But the air-raids often took place at three thirty sharp, as if the pilots were deliberately trying to ruin our routine. We would spring from the table thinking *not again* and run down to the basement.

Even our occasional baths were interrupted by the planes. Having a bath meant heating a few litres of water in a pot on the kitchen stove, taking it to the freezing-cold bathroom and crouching in the icy tub while pouring water over your body from a mug. Then you dried yourself as fast as you could and ran to the kitchen to get dressed by the stove. Once, on hearing the familiar rumble of the aircraft, Braco sprinted out of the bathroom as if catapulted and rushed down to the basement naked. We wrapped a blanket around him, and he spent the next half-hour shivering on the basement stairs, his teeth chattering with the cold.

On the street, between air-raids, people gathered to discuss following the fighters in an action on Skelani. Those who hadn't participated in the Kravica action had decided to go along, despite the fact that some of our neighbours had never come back from the last one. The famine raged; people had few options. I wondered how many would stay lying in the snow this time. As usual the four of us elected not to go.

On the day of the action I went to see Ćamil. I found him standing in front of his house with Fahro. While we stood there talking a truck came up the hill from the town centre followed by several more, and since they were not covered we could see the fighters seated facing one another. They sat with rifles between their knees, their heads bowed. It was so cold that I wondered how any of them would arrive in Jezero in a fit state to fight.

'There's Naser!' Fahro and Ćamil shouted in unison.

Naser was wearing a black woollen hat and was holding a machine gun in front of him. He seemed contemplative, a slight smile on his face. I'd heard from other people that he always smiled when heading into battle, no matter the circumstances. He was the commander, and that was his way of encouraging his men, I guess.

The attack on Jezero was a disaster. The outcome was the largest loss of life in a single day that the Bosniaks had suffered so far. Some of our best soldiers were killed up on the plateau, among them a man named Mirza, the commander of the Srebrenica military police. I'd seen Mirza on the street a few times. He used to wear a cowboy hat. His uniform always fit perfectly, his shirt tucked into his trousers and his trouser legs tucked into his boots. His complexion was dark, and his hair and beard were always neatly trimmed. He was in excellent physical shape. It was said that he had a black belt in karate.

Another casualty was a young guy, about twenty, whose courage had been the subject of many stories. With his long blond hair that fell over his shoulders he looked like the singer from the Swedish rock band Europe. Everybody called him Dulo, so I guess his name was Abdulah. He was from our area, from the village of Krivače in the Municipality of Han Pijesak. In August 1992, when the Chetniks attacked and burned Krivače, Dulo was among the last to retreat. They said that he ran from tree to tree with that girly long hair of his flying everywhere, shooting at Chetniks with some old revolver until he ran out of bullets. The Chetniks' machine guns, of course, did not run out of bullets. What an amazing guy! I'd heard fascinating stories about Dulo's courage from Sifo, an old schoolmate and Dulo's comrade in Žepa. I'd heard stories about Sifo's courage, too, and many similar tales of bravery during my time in Srebrenica.

The day after the Jezero attack I learned that Dulo was brought to the hospital with his belly slit open. Seeing his injuries the doctors said they could not save him. Dulo had apparently fired a rifle grenade into the treetop above his head. The rifle grenade burst and fatally injured him. What did Dulo know about firing rifle grenades? What did any of these brave guys, these Partisans, know about fighting?

Many fighters died in the battle, but even more civilians were killed by the shelling. The fighters were usually too close to the Chetnik positions for the Chetnik artillery to be able to fire directly at them, but the crowd that followed, always several hundred metres behind, was an ideal target for both artillery and heavy machine guns placed on the surrounding peaks.

The next day several of our neighbours came back from the action carrying their bounty, flour for the most part. Some of them were armed. They collapsed in exhausted heaps along the street, while those who hadn't seen the action gathered around. They informed us that they'd barely made it out alive. The Jezero plateau had been taken in a day, but Skelani was another story. Our fighters had entered the village but couldn't hold it, not even for an hour.

'The path from the plateau to the village goes down a very steep hill,' one of them said. 'While we were there an anti-aircraft gun started shelling us from Serbia. It was tearing up trees in the forest! A lot of people were killed. The Skelani Serbs were trying to escape over the bridge – we could see them – they were being killed on the bridge. Our people were being killed on the hill. You could tell the attack had failed, as our fighters started running uphill to escape. A number of them managed to enter the village, but they had to retreat pretty quickly.'

'This was the worst action I've taken part in,' another man added. 'Trust me, I had to run over dead bodies going up that hill. There were injured people everywhere – they were calling for help, but who was going to help them? We ran into several groups of Serbs who had seen that it was impossible to escape across the bridge and were running up the hill just like us, so we ran up together. Then the shooting started in the forest and hand-to-hand fighting – but you couldn't tell who was who.'

'I've never seen such a barrage of artillery fire,' a third witness said, 'as if the whole Yugoslav army was sitting on the other side of the Drina! But I've been told that our fighters had a mortar set up on the hilltop and that several shells reached Bajina Bašta in Serbia!'

'That's a first. Imagine that. Our guys shelling Serbia!' someone exclaimed from the group that hadn't been there.

That night there was a large crowd at house of our neighbour with the wheel-powered radio. We alternated spinning the wheel as we listened to a Serbian radio station that had a much stronger signal than BiH Radio. They said on the news that the Yugoslav army's military council had met in Belgrade and that Serbia had declared a state of war in response to 'an attack by Muslim forces on Yugoslav territory earlier that day'.

Soon after that, maybe even the next day if I remember correctly, we heard that Yugoslav troops had been spotted crossing the bridge from Serbia into Bosnia at Skelani. We weren't all that surprised. We already knew that Serbs from Bosnia and Serbs from Serbia were attacking us, but this was the first time that it had been confirmed officially. Years later the authorities in Belgrade would try to hush it up.

I was thinking: This time there will be a lot more of them. They will send the regular army, more tanks and artillery crews, special forces.

From the reports that reached us later we learned that this is exactly what happened.

During February and March 1993 the area became a living hell. Our lines fell one after the other, but a somewhat tighter line was formed in the region of Kragljivoda. The Chetniks launched their fiercest offensive to date on Cerska and Konjević Polje, attacking from the north and west.

After the war we would learn about the phenomenon of 'Weekend Chetniks', groups coming from Serbia to support the Bosnian Chetniks. They were apparently paid for their weekend 'jobs', probably not much but still something. Serbia was suffering an economic crisis, and this weekend activity must have been a useful source of income. Of course, money was not the only motivation; for some, helping their 'Serb brothers across the Drina' to kill 'the Turks', as they called us, was reward enough. And yet Serbia maintained diplomatic ties with Turkey during the war. Serbian tourists and business men and women still flocked to Istanbul just as they had done before the war to trade and smuggle goods.

Around that time Serbian radio reported that Libyan President Gaddafi had paid a visit to his pal Milošević and pitched his tent in the middle of Belgrade. I was very interested to hear if Gaddafi, being a Muslim, would demand that Milošević stop killing the Bosnian Muslims. But he didn't. Not then, not ever. Throughout the war in BiH and afterwards Milošević's Serbia also maintained very friendly business and political relations with Saddam Hussein's Iraq; even during the West's embargo Serbia was selling military equipment to Iraq, from mortar shells to spare parts for military aircraft. Serbia, therefore, with the blessing of their Orthodox brothers in Bosnia, was maintaining loving relationships with Muslim countries throughout the 1990s.

In Srebrenica during that horrible winter of 1993 we had no way of knowing this. Nevertheless, it was crystal clear then as it is now that for Milošević, Karadžić and the other architects of Greater Serbia the war in BiH had nothing to do with religion and everything to do with gaining territory, absolute power and money. But they were quite successful, at least for a time, in spinning a story to the West about fighting Islamic terrorists. And this despite the fact that well-meaning Westerners could see that genocide was under way in Bosnia.

KRAGLJIVODA

Routed at Skelani, and with the Chetniks launching major offensives capturing Konjević Polje and Cerska, the free territory was halved in a matter of days. Several thousand – some say ten thousand – people from Cerska and Konjević Polje rushed to Srebrenica. Only a few hundred of them were armed. I often went out to meet them; I wanted to know what was going on and whether I would meet anyone I knew, for many of these refugees were from the Vlasenica Municipality. I did see some schoolmates of mine, but they didn't recognize me. I identified myself to one of them, and he asked me with a teasing grin, 'For God's sake, what have you done to yourself?' He could barely restrain himself from laughing – as if my calorically restricted diet were a matter of personal choice. Then another classmate, a girl, actually burst out laughing. 'Hasko,' she finally managed to say, 'half of you is gone! You look like a toothpick.' They didn't look as thin, and I felt embarrassed by my appearance. I invented some excuse and took to my heels.

Several hundred of the newly arrived refugees ended up on our street. Over the next few days about a hundred or so more arrived from the villages along the Drina. These were families, carrying everything they were able to carry.

'All is lost,' a man leading a horse cried out as he passed by. His rifle was slung across his back. He was unshaven, and his long beard made him look like a Chetnik. 'All the Drina villages will fall, right up to Osmače!' He was yelling out pieces of information between asking around about a free room in the neighbourhood for his children and his wife.

Osmače was the largest village in the area. Those who spoke of it said they had tons of potatoes, and so my father had tried, before the new year, to trade some things we'd found in the Bašić household for food there. He took the VCR that Arkan's thugs hadn't stolen and fabrics for women's dresses. My father bartered these things for five kilograms of potatoes and had to give up on buying more because everything was so overpriced. Many others had the same experience. The newly arrived refugees were saying that Osmače was about to fall; if Kragljivoda fell, Osmače would, too.

'The people in Osmače thought that they would stay in their houses for ever,' someone said vindictively.

'It serves them right. Their village should burn,' another voice said.

'They'll have to leave behind the TV sets and video recorders they took from us for a kilogram of potatoes,' a third voice joined in. 'The Chetniks will have all the electronics they can get their hands on!'

Then a group of well-armed men rushed down the street. Somebody said they were military police. I went into the house and watched from the window. They stood among the crowd and ordered all the armed men to join in the defence of Kragljivoda at once. The meeting point was in front of the town hall.

Then someone came forward and stood in front of the military police, saying, 'What do you want from us? We've just brought our families to Srebrenica. We've walked from Konjević Polje through the snow. We barely got out alive. We didn't sleep a wink last night, and now you expect us to go and fight?'

'Listen,' one of the military policemen said, 'we all have to go. I'm not going to a Kragljivoda trench while you sleep here. I know you've got about twenty guys with you. Round them up, and let's meet in an hour. We'll be moving out before dark.'

The group in question soon collected themselves and headed to the meeting point.

'Take care!' someone shouted after them. 'It's total chaos up there. Kragljivoda is the front line.'

THE DEATH CAMP

Over the next few days information about the fate of Vlasenica began to arrive with the new wave of refugees. Since we'd left home on 12 April 1992 we had been hearing only horrible rumours. Among the refugees from Cerska I recognized Fatima, a woman about my mother's age, whom I remembered as a widow with a house in the suburbs of Vlasenica. She looked extremely gaunt and exhausted. Unlike my peers she recognized me immediately.

Fatima had received no news of her son since April 1992; her daughter had made it to Tuzla with her husband and children. Fatima herself had stayed in Vlasenica because she didn't want to leave her home. I invited her back to our Srebrenica dwelling. I told her my parents would be glad to see someone from Vlasenica.

After taking a rest at the house Fatima told us how she had survived the death camp in which she been lucky to spend only a few days. She said that all the young men and boys, as well as the young women, from Vlasenica had been taken to the camp. Fatima had heard rumours about their fate, but she couldn't learn much. 'I rarely ventured outside,' she said, 'and never went further than my next-door neighbours' house. If I went to see them I would stay the night. Just a few steps between houses had often proved dangerous enough.

'In September, when they came for the rest of us, there were only nine Muslims left in the whole neighbourhood! I really didn't care any longer whether I lived or died. I couldn't stand the waiting, and I couldn't bear not knowing what had happened to my son. I prayed to Allah for them to kill me or let me go. When they came for us they took us first to the police station. We asked whether we needed to give statements. They said no and took us to the Sušica camp in the middle of the night. There were about 250, maybe three hundred of us in the hangar, men and women together. We were all sitting against the wall, lined up along three sides. By the fourth wall there were two buckets in which we were supposed to relieve ourselves. The women did it in groups of three; two of them would block one from the view of the others. All night long the women were getting up to urinate out of fear, and the buckets were soon full. We had to do number two that way as well, in front of everybody. Diarrhoea was common; the poor hygiene spread diseases. Some people had been there for two or three weeks already, feeding on scraps thrown in by the guards. During the night the buckets overflowed and the floor became sodden, while the effluent flowed to the other end of the hangar where we were sleeping.

'In the morning they brought us a bit of rice floating in tepid water, which was supposed to be our breakfast. There weren't enough bowls, so we had to eat in shifts, waiting for people to finish their portions and pass the bowls along. During the day they let us out of the hangar to use the toilet – but only during the day.

'Later the healthier men were taken to work and would be given dinner on their return, but the rest of us wouldn't get anything to eat until the next morning.

'After three days they freed me, together with a number of other women and children, and they let us go towards Cerska. Some women were made to stay, including one who had been severely beaten. She rolled up her shirt and showed me the marks on her back. They'd thrashed her with a cable, first in one direction and then in another to create the mark of the cross. All the men were kept in the camp.'

In 2012 I asked Fatima to meet me to confirm some details of her story. There were dozens of witnesses who gave their testimony on the Sušica camp both to The Hague Tribunal and the BiH War Crimes Court in Sarajevo.

Sometime after the war I was visited at my Sarajevo apartment by a Serb who knew my father well having been in business with him. Among other things this man told me more about how the Chetniks had treated the Vlasenica Muslims during the summer of 1992.

'I was returning home one day,' he said, 'after my guard duty was over, and I found that all my Muslim neighbours had been executed in front of their houses. Their bodies were left lying by the side of the road. I believe their possessions had been taken as well.

'The Chetniks organized a brothel in town, with about fifty Muslim women forcibly kept there. The local Chetniks would invite those who were visiting, saying, "Just pick one, choose the one you want", but over time there were fewer and fewer women, as the Chetniks would kill them after they were done with them. They killed those women one by one, just as the whim took them, in front of numerous witnesses. They appointed one woman as a sort of manager, and they later shot her in the head in the middle of the street.'

The things this man claimed to have seen with his own eyes made me sick to my stomach. He said he was not a Chetnik, that he had been conscripted and didn't have a choice. He told me his father had fought the Chetniks in the Second World War; his father had been a Partisan, a communist.

In 1994 we would learn that the first suspect ever to be indicted by the ICTY was Dragan 'Yankee' Nikolić, who was charged with committing war crimes in the Sušica camp in Vlasenica.

It would not be until 2011 before one of the Chetnik butchers revealed the full details of the last days of the Sušica concentration camp. At the end of September 1992 twenty-nine Chetniks were killed during one of the fiercest battles for Cerska. In response, the Chetniks, in a single day, executed the 240 Bosniak detainees left in the camp. The same Chetnik butcher would also confirm that after the war the Bosnian Serb authorities had done whatever they could to prove that the twenty-nine Chetnik fighters killed in the battle had actually been civilians.

In Srebrenica back in 1993 we knew little, but we knew enough to consider ourselves lucky for having escaped Vlasenica when we did.

SMOKING KILLS

In March 1993 we could hear the rumble of big guns coming from the south. Walking around the city in search of news I learned that most of the men who had arms and responded to the call to fight were trying to halt the Chetnik breakthrough from the direction of the Drina.

Around this time I made friends with Azem. He lived on our street, and I found him one day sitting on a pile of firewood stacked in front of the house in which he was living. He was chain-smoking – not roll-ups but real, factory-made cigarettes. A half-empty and slightly crumpled red-and-white packet of Niška Drina, a popular Serbian brand, protruded from his shirt pocket. He was surrounded by a group of young guys from around the street. He smoked one cigarette after another, not offering them to anyone; they had been his reward for fighting at Kragljivoda where had held out for the entire seven days and nights in the muddy, snow-covered trenches.

I stood off to one side, close enough to hear what Azem was saying. I wanted to know whether our lines were stable or whether a massacre was imminent.

'So,' said one of the people around him, 'you're not offering round your cigarettes?'

'When you kill your own Chetnik and take his cigarettes you won't offer them round either,' Azem retorted.

'And did you kill this Chetnik?' I ventured to ask him.

'And where might you be from?' Azem asked, looking at me through the curtain of smoke.

'Vlasenica,' I said.

'Oh, from Vlasenica! How come you're here? I used to work in Vlasenica before the war. I'm from Nova Kasaba.' Azem's face brightened. He seemed glad that we were from the same area. Maybe that's why he decided to tell his story again. Meanwhile his audience had grown as a few more expectant neighbourhood boys joined in.

'I'll tell you, man,' Azem said, pulling on a cigarette, 'we're lying in a trench while the Chetniks shell us like crazy. They're killing us! There's a multiple rocket launcher firing at us non-stop, the tanks are firing at us, you can't stick your head out from under cover. I was thinking to myself, why stick my head out anyway? Why should I shoot when I've only got twenty bullets? I figured I would shoot if and when the Chetniks came within range and then get out of there!

'Guys are dying all around me. A man on my left is crying for help; some guy on my right has his arm torn off, blood gushing from the wound. A baker's van came from Srebrenica to pick up some of the injured. That can only have been Ramo – they call him the Breadmaker. He's the only one crazy enough to drive up there in that thing.

'That entire day a Chetnik transporter positioned itself in front of our trench. It nearly ran over us. Luckily one of us in the trench had a sniper's rifle, and, just as we thought we'd had it, he shot their gunner, and he fell from the turret. The transporter then reversed back behind their lines, leaving the Chetnik gunner on the ground where he had fallen. Their rocket launchers and the artillery never stopped firing, at least not before it got dark. They didn't give us a chance to breathe. I thought that was it, that we were done for. I thought I'd die in Kragljivoda, and it was the only time I'd ever been to the place!

'I wasn't thirsty or hungry even though I hadn't had any food for three days. I mean, you're so frightened you couldn't eat even if there were anything. All I wished for was a cigarette before I died, but if anybody had some they weren't sharing. Their infantry had moved their trenches closer to us; they were maybe a hundred metres away. And they stayed there during the night. I was sure they were going to attack our trench first thing in the morning. It was dark, but I could make out the ground ahead of us because of the moonlight. There was an odd shape poking out from behind a tree. I strained my eyes, and it dawned on me that it was the Chetnik we had shot. I figured he might have some cigarettes on him.'

Azem's audience was silent.

'So I took my rifle and started crawling. Some of the guys in the trench woke up. "Azem, where do you think you're going? Have you lost your mind?" one of them whispered after me. But I was determined to get my cigarettes. I went half a metre at a time, staying very still in between. I had to crawl for half an hour, but I reached the dead Chetnik lying under the tree. At least, I thought he was dead, but I'm not sure . . . I reached into his overcoat, and, searching him up and down, I found a packet in his pocket. Niška Drina. God, I was so happy!'

'Man, what about the other Chetniks?' we exclaimed. 'Didn't you think about them? Weren't you afraid?'

'We're talking extreme despair here,' Azem said. 'I was going to have a smoke or die. It took me another half-hour to crawl back, I think. My guys were all waiting for me, goggle-eyed. They were all like "Give me one, give me one", and at first I told them to fuck off and get their own, but then, of course, I gave out half the pack. What else could I do?'

Azem finished his story and continued to smoke in silence. We eyed the sniper's rifle beside him.

'Where did you get the rifle? Is that from Kragljivoda, too?'

'No,' Azem replied, 'I'd swapped it with Naser for an Uzi submachine gun earlier this winter in Nova Kasaba. Naser recognized the rifle the other day when we were ordered to Kragljivoda and remembered me. You know, when he jumped on our truck to wish us luck he realized that there were several pairs of brothers among the twenty of us sitting there ready to move out. So he ordered that for each pair of brothers one should get off the truck. He said that brothers shouldn't go Kragljivoda together.'

Around that time I ran into another of my old university mates. He had also been at Kragljivoda and was one that group who really surprised me by having become fighters because I had known them as quiet, withdrawn students. When we met on the street he seemed genuinely pleased. 'Hasko! Long time no see!' He was, incidentally, one of the few people who ever expressed any human feeling and warmth towards me during the war.

'Cigarette?' he offered, taking a packet of Vek from his pocket. Vek were apparently the favourite brand among Serb soldiers during the war. He'd always been kind to me, but I couldn't believe he would so casually offer me a smoke when a single cigarette had reached the price of ten marks. Ten marks – not for a packet but just for one!

'Where did you get these?' I asked.

'I took them from a Chetnik officer,' he said in the same casual manner with no trace of arrogance.

I stared at him blankly.

'He didn't complain. He was dead,' he added by way of justifying himself.

'Fair enough. Seems that nowadays you can only have a smoke if you take it from a Chetnik.'

'Yeah,' he said calmly, 'that's the way it is now.'

'I heard you were at Kragljivoda.'

'Yeah. After my own village fell my unit was sent to Kragljivoda. I've been in a lot of battles since the beginning of the war, but that was the worst yet.'

'I hear it was very bloody,' I said, trying to sound better informed than I was.

'It's worse than that. I've seen so much, but this . . . I was very nearly killed at Kragljivoda.'

'What? How?'

'The Chetniks attacked with their armour – a tank, a transporter – surrounded by infantry. No way you can stick your head above the trench! Half my unit was dead or injured . . . When the tank approached I stood up with another guy from my unit; we had an RPG and took aim at the tank, but the tank fired a shell and . . .' – he paused, his thoughts wandering – '. . . and it hit the guy beside me. Everything above his waist was gone . . . I reckon it was an armour-piercing shell, the kind that doesn't explode at once . . . His legs were still standing . . . I was covered in his blood. The rest of him had been scattered all over the place . . . I knew I had to collect myself or I'd die the same way. So I grabbed the RPG and took aim, not at the tank but at the APC. I could see the APC better. I held my breath and pulled the trigger . . . When the rocket hit the transporter I saw their gunner fly five metres into the air; the turret, too. Clouds of dust rose up around it. The tank stopped. The infantry stopped. There was silence. The attack stopped. That was it.'

I didn't notice that the cigarette had burned down to my fingers – without me taking a single drag. Who was this guy I was talking to? This giant of a man, fearless; a student of mechanical engineering transformed into something I was not and would never be. He looked at me. He seemed composed, prepared for a new battle.

As we were saying goodbye he added, 'Let me know if you ever need anything.'

Soon after that a story spread around Srebrenica of a BiH army helicopter landing somewhere near by. Everyone was excited. There had been a heavy snowstorm that night. I learned that the helicopter had remained only as long as was necessary to unload its cargo. Then it took off again and quickly disappeared into the night. But the news raised our hopes to the highest level. We started thinking that the BiH army, its headquarters, the BiH presidency – or whoever was boss in Sarajevo or Tuzla – had finally remembered us in Srebrenica and that some form of salvation was on its way. We started believing that the Chetniks would be stopped. At the same time I was thinking: Do such brave and crazy pilots exist? Who knew the Bosnian army had any pilots and helicopters at all? At least fifty kilometres separated the landing point to the nearest territory under the Bosnian army's control. That meant it had been one very risky flight.

I would learn later from some fighters that what the helicopter had actually delivered was ammunition, some RPGs and other weapons I'd never heard of before – some kind of grenade launcher. They were only given to the most courageous fighters. The grenades were highly explosive and burned and blackened everything, even the grass, the soil. Let's say a perfect weapon to use on the Chetnik trenches. That was supposed to be our artillery, I guess. The Chetnik artillery fired at us from a safe distance, kilometres away, but our fighters had to stand only a few metres away from the Chetnik trenches to use their newest weapons. And they did. I'd heard some of them boasting about the enemy losses they had inflicted this way.

Anyway, several days later word went around that a second helicopter had landed not far from the town. I found it interesting that information about attacks on Serb lines and villages always spread through town at lightning speed, but information about these helicopter landings seemed closely guarded, a real military secret. A group from the military and civilian leadership privileged with this information waited for the helicopter. Some were there with their families. About fifteen people boarded and flew off to Tuzla. Or so I've been told.

I wasn't angry when I heard this because it was perfectly in line with the law of survival that had governed relationships in Srebrenica from the very beginning. Some things were available only to those who gained their privileged status through direct participation in the fighting. I could only feel sorry for not having been in the vicinity that day to sneak on to the helicopter somehow. I was aware that this would have been impossible, but that didn't stop me from fantasizing about it. I imagined myself sitting in that helicopter, leaving all the chaos behind. My family wasn't in this daydream; I was the only one on board.

I'd also heard that the helicopter had brought other things that had inexcusably taken up space that might more usefully have been used for weapons and ammunition – such as cartons of cigarettes, chocolate, even tins of pineapple. Money, too. There were also personal effects, delivered by someone powerful or resourceful enough to sneak them on to a military helicopter. What was supposed to have been a military operation had turned into a circus, as indeed had been the case with many more initiatives related to the administration of support and aid in the pockets of territory under our control in eastern Bosnia. I heard that a lot of things unloaded from that helicopter ended up in the wrong hands. These may have been rumours, but even if they were only partly true, one thing was for sure: there was no order or discipline in Srebrenica

With the constant pressure of Chetnik raids and advances the crisis in Srebrenica was coming to a head. I had the impression that many people were ready to surrender to the Chetniks, to tell them everything they knew about Srebrenica's defences, anything just to save their own lives, just to leave that place and be *anywhere* but Srebrenica. I'm convinced that that is exactly what hundreds, if not thousands, of them would have done if only they could have been sure they wouldn't be killed, tortured or sent to detainee camps – but, of course, given the previous experiences of thousands of Bosniaks, of that they could not be sure.

The ideal according to which Srebrenica must be defended for the integrity of BiH was dead. Most were thinking: Take Srebrenica, take everything, just let me out of here so I never have to return. There were, of course, still people who were motivated by the idea of BiH, especially among the warriors, but even their number was dwindling as March of 1993 wore on.

A HALF-SLAUGHTERED OX

Biljeg, on the left flank of Kragljivoda and one of the most important positions in our defences, was lost to a much stronger Chetnik force. The commander of the unit that had held this position was Ahmo Tihić, my cousin Sabera's husband and one of the sons-in-law of my Aunt Mina and Uncle Asim who had been our hosts in Luka. Ahmo was one of the rare locals who hadn't forgotten my father's pre-war status. Apart from the whole carton of matches he'd once given us, he had come to our rescue with about thirty kilograms of wheat at a time when we were left without a single grain.

One day during the rush of refugees from the south, as Muslim villages kept falling to the Chetnik forces, my father ran into Ahmo in the marketplace. Ahmo had his whole family with him – his wife and our cousin Sabera, both their daughters, Senada and Adisa, Ahmo's father Mujo, Ahmo's brother Djemo with his wife and daughter. My father brought them all home. They had a lot of belongings with them – by refugee standards they were well off. My father said they were going to move into the first floor of 'our' house.

The family from Višegrad, who already lived upstairs, now had to squeeze into one room so that Ahmo's large family could take over the remaining two. The twenty or so of them had to share a single bathroom and toilet. As mean-spirited as it may sound, the four of us were happy that no one asked to move in with us downstairs where we retained the privilege of having the second bathroom and toilet just for ourselves. From that day on about twenty-five of us lived in the house that Veljko and Razija Bašić had built for their four-person family.

The new inhabitants started to bring in their possessions. It took days, so we couldn't wait for the confusion to end. We could see they had loads of food – including several hundred kilograms of corn and wheat, flour, beans. They also had several cows and oxen. They never offered us any of their supplies, nor did they ever ask if we were hungry – and we were hungrier than ever. All we had at the time was about two hundred marks, enough for fifteen or so kilograms of corn.

Soon after Ahmo's family moved in, two of his men appeared on our street with a huge ox they intended to slaughter right there and then. The town was heavily shelled that day, but the blood pouring down the street was bovine not human. I watched as the men tied all four of the animal's legs with rope, then the largest man struck it right between the eyes with the poll of an axe-head. They plunged a huge knife into the ox's neck and opened its throat – at first the blood spurted upwards like a fountain and then started to flow down the street like a crimson stream through the snow. But the wounds the ox had received hadn't killed him; he was so strong. He jumped up, broke loose, kicked off the ropes and rushed down the street staggering like a drunk. The men ran after him with knives in their hands, axe, rope, trying to catch the ox with the half-slit throat. The scene made me sick to my stomach because it brought back to my mind the story of the slaughter on the Višegrad bridge. The man who had witnessed it and had hid in the grass for three days said the Muslims taken to the bridge had all been thrown into the river, some dead but others half dead with their throats half slashed. I'd heard similar stories of several surprise Chetnik attacks on Muslim villages during the summer of 1992 when people with their throats slit – but not entirely – would suddenly break loose and start running with blood pouring from their necks.

I didn't see where and how they subdued the ox, but soon they were skinning it and butchering it in front of the house. I heard somebody say it was a seven-hundred-kilogram animal. Our neighbours watched from their windows. Many of them couldn't remember the last time they'd tasted meat, although it cost less than grain. But bread was our lifeline, the only food we couldn't live without. During the war I realized that, rather than being carnivores, humans were herbivorous by nature – or, more accurately, panivorous: bread eaters.

Speaking of which, something incredible was going on. Given the total lack of baking powder and yeast in Srebrenica, people started using the dry powder from fire extinguishers as a raising agent. Fire extinguishers weren't in short supply. Every building had them, every office and factory. All the extinguishers were picked up and smashed, the powder taken out and sold in the marketplace. To this day I have no idea what kind of chemical it was and what possible long-term consequences it may have had on our health. In a similar vein, all the electrical substations in the free territory were demolished and the oil drained from the transformers. The few people who still had cars or trucks used this oil as fuel. The stench was terrible, with the exhausts smoking and exploding, but the vehicles kept moving as long as the oil lasted.

Anyway, Ahmo's men finished butchering the ox. Some pieces of meat were given to the neighbours and the rest of it was piled up, steaming in the cold, in the hallway where we left our footwear. While moving our shoes – I didn't want them soaked in blood – I caught my mother in the kitchen holding a large knife. She – like a hawk or, rather, a vulture – looked left and right and rushed past me with her sleeves rolled up and the knife in her hand. She'd been waiting for Ahmo's men to leave the house. She swiftly cut a piece of beef from the huge mound in front of her then whispered my name saying, 'Quick!' and passed me the piece she'd taken before hacking away another. She did it without anyone noticing. We closed the door to the kitchen and stared at the heap of meat on the table, free from sinew, gristle and fat. Braco joined us. My father was not at home.

'Don't you think they're going to notice?' Braco asked anxiously

'Don't worry,' I said. 'How could they notice when there's half a ton of meat out there.'

Soon there was a knock at the door. It was Sabera, Ahmo's wife and our cousin, with a piece of meat in her hand. 'Here's some meat for you,' she said and left.

My mother roasted about two kilograms of the beef with no condiments, no seasoning, no onion, no potatoes, no nothing. When my father came home we had a feast of unsalted roast beef – our first substantial meal in a month. Every tasteless bite we chewed in silence, convincing ourselves that the only thing that mattered was to fill our stomachs, where it sat like stone. Afterwards I lay down for several hours with my eyes closed, feeling my stomach digesting chunks of ox. I could sense life starting to surge through my body.

It was in Srebrenica that I learned for the first time that cattle need salt the same way humans do. I also learned that the meat of animals lacking salt was tough and tasteless. Several years after the war I was shown a document discussing the annihilation of Srebrenica's Muslims, apparently a plan designed with the help of experts from the Belgrade VMA, the Military Medical Academy. In Tuzla the now-deceased Dr Nedret showed it to me during one of our meetings. According to the paper experts at the VMA confirmed that a population long deprived of salt would suffer complications. So, accepting this as one of the methods of liquidating Muslims, it was decided that salt should be prevented from entering Srebrenica at all costs. The paper mentioned side effects of salt deficiency, including goitres, hallucinations and aggressive behaviour.

I saw the document, but I don't have it and cannot comment on its authenticity, but if anyone is interested in checking there are institutions that have access to it.

CLINTON

At the end of February, I don't remember the exact date, we heard on the radio that the Serbs had allowed a UNHCR food convoy to reach Žepa. Srebrenica had received its first and only food convoy back in December 1992, and this was to be the first to Žepa. All that time the people there, at least those who still had German currency, had been travelling to Srebrenica to buy grain, returning with it on their backs. It was a long, tedious and dangerous fifty-kilometre journey across the same mountains and precipitous trails that my family and I had taken to get to Srebrenica.

There were about fifteen thousand people in Žepa then, while the population of Srebrenica had risen to sixty or seventy thousand after the fall of Cerska. These are estimates I would hear much later – there was no way of making a more precise calculation at the time – but it was evident that both these enclaves were crammed with refugees. The change in the US administration, they said on the radio, would bring change for the better in Bosnia. After President Clinton assumed office we all started listening to the news again, gathering around the few transistor radios that were available. Our hopes rose once more, and this despite our hunger and the fact that our fighters were struggling hard to maintain the existing lines of defence. The free territory was getting smaller by the day.

It had been snowing for several days when we heard about the Žepa convoy. My family's supplies of rotten cornmeal had come to an end, so I suggested that my father and I go to Žepa to try to obtain some food from the convoy. Unlike all my previous ideas this one was accepted by my father simply because we had run out of options.

We set off early the next morning. I didn't have a woollen hat, so I wrapped my head in a thick scarf – from a distance one might have mistaken me for a woman. My father did have a cap, but his blue jacket was too light for winter and for this trip. My jacket was more appropriate, and underneath I wore a thick Shetland sweater I'd bought in Sarajevo before the war. I also had some long-johns and a pair of warm black trousers that I'd found in a wardrobe in our accommodation.

We were already hungry and exhausted by the time we started climbing the hill above Srebrenica. I was walking in front of my father. I set the pace, and he barely managed to keep up with me but did so none the less despite his hip troubling him. Somewhere along the way I saw him picking leaves off a bush and putting them in his pocket. He hoped to roll them up as a tobacco substitute. I knew he had torn out a page from a book for this very purpose. His attempts to smoke anything he could get his hands on annoyed me. I hadn't smoked for months, and I couldn't understand how, given our situation, he couldn't give up. But that was something he wouldn't discuss.

The snow had stopped the night before, and the sky had cleared a bit, but everything was frozen. The two small pieces of cornbread my mother had packed for us were hard anyway, but now they were stiff with cold. The thick clouds appearing over the horizon promised a new storm, and I was conscious of having to move as swiftly as we could manage to avoid it. The wind whistled noisily around us, and the snow crunched beneath our feet. Thinking of the food we would eat in Žepa and what we would bring back to Mother and Braco, I was able to muster every little bit of energy I had.

My father told me he feared Chetnik ambushes more than being trapped in a snowstorm. After two hours, pushing our way through the deep snow, we arrived in Zeleni Jadar. Several dozen refugee families had been living there for months in the ruins of houses and in the buildings of an abandoned and charred chair factory. During the 1970s my father had been one of the factory managers, but I don't believe that this was on his mind as we approached one of the buildings. We were both freezing, and my father wanted to ask directions, whether anyone else had passed towards Žepa before us and if there were Chetniks in the area.

To our surprise the man who answered the door invited us in. The building was full of refugees, all of whom were huddled around a stove. We warmed up a bit. It turned out the man had a cow, and just as we were leaving his wife appeared carrying a bucket of fresh milk. We were offered a cup each – a very welcome pleasure that unexpectedly invigorated us.

We set off on the next leg of the journey, over ten kilometres across difficult terrain. Not long after we came across several groups of people, some of whom were leading horses, heading to Žepa. We were glad we wouldn't be walking alone, especially because some of the men had weapons.

After an hour or so we arrived in a clearing behind Mount Jasenova. There was no path through the snow, which suggested that no one had passed here for quite a while. Kilometres of white wasteland lay ahead of us. We formed a column and began wading through the knee-high snow that, in some places, rose to our waists. With my feet in so deep I had to lift my knees high to take the next step, which felt as though I was participating in some peculiar parade march; it was exhausting and caused a severe pain in my groin. My father didn't seem to have this problem. Under the circumstances his leather boots – even though they were disintegrating – proved more appropriate than my oversized rubber fishing footwear.

The men behind me began to complain at my slow pace, and the horses grew restless and whinnied. Somebody suggested we should let the horses go in front. That was a bad idea. The horses were much heavier, and the surface area of their hooves was much smaller than our boots, so they sank deeper into the snow. I found myself confronted by a series of deep narrow holes that were hard to avoid. My feet kept plunging into them, and with each step I found it increasingly difficult to pull them out. To make matters worse the tops of my boots were wide and soon filled with snow. I was moving with extreme difficulty anyway, and the whinnying horses ahead of me and the protesting people behind didn't help. My father looked very worried. He was as pale as a ghost, and I was as tired as a dog. It seemed we were getting nowhere.

People began to disregard the rules and order of the column, pushing past and swearing at me. After realizing the horses were making progress more difficult they forged new paths through the snow, their rifles slung on their backs.

I had to stop treading in the hoof prints, but that was easier said than done. I was exhausted and hungry and frozen right through, and now that I was making my own path through the snow the thought of mines troubled me. At least walking behind the horses had saved me from that concern. By the time the column stopped for a break I was in agony. Some of the armed men went forward to scout for signs of Chetniks. We ate our meal in silence, doing our best to chew the frozen bread and the few pieces of dried meat my mother had packed for us. When I tried to quench my thirst with snow I was told not to do that as it would only make me feel worse.

Even my leggings were wet – partly from the snow and partly from sweat. I took my boots off and knocked off the snow, but the boots were cold and wet inside. The bottom half of my trousers was frozen stiff.

Somebody said that we were close to Šarena Bukva, the mountain pass that the men from Luka had barricaded, a place to which I had sworn I would never return. Now nothing seemed familiar under the deep cover of snow.

It was decided that we would continue in smaller groups because of the danger of Chetnik patrols in the bordering woods – they knew this was the only way to get to or from Srebrenica. When we started up again the pain in my groin quickly became unbearable. With every step I bit my tongue against the pain, and when, finally, I could not stifle my groans any longer everyone turned their heads to see who was making so much noise. The Chetniks would hear us if I didn't keep quiet, they swore at me. I had fallen behind a line of people who moved on without looking back – I understood that they did not intend to help anyone who fell behind. The days were short, and it was about to get dark. To stay in the snow meant certain death. My father was about ten metres ahead of me. He stopped and looked from me to the column that was now so far ahead that we could hardly see it. It occurred to me that we might be attacked by wolves, although wolves seemed a rather harmless prospect in comparison with the Chetniks.

I tried to step forward, but again I groaned in pain.

My father railed at me. 'What are you playing at?'

I hadn't seen him this angry for months. He hesitated, looked towards the column, went back and forth and finally approached me. I was on my knees, literally.

'Get up, get up!' he screamed. He was afraid we would be left alone and couldn't grasp that it was impossible for me to go any further. 'You persuaded me to do this. Now get up. We can't stay here. We have to keep moving.'

I fell on to my back. I remember seeing a piece of sky and then my father bending over me. His face retreated. I heard him swear and spit, which was his way of expressing frustration or disappointment. And then I fainted. I don't know how long I was unconscious – maybe just a few minutes – but when I came to my father was half carrying, half dragging me through the snow. Luckily Vukoljin Stan was not far from Šarena Bukva. To our great surprise people were still living in the shepherd huts there. We staggered through the snow towards the nearest one. It was already dark when we arrived at the door.

A group of men, women and children stood in front of the hut. They just stood there waiting for us. One of them apparently recognized my father – it might have been a relative of ours or someone who used to work with him. I heard nothing about that anyway. I couldn't wait to collapse somewhere. We were shown into a room where we could spend the night. It was warm; a fire was burning in the stove. We dried our clothes – or, rather, my father did because I was on a mattress in the corner, motionless.

An elderly woman brought us some herbal tea. 'It's bitter,' she said. 'We haven't had any sugar since last summer, but it will help you feel better, son.'

There was a lamp on the table. It was what they called a tallow lamp. You soak a cloth in animal grease, then it burns slowly. Watching the flickering light and sipping my tea made of who knows what kind of herbs, I quickly drifted off to sleep.

My father woke me at dawn. 'Get up,' he said. 'Are you going to stay in bed all day? Come on. We have to go.'

I stood up cautiously. To my great surprise and pleasure I realized that the pain had subsided considerably.

'I'm OK,' I said, 'Let's get going.'

We got dressed immediately and were ready to depart. Our hosts offered us some more bitter herbal tea for the road.

As I stepped outside I was blinded for a moment. The whiteness was dazzling, although the sun was only just breaking through the clouds. Even the trees were almost entirely covered in snow. There was endless pure white everywhere I looked. It was the kind of scene you usually see in movies with Santa's sleigh and his reindeer flying through the sky.

Ten minutes later, my father and I stood at the foot of Mount Javor.

We followed the tracks of yesterday's column until we reached the forest. There was no sound there except for us shuffling over the frozen snow. No path was visible now. Either it had magically closed behind our fellow travellers or they hadn't passed this way at all. There were no signs of any animals either. At times it seemed we would be marooned on the steep icy slope for all eternity. The snow was waist deep in some places, and there were snowdrifts taller than us, especially around the bigger trees. After two or three hours of incredible effort we reached the summit. There we paused, utterly exhausted but too afraid to sit down in case we sank too deeply into the snow.

Then we heard singing.

Three women appeared in front of us, coming from the direction of Žepa. They were pushing through the snow, one behind the other, singing. Each carried a sack over her shoulder. When we came nearer they gave us room on the path for us to pass but remained tight lipped. They were in a hurry to reach Srebrenica. Three women alone on the mountain, apparently unconcerned and, I noticed, shoeless! All three of them had only thick woollen peasant socks on their feet. From Srebrenica to Žepa and back, across snow-covered mountains, wearing only woollen socks!

'What are you carrying?' we asked.

'Food,' one of them replied cheerfully. 'Aid from the convoy. There's everything from flour to tins to cheese!'

My face brightened at once. I looked at my father; it seemed that his mood had also changed in a flash.

'And where might you be going? To Žepa?' the other woman asked.

'Yes. We hope to get some food as well.'

'And have you got your papers?'

'What papers?'

'The certificate. That you are registered as refugees in Žepa.'

'Well, the three of you are obviously heading to Srebrenica, so you're not refugees in Žepa either,' we argued.

'True, but we are registered in Žepa. No paper no food, I'm afraid,' one of them said, taking a piece of paper out of her pocket to show us. The paper was torn along the folds. I didn't bother to read the short paragraph, but I saw a stamp under the text – it looked official enough.

My father scowled at me. Sometimes it seemed that we could communicate telepathically. This was one of those occasions. His eyes said, 'You and your bright ideas!' Mine retorted, 'How was I supposed to know that we would need a piece of paper we don't have?'

'All right, off we go then,' they said, carrying on down the slope. They were soon out of sight, but their song seemed to echo around the mountain for a long time.

They had every reason to sing for joy, I thought. Each one of them was carrying about fifteen or twenty kilograms of food on her back. That was much more food than we'd seen in months.

My father and I continued across the Mount Javor plateau. Neither of us said a word. I could feel his anger growing with every step. He was angry at everything and everyone. He was angry at himself, at the war, the Chetniks, the mountain, the snow, our fate. He was angry with the officials in Žepa who required a piece of paper. And he was angry with me. Soon we found ourselves in the middle of a snowstorm. With the snow blowing into our eyes we could see nothing ahead of us. We lost our bearings and no longer had any idea which direction Žepa was in. My father was growing more furious with each passing moment. And more desperate. He was furiously desperate, or desperately furious. I couldn't tell which it was.

We fought the snow and the wind for quite some time, and by the time the Žepa valley finally appeared in front of us we were both exhausted. We were physically and emotionally drained.

'We will get nothing,' I muttered through my teeth, breaking the silence between us.

'This is all your fault!' my father yelled. 'We should never have set out! Here's your Žepa now! Look!'

I was livid. My stomach turned with rage. I was frustrated with every aspect of this life, but I was most infuriated by my father. A deep cry erupted from the depths of my being. The words came out that I'd been wanting to say to my father all this time but could not. 'You!' I cried. 'Your fault, nobody's but yours! Yours! It's because of you that we didn't leave Bosnia! It's because of you we didn't go to Tuzla! It's because of you that we're stuck in Srebrenica! You!'

The mountain echoed with my cries.

My father's arms shot out for my throat, but I grabbed hold of both his hands. We pushed against each other, locked in each other's grip, neither of us able to shift the other. Time seemed to stop. I looked at him. He was squeezing my hands, grimacing and growling behind clenched teeth. Then he slipped and fell to one knee. The strain was too much for him. It brought tears to my eyes to see my father kneeling in front of me. Defeated by life. Brought to his knees by his own son.

We both let go. I took a step back. My father was staring straight ahead, speechless, crying.

I thought: What have you done, Hasan? You've brought your own father to this. Look at what you've become. Look at what the war has done to you.

And look at what the war had done to my father.

But he recovered sooner than I did. I was still whimpering when he straightened up and composed himself. Without saying a word he began to descend, skidding down the frozen slope towards Žepa.

My father and I exchanged no words. We spoke only to ask the locals we came across for directions to the food delivered by the UNHCR. The village was teeming with people carrying sacks on their backs. Some were even loading ox-drawn sledges.

We were directed to a warehouse. The snow was falling relentlessly.

My heart pounded with excitement as we found ourselves in front of the warehouse. An ex-colleague of my father's, a man named Bekto, was standing by the door. He didn't so much as flinch when he recognized us. The verbal exchange between Bekto and my father confirmed what the singing ladies had already told us: no certificate no food. While this was being established I stared over Bekto's shoulder at the stacks of food in the warehouse.

This could be a death sentence for the four of us.

My father just turned his back and walked away. I followed. We were moving up the hill again. Each time I asked where we were headed he would tell me just to follow him. I wondered where he got his energy from. He was twice my age and marching uphill, while I felt as though at any moment I could collapse in the snow.

Were we really to starve without anyone doing anything about it? I had the impression that if we collapsed there and then people would just push us into a ditch and let us die. I vowed that I would knock Bekto out if I ever saw him again – that is, if I survived the war.

'We aren't going straight back, are we?' I asked my father.

'We're going to find some food,' he replied.

I'd always been aware that my father was well known in this part of the country, but for the most part that had meant little during the war. I didn't ask any more questions. We clambered up a steepening hillside for at least an hour. Getting out of the Žepa valley is by no means an easy task, for it is a pit rather than a valley. We arrived, covered in sweat, at the next village. My father walked to a house near the road and called out. The woman who appeared at the door waved us in. It was warm inside. We were invited to sit at a table with several silent men whose wet clothes suggested they were in a situation similar to ours. The woman brought in a bowl of steaming-hot polenta and put it on the table. It was topped with some cottage cheese. She put a spoon in front of each of us, sliced an onion, left it on the table and disappeared. We exchanged a few bashful glances before grabbing our spoons and ravenously attacking the polenta which had to go around half a dozen men. We each had a few mouthfuls before it was gone. One man took the bowl and picked at the residue in the bottom. I felt hungrier than I'd been before.

We thanked the woman and left the house. I asked my father where we should go next, and he mentioned a name, Čavčić. My father had learned that this man was the local humanitarian-aid administrator, not that there had been any humanitarian aid before this UNHCR convoy. At any rate, this man was responsible for distributing the aid brought in by the UNHCR in this part of the Žepa valley.

My father entered the courtyard of Čavčić's house while I, not believing we would get anything anyway, headed off to look for a toilet. While I was undoing my trousers I happened to see the contents of the cesspit and couldn't help but exclaim aloud, 'Wow, these people clearly eat well.' When I came out I felt deeply embarrassed because Mrs Čavčić was standing just outside talking to my father.

But the woman gave me a smile and asked him, 'Is this your son? Do you have any other children?' She went back into the house and brought us two cups of herbal tea. 'To get you warm,' she said. I expected the bitter stuff I was used to by that point, but the tea was generously sweetened. I practically gulped it down, and almost instantly my vision cleared. It was as if I'd been watching a fuzzy television screen and suddenly somebody had adjusted the aerial.

'Ibro, why don't you come in? It won't be long now before Mehmed gets home.'

My father accepted the invitation, and we went into the nice warm house. There were three children inside, and as soon as their father arrived he told his wife to offer their guests some bread and chicken pâté. I was like a hungry animal, my eyes wandering around the room in search of food. The woman brought in half a huge round loaf of white bread, steaming hot. When she put a tin of chicken pâté in front of each of us I couldn't believe my eyes – I'd never seen one that big. It must have weighed at least half a kilogram. My father and I exchanged looks, but, as if reading each other's thoughts, neither of us touched the food. The white bread – real bread – was something we hadn't seen in months. Actually, we hadn't seen any food in such a quantity or of such quality in a long time. We certainly hadn't seen tins of chicken pâté. Looking at the food on the table in front of us we were conflicted by thoughts of my mother and brother in Srebrenica.

Mehmed was obviously confused.

'Look, Mehmed,' my father started to explain, 'my wife and my younger son are in Srebrenica and . . . Look, Mehmed, the situation is very difficult. You see . . .' The words got stuck in his throat.

'Ibro, help yourselves. Please. Don't worry, we'll pack something for the two of them.'

We ate. It tasted like heaven. Hot bread? Chicken pâté? My stomach seemed surprised.

My father briefly recounted our story. Mehmed's wife put mugs of hot milk in front of us.

Mehmed said that there was nothing he could do to help us regarding the UNHCR food aid. The rules were strict, and everything was precisely measured. 'But', he concluded, 'Clinton has promised that food will be delivered to Srebrenica by air. And to Žepa and Cerska as well. That's what they've said on the radio. If it happens, good. If it doesn't happen, you come back here and I'll give you an ox, a five-hundred-kilogram ox. You can get two hundred kilos of grain for that.'

That was a moment of indescribable relief. For the first time in months we thought there was some hope for our survival.

Things would change, and we'd never consider going back to Žepa, but I'm sure Mehmed would have kept his word had it come to that. The thought of his promise would make it easier to live through the events of the next few weeks.

We'd eaten well that evening, and we stayed awake for quite a long time, my father deceiving his cigarette cravings by rolling up the bush leaves he had in his pocket. Mehmed spoke for a long time about something that had happened in 1945 that he'd never forgotten. He had been a child then, but, as I understood, his hospitality had something to do with what my Grandpa Hasan had done for Mehmed's father forty-seven years ago. Mehmed was, in a way, repaying the family debt.

In 1945, when the Yugoslav Department of National Security, the OZNA, began arresting alleged members of the so-called Muslim Militia, they had surrounded his family's house and demanded that his father surrender and give up his weapons. His father refused. Mehmed was sure that the OZNA would have broken into the house and killed his father in front of them all were it not for my Grandpa Hasan. During the Second World War Grandpa Hasan had acted as a liaison between local Partisan groups loyal to Tito, which was a dangerous job. He had even managed to escape a Chetnik firing squad. He had been rewarded for his service in 1945 and made commissioner for the Žepa District.

'All of a sudden he appeared, your father,' Mehmed said to my father. 'Those OZNA people respected him, and my own father trusted him. Your father convinced my father to surrender his arms, guaranteeing with his life that my father wouldn't be arrested. I was five then, maybe six, but in my mind it is as clear as if it were yesterday.'

As I was listening I had the impression that Grandpa Hasan was sitting with us or watching us from a corner of the room.

So many times, especially during the war, I had heard people say, 'As you sow, so shall you reap.' My father had done so many favours before the war, and yet I had rarely seen him reap anything. Now we seemed to be reaping the good my grandpa had sown.

We got up at dawn and decided to set off at once. We had to cross two mountains on our return journey, and you never knew if it was going to snow. Breakfast was waiting for us on the table, which we didn't expect, and food to take back to Srebrenica. There was a kilogram of powdered milk and a kilogram of powdered fruit juice, a few kilograms of flour, a loaf of bread – and a tin of chicken pâté for each of us. This was nothing in comparison with the individual provisions from the Žepa food convoy, but for us it was a lot. With the scant rations we were used to, this would be enough to last seven days. We were happy just imagining the joy we'd bring my mother and Braco.

My father suddenly stopped loading his backpack with the donated food. He sat down, covered his face with his hands and broke down, sobbing like a child. Everybody was silent. I'd never seen my father cry like that. Trying to comfort him, Mehmed put a hand on his shoulder.

'Ah, Mehmed,' my father gasped through tears, 'see what's become of me. See what I'm reduced to. God forbid that anyone should have to experience this.'

It seemed like he wouldn't stop crying. When eventually he calmed down we thanked our hosts, said our goodbyes and left. The sun had not yet come out, and the temperature was well below zero. The mountains were ahead of us, a fifty-kilometre snow-covered track. The Chetniks were lurking somewhere along the way. But we felt much better than the day before, and we walked quickly and decisively. I was so buoyed by the food we were taking back that I don't remember any details of the return journey except that, luckily, at about the halfway point we found another group returning to Srebrenica and travelled together.

We arrived very late. It had already been dark for some time when we reached home. My mother and Braco were waiting. We unloaded the food together.

Despite the deep snow, my father and I had made it all the way from Žepa in one go, or, at least, that's how it felt that day.

FOOD FROM THE SKY

My father received a message from Žepa, an invitation to come as soon as he could to discuss his appointment to the War Council there, either as its head or a member. As Zoran had made clear, someone or some group had nominated him, although I never learned the exact details. Either way, my father decided to go. This time my father decided to take Braco with him; my mother and I stayed in Srebrenica.

Shortly after midnight the next day we were awakened by a roaring sound overhead. At first we thought Chetnik planes might be attacking by night, something that had never happened before, and we headed for the basement, but some minutes later we heard a commotion in the street, and we ran out to see what was happening. Everybody was looking up, and there was an amazing sight in the sky. At first we saw the glint of hundreds of falling objects and then parachutes opened. We couldn't see the planes, although there was some moonlight, but the sinister sound was so resonant that everybody had the feeling they were flying just above our heads. We could feel the vibrations in the air; it was clear that several huge aircraft were flying above Srebrenica.

As they neared the ground the parachutes started whistling and fluttering. We were all watching the sky as if hypnotized; hundreds of mesmerized people all along the icy street. Somebody shouted that Clinton was sending food by air. All at once everybody was running to where the parachutes might land – up the hill, up another hill, down the street – but the wind could take them anywhere, including to Chetnik-controlled territory.

'Hasko,' my mother called to me, 'you shouldn't go immediately, you know. It may get rough. Let's go home and see if we can find anything in the morning.'

I was so excited that I hardly slept. The next morning my mother woke me up at first light. As soon as I went out on to the street one of the neighbours shouted from their veranda that the parachutes had landed around the Guber Spa. I hurried up the hill, since the spa was only a few kilometres away. When I arrived at Guber I noticed three men climbing a very steep slope. One of them was carrying a rifle. I decided to follow them. The snow was so deep that it took us half an hour to progress a hundred metres. We climbed on all fours. The three men looked back at me on several occasions.

'Hey, you,' one of them finally yelled. 'Where do you think you're going? Why are you following us?'

He sounded aggressive, and I wasn't sure how far they would go to force me to stop following them.

'I'm looking for the parachutes,' I answered.

'Go and look on your own then,' they shouted angrily. 'Leave us alone. Don't come this way.'

I hesitated a moment before carrying on. They stopped looking back.

I knew that in all likeliness there were Chetniks on the other side of that hill; on several occasions they'd even been seen on this side. A certain Dušan, if I remember correctly, wrote his name on the walls of the ruined Guber restaurant every time he came over. People said that he was from Srebrenica and that, apparently, he had become a Chetnik *vojvoda*, a warlord.

At the very top of the hill a pallet was sticking out of the snow. It was a cube, a metre and a half, maybe two metres, on each side. The three men forgot about me. They busied themselves with cutting the straps attached to the parachute. Their hands trembled with excitement. Nobody had the patience to unbuckle the straps the normal way. When they removed the canvas cover a load of cardboard boxes appeared. Later I would learn that each pallet contained six hundred kilograms of food packed in fifty boxes and that each box contained twelve lunch packs, that is twelve lunch packs for one person. But the first time I saw it the pallet looked surreal to me, strange and mysterious. It was as if a UFO had arrived from some distant planet.

The four of us were nervously looking around, fearing that someone else might come up from the valley. They could easily have followed our footsteps. At first my three companions tried to carry as many boxes as they could pile in a bundle, but they soon realized that wouldn't work. Then they tried to roll the boxes down the hill, but that didn't work either, and they hurried down to retrieve those that had become stuck in the snow. It would be impossible to carry more than one box at a time down the hill. I went to the pallet, opened a box, took out a pack – a dark-brown plastic container – and tried to open it, but I couldn't.

One of the men approached and cut the container open with his knife, saying, 'Go on then, eat!'

The three of them had opened packs for themselves already and were sitting in the snow studying the contents. As soon as I finally managed to unwrap something I thought might be chocolate I enthusiastically bit into the light-brown bar expecting the wonderful flavour and taste of food that had fallen to us from the sky sent by Americans or Germans or whoever.

But it tasted so nasty I had to spit it out. 'What is this stuff?' I asked the three of them. They were still chewing it and asking themselves the same question.

'I have no idea, mate,' answered one.

'But it tastes horrible,' added another.

'No sign of any bread. What were the Americans thinking when they sent this?'

I took the thick foil wrapping, turned it over and read: 'Chicken Stew'. I knew what *chicken* meant, but I had no idea what *stew* was.

I gathered up the box and said, 'I'm off.'

As I was leaving one of them yelled after me, 'Hey, you! Better watch out for the military police. They're down by the hotel confiscating everything. They say the food is for the fighters.'

The military police were indeed where he said they would be. I would later learn they were confiscating large amounts only, but I was fearful after my companion's warning and hid ten packs in the ruins of the Guber restaurant. Putting two more under my jacket I hurried home walking in a wide arc to avoid the military police. As soon as I arrived at the house I asked my mother for a knife, opened both packs and shook out all the contents on the table. Delighted and curious, my mother and I examined the contents, which were the same in both packs. These were Meals Ready-to-Eat (MREs), basic field rations for US soldiers.

The contents of an MRE included a main course (mashed or pressed and packed in a plastic bag fifteen centimetres long, five centimetres wide and about a centimetre thick, the instructions for which said to leave the bag in hot water for a few minutes), tiny sachets of peanut butter and jam, a dessert (a chocolate bar or something that looked like it labelled as an energy bar), a tiny sachet of instant coffee sufficient for one cup and two tiny sachets of sugar. There were also some matches and a plastic knife, fork and spoon. And that was it, as far as I remember.

My mother was particularly thrilled with the coffee. She immediately heated some water, and for the first time in ten months we had coffee – with sugar, no less!

'What a shame', I said, sipping the aromatic drink, 'that they don't include at least one cigarette, say a Marlboro, to go with the coffee. What kind of people are these Americans if they don't offer a smoke to their own soldiers?'

'We have to be careful to leave one pack for your father and brother when, God willing, they return from Žepa.'

'Don't worry, you can have another cup while I go and get the rest,' I said, leaving in a hurry, for in the meantime it had begun to snow again.

As soon as I approached the ruins of the Guber restaurant I realized that hiding the packs there had been a huge mistake. A bald man in his fifties, our neighbour on Crvena Rijeka Street, not a refugee but a Srebrenica local, was stuffing his jacket with the packs I'd hidden there.

'Hey, you!' I shouted running towards him. He raised his head, an aggressive expression on his face. But that was not what brought a lump to my throat; I realized he must have seen me hiding them and taken advantage of my absence.

'Man, those packs are mine,' I uttered the words with extreme difficulty, although I shouted. 'Do you know what I had to do to get them?'

'And now they're mine. I found them,' he said. 'Can you prove you left them here?'

He just stood there looking at me, annoyed. I could barely keep myself from punching him in the face. I clenched my fists in frustration while tears filled my eyes. He didn't seem like someone who would yield, even if punched. So I restrained myself.

'Listen, here, take this,' he offered, pulling out a pack from under his jacket, then he walked straight past me, saying as he went, 'That's fair, isn't it?'

At that moment I felt truly sorry for myself and for humanity in general, for there were so many greedy, cruel people in the world. Definitely too many. Something hurt in my chest. I felt a crushing pain.

The man was utterly appalling; I really hated his guts.

HUMAN STAMPEDE

The next day my father and brother returned from Žepa. Nothing had come from the whole affair with the War Council; apparently someone had managed to convince everyone else that my father wouldn't be the best person for the position after all. My father didn't know why or what had been said.

Given this and, more importantly, given the prospects of food drops in Srebrenica where we at least had a roof over our heads, we decided to stay where we were. Like everyone else we hoped that this was the beginning of better days to come. We saw the drops as a sign that the world had not forgotten us. We thought that after this spectacle something even bigger would happen that would change the situation for the better.

The next time our food supplies dried up we had something to hope for. We eagerly expected to hear the roar of planes followed by the sight of parachutes. A few days later it did indeed happen again, and the routine continued for several consecutive nights. The planes – a whole squadron of giant aircraft – always appeared after midnight but never at the exact same time or place. None of us had actually seen them as they flew only at night – and I heard on the radio that they flew at an altitude of ten thousand feet, or about three thousand metres, apparently to avoid the Serb anti-aircraft guns. But this was anything but humane. There were several instances of parachutes not opening and pallets simply crashing to the ground. Sometimes they fell on those waiting for them. I heard about one landing on a woman and killing her; it hammered her straight into the ground.

However, no matter how terrible, dangerous or unpredictable, those February and March nights seemed beautiful, and we couldn't wait to hear the roaring from above. They seemed beautiful because we, as hungry and miserable as we were, thought of nothing else but how to fill our empty stomachs. Our minds were consumed by those pallets and boxes, where they would fall and who might find them. We were anxious, as if this were a lottery and we couldn't wait to see who the lucky winners would be.

We agreed that my mother shouldn't participate in the nightly parachute hunt. My father, my brother and I used to go to bed early and get up as soon as we heard the planes. We would rush into the night, at times all three of us running in the same direction, at other times deciding that our chances were better if we split up. But other people were already positioned on the hills, having decided to stay awake all night. Maybe they slept during the day.

The planes flew regularly, regardless of the weather. During the moonless nights the hunt for parachutes would become a dangerous groping through the deep snow in the pitch darkness. Led by the hubbub of voices I would always end up with thousands of other people. If I heard someone mentioning a specific location I would start to run towards it through the snow, through thickets, ditches, streams and over rocks. And I would end up all alone in the dark woods above the town. But most often I would run to where everybody else was running. We would push each other in the dark, mostly by accident; every now and then someone would grab you to save themselves from falling, but sometimes they would do so to prevent you from arriving ahead of them. Some would carry weapons, and these were people with whom I never competed. Gun shots often echoed through the night, single shots as well as bursts. Every time a group of people reached a pallet at the same time there would be a brawl.

In this chaos people would pull out their knives as soon as they spotted a pallet. They would jump on it, trying to cut the straps. Blades would flash in the darkness, and you never knew if someone would cut you, accidentally or deliberately. I used to stand aside and watch – that is, mainly listen, as I couldn't see much in the darkness. Every time I finally dared move closer I would stomp on empty cardboard boxes and stumble over the remains of the broken pallets.

Hoping to find any leftovers of the main catch I would frantically sift through the mud, snow and dry leaves, my hands fumbling against other desperate hands. I still wonder how those who got there first managed to empty a six-hundred-kilogram pallet in a matter of minutes. Somehow they managed to remove it all before the crowd arrived.

I remember on one occasion a pallet landed right on our street, some two hundred metres from the house. I started running the moment it became clear where it would touch down, but by the time I arrived I found at least fifty people around it, men, women, elderly people, children. There were armed people and unarmed people. Everybody was shouting, swearing, pushing... I stood there confused, wondering if there were any way to approach a pallet surrounded by a crowd of people five-metres deep. And then I witnessed a kind of athletic feat; it was like a scene from a movie. One guy came sprinting past me – uphill, no less – and launched himself over several heads and landed on top of the pallet. Immediately somebody shouted, 'Knock him down! Knock the bastard down', and at once handguns and knives were drawn and shots fired into the air. I turned and went home without looking back.

During that time I used to join Braco and his friends, who had taken to hanging out on the street in the evenings. I would stay with them all night long waiting for the planes. Sometimes we would wait in vain, standing in the cold, shivering.

One evening my brother and I left the house together; we'd heard that the parachutes would land around the Old Town that night, so we decided to wait up on a hilltop near the fortress. The planes started to arrive just after midnight, and it seemed as if there were more than usual. There was a moon, and we could clearly see the parachutes as they started dropping, the sky was full of them. The wind took them towards the mountain above the Old City, and Braco and I did our best to get there before anyone else. While the parachutes fluttered above our heads a crowd of several thousand materialized around us, breathless, panting, gasping. We knew that our father was somewhere among them, but we couldn't see him. Then, all of a sudden, there was a terrible thud, and the earth shook. Another thud. And another. We were too close; six-hundred-kilogram pallets were falling right on top of us, their parachutes having failed to open. While looking for shelter I instinctively hugged Braco and covered his head with my arms. We crouched beneath a plum tree, which was actually no protection at all. If a parachute didn't open a pallet could land with enough force to split a metre-thick beech tree – I'd seen it with my own eyes.

'We're going to die here!' I cried as I held Braco's hand. He was numb with fear. I really thought this was the end for us. I prayed for the planes to leave or stop dropping their loads. I kept muttering, 'Please God, make it stop. Even if we don't find a single box ever again, please just make it stop.'

The pallets fell for several minutes. As soon as the planes stopped dropping them the crowd swarmed the hill. Running as fast as we could, but not seeing well in the dark, Braco and I fell into a deep stream, and it took us a long time to get out. The slope was so steep that we had to climb up it on all fours. The crowd was so huge that the snow melted under their feet, and we floundered through the mud.

We heard the brawl begin along with the sounds of a pallet being taken apart. Several voices yelled the same thing, 'Leave it alone, I tell you! Leave it alone.' I grabbed Braco to stop him from moving forward. I was afraid we might meet a knife in the dark. I felt a cardboard box in front me and plucked at it with my frozen hands. It was empty. When the noise subsided it became clear that all the boxes were gone, so we decided to leave empty handed. On the way back we managed to avoid the stream and, groping through the woods, reached the main road. The whole landscape was lit up by the moon, so we could see the lucky ones with the MRE packs they had found. Some carried many more than one. Some were even eating as they walked. Every now and then someone would break off from the party to open a pack, take out a bag and, without knowing what it contained, empty its contents directly into their mouths.

There were those who made fun out of it all. 'Have you heard that some guys found powdered beer down by the stream?' someone shouted.

'Here, mate,' another shot back, 'I'll give you all this stuff for a pack of that beer!'

There will always be gullible people who believe anything they hear. One man handed over his haul for the box of beer only to discover that it was full of medical supplies. He swore loudly, 'Damn you! What am I going to do with this? There's no beer in here!'

You could find lots of medical packs along the road as people only looked for edible things, but I heard later that some of these packs contained sedatives such as morphine. In a few months there were a number of junkies in Srebrenica; you could spot them by the look in their eyes.

Satisfied with what they'd found, many people sang and chatted along the way, but others looked very tense, fearing that somebody might seize their goods from them. This was not an unfounded fear. A man would push another man into the snow, take his food and disappear, leaving the wretch weeping in the snow. Only the law of the strongest applied. Literally.

Although my father, Braco and I would participate in the parachute hunt each night we never managed to get hold of a single pack, while some people apparently managed to make off with entire pallets.

One evening a pallet fell directly on a house in town, causing its roof to collapse. Luckily nobody was hurt – and the inhabitants didn't mind at all, as they had six hundred kilograms of food delivered direct to the ground floor of their house. Mending a roof was much easier than finding food to feed your family.

After the pallet hunt people would get some sleep before heading out into the streets to barter various bits of their meals. The American MREs had twelve different mains packed in brown retort pouches: meatballs with tomato sauce (nobody ever asked what kind of meat it was), chicken with a side dish, turkey with potatoes, corned beef, shepherd's pie, sliced ham (pork, that is), macaroni cheese, spaghetti Bolognese and a couple of others. People would try to swap the meals they didn't like for those they did. Not all the MREs were American. Sometimes pallets were dropped containing Italian, French or German MRE rations. All being armies of NATO countries the contents were more or less similar, but the Italian ones were everybody's favourite. Apparently the German MREs were not bad either – in fact, many people loved the German packs because the dessert was always a bar of chocolate. The bars were tiny, but the chocolate was real. Many used to complain about the French ones, however. What all the MRE packs had in common was the sachet of coffee or tea, the tiny bag of sugar and the set of plastic cutlery.

At first people would eat the MREs as they found them but eventually figured out that they were much better and tastier when reheated. When they finally understood this the lucky ones started having real feasts. You could tell morale was considerably higher than before.

The fighters received their share of the meals even when they didn't manage to get hold of them personally, although we did hear rumours that they were coming to town every night and leaving the lines exposed so they could try their luck in the food hunt. People started saying, 'Huh, if the Chetniks knew this, entering the town would be child's play for them.' The commanders apparently had a very hard time convincing the fighters not to leave the lines exposed, but they had families to feed.

After a time the radio communications centre in Srebrenica managed to let UNHCR know that the pallet dropping, besides being dangerous, was not particularly efficient, and that many people were left with no food at all. In ten days or so NATO and UNHCR came up with a new way of delivering food. Individual packs, we were told, would now drop from the skies. We were not really sure how that would work, but we couldn't wait to find out.

'Here they come!' somebody shouted. Everybody started running in every direction.

A very unusual sight appeared in the sky: thousands of objects glistening in the moonlight. Whistling and fluttering on their way down, countless packs fell from the sky one by one in free fall. We took cover. Even if each package weighed only half a kilogram, if it were dropped from an altitude of three kilometres there was no way such a blow could be harmless.

Then: *thump, thump, thump, thump, thump, thump* . . . each pack slammed into the snow and disappeared under the surface. Whether it was dangerous or not, people joyously dived in after them. I would thrust my arms into the holes in the snow but would find nothing at the bottom. Together with a hundred or so other individuals I started digging into the snow with my hands, feet, any way I could think of. Soon the frozen grass became visible. In a matter of only a few minutes the whole plain was cleaned of snow, and I hadn't found a single pack.

Then another plane arrived, and another hard rain of MREs followed. I took cover again, but this time a pack hit me directly on the head. The pack bounced off and landed in the snow. I was sure that my skull was cracked, but there wasn't any blood. In the meantime a small boy had appeared out of nowhere and taken the pack.

'Hey, you! Stop!' I yelled after him. 'It's mine. It hit *me* on the head!' I furiously rushed after him yelling, 'You little bastard,' but he was already too far away. As I watched him disappearing with my pack under his arm I could do nothing but swear at him.

That night I came home with nothing, as I had every night. My father and Braco were equally unsuccessful. We went to bed exhausted and hungry, but the next morning my brother woke me up shouting, 'Come, quick!'

I stepped outside to a wonderful sight. The thirty centimetres of snow on the roofs of the neighbouring houses were full of holes where the packs that had clearly fallen on them and then slid down the tiles leaving a trail in the snow. Those had already been picked up, but some were still up there. My mother appeared from the garden, smiling, presenting an armful of packs she'd gathered.

'See, I didn't have to go further than the garden,' she said happily.

Braco and I agreed that I would go up to the attic and push the packs down off the roof while he waited below to collect them. As I removed the first tile he shouted, 'You're nowhere near. Go lower, more to the left.'

I put the tile back in place and removed another as directed.

'Not bad!' he shouted. 'Just a bit lower, you can easily reach it.'

That day I managed to get three packs from the roof, the only three I ever managed to collect during the forty days and forty nights of hunting the food that fell in abundance from the sky. Between us we had ten or so, which meant that we were not going to be hungry for several days.

Our hunt for food continued over the following nights. I was sure I'd broken all the records in running uphill; I had no idea where my strength came from. However, after a few nights something happened that made no sense at all. Nobody knew whether it was down to a mistake made at the NATO or UNHCR offices or wherever the planes had been loaded – or maybe it was someone else's fault entirely.

I was waiting on a nearby hill. From there I could see Bojna Hill where, for some reason, the largest crowds would gather to wait for the planes. People improvised torches of various kinds so they could see where they were going. Most often it would be a piece of plastic or rubber strapped to a wooden stick. You had to be careful with the timing of ignition because plastic and rubber burn quickly. As the flames flared on the makeshift torches the burning rubber often poured down the sticks and on to the hands of those holding them or sometimes spat in their faces. During the day I saw more and more people with burned hands, but nothing could stop the human stampede. Every time I saw Bojna Hill with ten thousand torches burning brightly I thought it looked as I imagined New York City might by night. I'd heard others say the same thing. If the drop spot happened to be on the far side of the town the mass of torch lights rushing in your direction was quite a sight.

That night the sound of the objects raining down on the hill was different, more muffled and more frequent. Groping in the dark, feeling the ground with my hands, I found several potatoes! They were falling all around me. A bit later someone found a whole sack of potatoes, and then a whole sack of rice. Then it rained grains of rice. The sacks were obviously tearing apart in mid-air. But then something even worse happened: it started raining tin cans. Actual metal cans were falling on us from the full altitude of three thousand metres! A man standing near me was hit on the shoulder; he screamed in agony. I took off headlong down the slope, desperately looking for cover. I skipped over the tins lying on the ground. Unwilling to have my brains smashed out by a tin of beef stew I didn't stop to pick any up, and I managed to reach the first houses unharmed.

The next day I heard that many people had been injured and that there had even been casualties. None of this would have happened if we had all stayed home waiting for the food to be dropped and for the planes to leave. But there was no reasoning with starving people.

Who knows why, but my father, Braco and I had none of the luck. If the food drops had continued for ever we would still have been the last people to eat a full meal, and then only after everyone else had stuffed themselves. But I cannot say that we went completely hungry in those days. After a few weeks of unsuccessful hunting Braco appeared one night with a whole sack of powdered milk: twenty-five kilograms. Our happiness knew no bounds. This amount of powder apparently made 250 litres of milk. We mixed the powder with water and drank it throughout the day hoping it would help us to overcome fatigue and regain our strength. My mother even tried mixing it with cornmeal in the bread she baked.

MORILLON

When March arrived the Chetnik offensive was still in full swing. Our lines were falling one after the other, and the Chetniks were getting ever closer to the town. The greatest threat came from the south. Kragljivoda had fallen and so had Osmače. The lines around Zeleni Jadar were barely holding. The Chetniks were in the same position they would occupy two years later when they attacked Srebrenica for the final time.

It was my turn to look for firewood. It was snowing like crazy, and I could hardly move through the forest. As luck would have it I soon found a suitable tree on the hillside. I was lacking strength, and it took me a long time to cut it down. Just when I had finally succeeded I heard noises coming from the bottom of the hill. My first thought was that the Chetniks were attacking.

I heard a voice saying, 'There's a UNPROFOR general in town.'

I was immensely excited by the news. I abandoned my tree and rushed down the hill to see what was happening in town. I ran all the way to the post office. As I got closer my heart started beating out of my chest. The Chetniks weren't shelling; it must have been because of General Morillon.

The white UNPROFOR vehicles were visible from a distance. Several of them were parked in front of the post office. There were a few APCs and jeeps surrounded by a crowd of several hundred people, mainly civilians, who had gathered spontaneously in front of the building. The few armed fighters were there to secure the building in which Morillon was having a meeting with Naser and the other commanders.

It was already dark. Hoping for a cigarette I approached an APC with several UNPOFOR soldiers sitting on it. This was also a chance to practise my English.

'Hey,' I addressed the soldier, 'can you give me a cigarette?'

The soldier gave me a blank look.

'Where are you from?' I asked in English.

'I'm from Srebrenica,' he answered in English.

'No shit!' I exclaimed in Bosnian as the guy burst out laughing. His name was Senad, and I had, in fact, seen him around before. Having fled to Germany he had returned to Srebrenica in the company of a German photographer, Philipp von Recklinghausen. From Germany they had travelled to Tuzla then walked to Srebrenica, where Senad's mother was still living. I'd occasionally spotted the pair walking around town. Philipp wore a fez the whole time, and Senad wore a uniform, very neat, with a helmet and flak jacket. None of the fighters had anything quite as protective. Senad had purchased his kit back in Germany. He was now sitting on the APC talking to the UNPROFOR soldiers in English and German. He was fluent in both, and, dressed in a proper uniform, he didn't look any different from the others, so no wonder I mistook him for one of them. I hadn't noticed that his helmet was green and not blue like theirs.

I was so excited and happy that the UNPROFOR general was in Srebrenica that I didn't go home for hours despite the cold. And I wasn't the only one. I hung about with a hundred other people waiting for someone from inside the post office to bring us good news – that the Chetnik offensive was going to be stopped or that food convoys were going to arrive. In the end no one came out of the post office, and I went home around midnight.

The streets were again full of women and even children. The refugees from Cerska and Konjević Polje lit fires along the streets. Many of them didn't have any accommodation yet; the houses were overcrowded.

The next day I tried to strike up a conversation with the UN soldiers, believing they would transmit our story to the world; the story about the hell in which we lived.

Morillon appeared at the entrance of the post office. He looked angry and indignant. The crowd came closer, forming a semi-circle around him. Morillon apparently didn't want to go back into the building, but he also couldn't move forward since we were blocking his way. The most vociferous was a group of women with children. They claimed they would prevent the UNPROFOR vehicles from leaving with their bodies if necessary. I didn't understand what was going on. Then one of the fighters told me that there had been a disagreement between Morillon and our representatives at a meeting the night before. Morillon had told them that he would be meeting Milošević in Belgrade next. Our representatives, however, considered the whole thing a deception, for if Morillon left Srebrenica the Chetniks would continue their offensive. 'The town would fall and there would be a massacre. The people won't let you go,' they'd said. 'You're staying here with us.'

I walked closer to the entrance of the post office. I was standing less than a metre away from Morillon. Only his interpreter stood by his side. The interpreter was dressed in the same uniform as the general, that is, in a French army uniform with a blue beret. He spoke our language with a Macedonian accent; I noticed this immediately. Morillon addressed the crowd; the interpreter translated. He confirmed that he needed to go to Belgrade to meet Milošević. He said that this was the only way to save Srebrenica, and he also said that he knew what was going on, that he was aware Srebrenica was about to fall, that people were starving and that the refugees who'd arrived most recently were sleeping in the snow-covered streets. Then he said that the food convoys were ready to enter Srebrenica but that wouldn't happen before he left. He needed to report to the world what he had seen here. He repeated that it was necessary for the people to move out of the way in order for him to go to Belgrade.

But the crowd reacted negatively to every mention of Belgrade; the very name suggested deception.

'You will not pass!' the women shouted, and they sat down in the snow in the middle of the street. Some of them were weeping, waving their arms, beating their chests, yelling, 'If you leave the Chetniks will kill our children! You have to stay with us!'

This went on for an hour or so, then Morillon went back in and, after some time, appeared at the window holding a megaphone. He addressed the crowd with a single sentence that would become a historic one. 'You are now under the protection of the United Nations.' He uttered that sentence and then had the UN flag raised on the roof of the post office building.

Little did we know then that this was Morillon's own initiative and not approved by any UN resolution, and it would cause major problems for the general. I would learn all this only after the war while researching the UN's and the West's decisions during that period. The UN and Western diplomats and politicians would later say that Morillon's promise could not be fulfilled, that it was not his promise to make. They tried to produce a working definition of Morillon's commitment and the international community's obligations to us. What they came up with was very different from what Morillon seemed to have in mind. What they came up with was a lot of empty words. The people of Srebrenica clearly believed Morillon; they let him go the day after his pledge. But after he departed Srebrenica was anything but a protected zone.

Morillon left some of his troops in Srebrenica – as a guarantee that he would be back, I guess. And so Srebrenica got its first UNPROFOR soldiers: ten or so members of the general's escort plus a three-member team of UN Military Observers (UNMOs). If I remember rightly a food convoy entered the town the very same day the general left, but the Chetnik offensive continued with even greater intensity. It was as if Mladić believed the UN would indeed declare Srebrenica a safe zone and decided to act before it happened. He must have figured that once the town had been taken the UN could declare whatever they wished.

MARCH AND APRIL 1993

One day in March I noticed from my window that a long line of men was moving from the town centre up towards the ruins of the Old Town's medieval fortress. I tried to count them but stopped after realizing that there must have been more than a thousand. From what I could see, every fifth man was armed; later I would revise that to one in every ten. I would spot a piece of camouflage every now and then, but mainly they wore civilian clothing. The scene reminded me of every Partisan film I'd seen as a child. The people seemed miserable, tired, demoralized. Nevertheless, they slowly but steadily progressed up the hill.

I went out into the street and started talking to a few people from the neighbourhood.

'You know where those people are headed?' I asked.

'To Osmače. Haven't you heard?' Our commanders had apparently made a decision the previous night. 'They're going to chase the Chetniks out of Osmače. This is our last chance to defend Srebrenica. If they fail the Chetniks will be here in no time.'

Looking at that long line of people I envisioned a great battle at Osmače, a battle of historic proportions that would stop the Chetnik advance, or so I believed.

The next day I heard that there had been no battle but, rather, a skirmish near Osmače between the Chetniks and one group of our fighters. But then, much to the surprise of those who reported this to me, an order came for everybody to return to Srebrenica.

Although the Chetnik troops were advancing on all fronts Mladić had finally decided to let a food convoy enter Srebrenica, which surely must have had something to do with the UNPROFOR commander's visit and his subsequent meeting with Milošević.

At the end of March a huge convoy of some twenty trucks entered the town. The food was distributed quickly, but it was a small quantity per person.

For some reason all the UNHCR convoys entering Srebrenica at the time were Danish. The drivers were Danish and so were all the support staff. One night, when the convoy arrived late, I was still standing in front of the department store along with several hundred others. It was still snowing. A few Danes got out of a jeep and began to assemble a device right there, in the middle of the street. They first set up a stand and on it they mounted a satellite antenna. It was a circular dish; the whole thing looked surreal to me. It was something I'd previously only seen in the movies. Then one of the Danes connected a telephone cable to it and made a call, just like that, standing in the street. At the time we hadn't had any telephone service for a year, ever since the Serbs had cut the lines. To the best of my knowledge mobile phones were things you saw only in science-fiction movies. I spoke to one of the guys in my broken English. I wanted to see if I could communicate in that language and find out whether these foreigners, these Danes, knew what was going to happen to us, to Srebrenica, to all these people. But the main reason I wanted to talk to him was because I secretly hoped the guy would let me use the satellite phone to call my girlfriend Mirza. It had been almost a year since we'd heard from one another.

When I told him what I was hoping for the Dane smiled. He must have thought I was joking.

'Do you know how much one minute of conversation would cost?' he asked.

'No.'

'You don't want to know,' said the Dane, turning his back to me. He then dialled a number and spoke to the outside world, a world that seemed so very far away.

I remained standing there on one of Srebrenica's frozen streets, listening to the beeping sound of that amazing satellite phone. The atmosphere seemed unbelievable and bizarre; that device, the jeep, the huge trucks . . . the whole appearance, robust and modern, of the Danish convoy. Even the smart winter uniforms, all blue, their nice warm jackets and the special boots filled me with hope that the mighty world, the mighty UN, mighty Europe, would save us after all.

I asked the Dane if he would mail a letter for me. He agreed.

I ran home, hastily wrote a few sentences and ran back just in time to hand him the letter as the convoy was about to leave. I folded the sheet of paper in half and wrote Mirza's address on the back. The Dane put the letter in the inside pocket of his jacket. I felt happy watching the trucks reversing one by one and driving off. I imagined Mirza receiving my letter.

A few days later, when the next convoy arrived in Srebrenica, more than ten thousand people were waiting for it. The square in front of the department store was in a state of complete chaos. Learning that the Chetniks had entered Zeleni Jadar, just five kilometres south of the town, panicking people had gathered up their families and hoped to flee. But there was nowhere to flee to. We were besieged. Srebrenica was about to fall.

The people were told that once the food was unloaded the Danish convoy would let women and children on board and evacuate them. The news travelled through the town at the speed of light. People rushed out of their houses leaving everything behind. Great crowds of women were running with their children. Men forged a way through the masses, trying to get their own families on board the trucks. The crowd was so agitated that they rocked the huge vehicles.

Then somebody started shooting into the air. There were armed fighters in the crowd who also wanted to send their families to safety. But not everyone was prepared to let their loved ones go because nobody had actually guaranteed the safe passage of civilians through Serb-controlled territory. We knew from experience that anything could happen on their journey.

Only a few men considered leaving. Everyone remembered Bratunac in May 1992 when Bosniaks from the town and the surrounding villages were brought to the stadium, the men separated from the women and children, and several hundred brutally tortured and killed. There were no guarantees that the same scenario wouldn't be repeated here. The Danish convoy had to pass through both

Bratunac and Vlasenica – the latter the location of the notorious Sušica detention camp.

Never had I seen such turmoil. People were throwing their children towards the trucks over the heads of the crowd. The trucks were so heavily laden that people were practically sitting on top of one another. This caused even greater panic, as it created the impression that the Chetniks were already entering Srebrenica, which was not the case. A group of armed fighters tried in vain to create some semblance of order. Some women and children were trampled under the feet of the crowd. The fighters kept firing their machine guns into the air to bring the crowd to reason, but that seemed an impossible task. The human stampede, like some gigantic river of bodies, flowed back and forth. Hands kept springing out of the crowd, clutching wads of German banknotes. People were willing to give away everything they had to get their families out.

The Danes were perplexed. The drivers sat in their cabs not knowing what to do. Then they were ordered to move the trucks no matter what. I still don't understand how they managed not to kill anyone.

Thousands of disappointed people remained on the square in front of the department store that day. Many were weeping. Somebody said that soon more convoys would arrive – and, indeed, the next convoy did arrive a few days later. The Danes showed up early in the morning, but it didn't take long for thousands to gather in front of the department store again.

Braco, my father and I had been trying to convince my mother to leave Srebrenica with the convoy. In the late morning the convoy was still there, and the four of us were still sitting at the kitchen table deep in discussion.

'I can't go without you,' my mother said, her eyes full of tears. 'How can I leave you here?'

'Mother,' my brother and I tried again, 'if we end up deciding to escape over the mountains it will be easier for the three of us if you're not with us, if we know that you're safe.'

'I know, but we've been through all this together, and that's how we should continue. What are you going to eat without me to cook for you? Now that the convoys have started arriving we won't be hungry any more. Maybe the shooting will stop, too. It will be better, I'm sure.'

'Don't you see that all the women and children are leaving?' my father asked. 'Don't you worry about us! We'll manage.'

'I'm not leaving without you. It's not happening. How could I even think of saving only myself? If anything should happen to you I wouldn't want to go on living. So what's the point? I'm not leaving without you.'

Then my father mentioned his eldest brother and his wife. 'Well, Hasib and Zehra are leaving,' he said.

'Are they really?' I exclaimed. 'But they have plenty of food! They can't be taking it all with them. I'll go and see what's happening.'

I rushed out the door and ran all the way to their house. I arrived just in time. Hasib was locking the door. Aunt Zehra was standing at his side.

'Oh good, here comes our Hasko to help us! Come with us. You know how this goes, and you speak that foreign language. I thought you might ask one of the drivers to let us sit in the cabin with him. What do you think? What if we offered them some money?' he said, taking out a few blue banknotes from his pocket. 'I could give them all that's left of it.'

'I'm afraid that's out of the question,' I said. 'We could try the back of the truck, like everyone else.' I knew that Hasib had slaughtered a cow last autumn. He had a pile of dried meat somewhere in the house. I was hoping that the two of them hadn't finished it all. They must have left some flour, sugar and other bits of food, too, that they had traded for some of the meat.

I walked them to the square. We approached a truck around which the crowd didn't seem quite so thick. To my surprise the entrance to the trailer was not blocked, and I managed to get the two of them inside.

'What if the Chetniks take you off the truck in Bratunac?' I asked.

'Let's hope they won't,' Hasib said. Aunt Zehra was silent.

When the engine had started, just before the truck began to move, Hasib slipped a key into my hand saying, 'Take the food that's left in our room. There's quite a lot there.'

As soon as the truck turned the corner I sprinted back to the house. But, by the time I got back, the room had been ransacked. It had happened so quickly that I only managed to see the back of a cousin whose name I won't disclose here. He had forced open the door and looted the most valuable items from the room, a couple of sacks of flour. He must have seen me leaving with my uncle and aunt and seized the opportunity.

My vision blurred with tears of anger, of self-pity, of despair over the fact that the thief was one of my favourite relatives. I shouted and cursed him as he raced away. He never turned to look back.

Still weeping, I entered the room and saw that almost everything had been taken. After a thorough search I found two kilograms of sugar and a few kilograms of wheat flour. Besides a little sachet in the MRE we hadn't tasted sugar in months, so I hoped it would energize us a little bit at least.

That evening we savoured the taste of sweetened powdered milk until late into the night.

UNCLE HASIB

Nobody could know whether the Danish convoy would pass safely through the Chetnik checkpoints. Uncle Hasib and Aunt Zehra couldn't be sure they wouldn't be killed that day, but since their son's death they seemed not to care whether they lived or died.

Hamdo had joined Akif Ustić's militia unit. 'They get two meals a day,' he'd told me when I ran into him in Srebrenica.

He was forty years old. Soon after I saw him he joined another militia unit in Biljeg, about twenty kilometres away towards the Drina. Once or twice he dropped by the house to see us. He said that Biljeg was one of the more dangerous places, but 'food-wise there's no crisis with Ahmo Tihić, the unit commander. His fighters always have regular meals.'

At the beginning of March, during the massive Chetnik offensive, Biljeg fell. We'd heard that Hamdo had 'stayed in the trench' after the Chetniks' armoured vehicle had reached it. This could only mean that he'd been killed. It could be that the Chetniks had captured him alive, but there was no chance that they would have kept him alive. No one dared say this to Aunt Zehra. When I went to visit them Hasib and I had to whisper if we spoke about his son.

'Oh, dear God,' Uncle Hasib sighed. 'Who would've thought this would be possible? This is even worse than the last war.' Then he proceeded to tell me a remarkable story. 'In 1943, when your father was born, I was thirteen. My father, your Grandpa Hasan, was hiding in the forest after escaping a Chetnik firing squad. Without him my mother was on her own with seven children. Then one day a group of Chetniks broke into our house. They were from Mislovo.'

'Where's Mislovo?' I asked. This was the first time I'd heard about all of this.

'It's on Mount Devetak. You can see it from Stoborani, off in the distance. It's a Serb village. So they drove us all out of the house,' he continued, 'us and everyone else in the village. They made us walk to the centre of Stoborani and forced us all into a cowshed. All of us – men, women, children . . .

'My mother had a newborn baby in her arms, Ibro, your father. One of the Chetniks shouted at my poor mother that she was feeding a little Ustaša; swearing at her and calling her a Turkish bitch, he slapped her across the face so hard that she fell to the ground. Then the Chetniks started piling hay around the shed – I remember this so clearly, as if it happened yesterday – they started piling up the hay, intending to burn us alive. All of a sudden we heard gunfire coming from somewhere in the direction of Jelovci. What had happened was that the Jelovci Chetniks had entered Stoborani firing from all sides; that scared the hell out of the Mislovo Chetniks, and they eventually ran away. The Jelovci Chetniks' *vojvoda* came running and shouted at the Mislovo Chetniks. He called them names and cursed at them and swore, pardon me, at God and – of all things – their Chetnik mothers! "What do you think you're doing? What do you think you're doing?"'

I couldn't believe my ears; the same Chetniks from Jelovci who had wanted to kill my Grandpa Hasan but had failed because he had escaped into the forest, those same Chetniks saved the Stoborani villagers from the Mislovo Chetniks!

'Eh, that's how it was. They didn't let those other Chetniks burn us alive,' Uncle Hasib concluded. 'While now, this war . . . they'll kill whoever they can, burn whatever they can.'

After the war in the 1990s I would learn about a little event that had happened in Jelovci on 4 June 1992 as the Chetniks were about to set off to attack Žepa. A certain Dušan had apparently stood before the column of Chetnik soldiers and said, 'Don't go there, my children. The Žepa Muslims are dangerous. You will not return alive. They don't bother us, and you shouldn't bother them.' This Dušan was a son of Đorđo, the Chetnik who wanted my Grandpa Hasan dead in 1943.

During the war in the 1990s I rarely gave much thought to that 'other' war, the one that had ended twenty-three years before I was born, but I cannot agree with those who claim that the 1990s war was a continuation of the previous one. I didn't agree then, and I don't agree now. I simply find my Uncle Hasib's story interesting because it's something you cannot read in history books.

'So tell me,' I prompted, 'how did this thing go with Grandpa Hasan and this Đorđo? How did Grandpa manage to escape?'

'Well, it's a long story,' Hasib said, 'but I'll try to make it short. Two men on horses arrived at our house, and they asked for Grandpa Hasan. They claimed they'd been sent by Petar Kosorić, who wanted my father to come and see him.'

'Who was Kosorić?' I asked.

'He was like a communist, a Partisan. Grandpa Hasan used to help communists even before the war, even during the Serb King Petar's rule.'

'What do you mean by *help*?'

'Well, he was in the Comintern. He went to Sarajevo and organized strikes along with the communists for workers' rights and suchlike. And then, after the war began, he maintained contact with the communists up there on Mount Romanija. The Chetniks knew this, and that's why they wanted to kill him. And so the two men came on horseback saying they would accompany Grandpa Hasan to Petar Kosorić. That's what they said, and naïvely my father believed them. He got dressed and foolishly went off with them. They brought him to none other than this Đorđo, who assigned three men to escort him on his way to Petar Kosorić.

'Well, that was a lie! Two of the escorts walked in front of my father – that's what he told me later – and one walked behind. Then, somewhere in the middle of the forest, one of the guys in front turned and pointed his rifle at him! The guy shot Grandpa Hasan through the shoulder, but he managed to dart into the forest, even with his wound. It was winter, and it was very cold. They chased him all night long, but they never caught him. By the morning he had somehow managed to reach the house. He was all bloody and frozen. I helped make a shelter for him in the woods, and that's where he hid. The Chetniks returned every day to look for him. They put guards around the village. They would harass my mother as well as us children. 'But they weren't killing women and children around Stoborani then like they are in this war. So one day I'd just let the cattle out – we had around twenty at the time – and the Chetniks were there looking for my father, but they left me alone. They didn't ask me anything. But then Đorđo told two of them to take two of my oxen, and I stood in front of him begging him not to do it. I had known Đorđo from when we dragged logs from Radava together. But Đorđo struck me across the face with his fist. I found myself on the ground. Then they took the oxen away.

'Anyway, my father couldn't leave the shelter as the Chetniks were all over the village – but they didn't burn houses then as they do now. In that war only two houses were burned in our village. So, since my father couldn't hide in the forest for ever, one day he fled to Srebrenica. From there he went to Tuzla and eventually to Sarajevo. And then came the end of the war.'

'And what about later?' I asked. 'Why did Grandpa Hasan end up in the Goli Otok prison camp?'

'Well, during the war my father was what they used to call a guide. The Partisans, you know, had one in every village to guide them around the area, and my father was the guide for ours. On one occasion a Serb woman, who was a Partisan, had somehow lost her group, and she was injured. My father helped her. He hid her in our house, otherwise the Chetniks would have found her.

'Then after the war, when my father realized that some Chetniks from Han Pijesak had been awarded medals as freedom fighters, he went to Sarajevo to protest, but they accused him of being a Comintern supporter, a Stalinist, and sent him to Goli Otok where they kept political prisoners. At Goli Otok he spent days standing in deep water, up to his waist in water, so he contracted pneumonia and was sent to hospital in Rijeka. And the inspector who was sent to question him was none other than the Serb woman he'd saved, the Partisan.'

'Did she recognize him?'

'Not immediately, but as they talked she realized that he was the one who'd helped her, and she released him. She told him he was free to go; she even gave him a police escort.'

If it weren't for Uncle Hasib I wouldn't know all this. The Chetniks were defeated in the Second World War, and, although they had killed thousands of Muslims in eastern Bosnia, several hundred thousand Muslims continued to live there after the war. This time the Chetniks had tanks and military planes behind them, they had the support of the fourth-biggest army in Europe.

The Danish convoy my Uncle Hasib joined in 1993 wasn't stopped by the Chetniks after all, and after the war I would ask him to refresh my memory about the story of Grandpa Hasan.

THE APRIL MASSACRE

After General Morillon's visit I would often hang around the post office. Morillon's escorts who'd been left in Srebrenica and the three military observers seemed to have bonded with the postal employees. Apparently, part of the military headquarters was located in the same facility.

One of the employees, Naser Sulejmanović, would later become a very good friend of mine. Naser had survived a firing squad in 1992 when the Bratunac Chetniks took him outside town together with ten or so other Bosniaks.

'I said farewell to life,' Naser told me. 'They shot us from behind. I fell with the rest of them, but after a few moments I realized that I hadn't been shot at all, so I pretended to be dead, and the Chetniks left. I'd known some of them; they were my neighbours.'

Naser also told me about how, although he didn't speak a word of English, he'd become friends with the Canadian soldiers from Morillon's escort group. 'My colleagues and I used to set up a chessboard in the office. We played chess quite often, and there was this nice UNPROFOR soldier who would always stand in the corner and watch. He used to smoke one cigarette after another even though we didn't have any ourselves. So on one occasion this guy and I were alone in the office. I was craving a cigarette, but I felt it would be rude to ask for one, then he gestured that he'd like to play a game. Why not? I thought. I checkmated him in a few moves – it was child's play. Then again and again – five times in a row. I began to feel sorry for him. He was really nice, and I let him outplay me. He cheered up at once. He said something in English and took a packet of cigarettes from his pocket. He offered me one and then lit one himself. I figured out he would offer me a smoke every time I let him win a game, so I lost until we emptied the packet.'

Morillon never came back, but the small UNPROFOR team stayed in Srebrenica for all of March and the first half of April. During that time the Chetniks captured the last Bosniak villages around Srebrenica and the planes from Serbia bombed the left bank of the Drina several more times. The three military observers were taken there to observe one of the attacks. They witnessed the event and they sent a report to their headquarters. We never learned what was written in the report nor if the information was ever acted upon.

The presence of the UNPROFOR soldiers in our midst, no matter how tiny their group, seemed to make people feel safer. They started moving around the town more freely, so much so that on 12 April a soccer tournament was organized, despite the fact that gathering in large groups was prohibited because of the frequent shelling.

I was at home when I heard a large explosion. Word spread quickly of a massacre at the soccer ground. The Chetniks, being on the higher ground around Srebrenica, must have seen the crowd. They fired a salvo of three 120-mm artillery shells, which all landed on the concrete base of the playing field. The huge explosion and the shrapnel flying everywhere killed all the players and everyone who was standing near the field, more than a hundred people in total. Almost as many were wounded. Pieces of human bodies were caught on the fence that surrounded the schoolyard. The dead and wounded were transported to the hospital by UNPROFOR vehicles. Volunteers collected the severed limbs and loaded them on to trollies to bury them in a common grave somewhere behind the hospital.

The 12 April massacre would be forever overshadowed by the much greater one that took place in July 1995 and is thus rarely, if ever, mentioned in either media or official reports.

The victims were made up predominantly of those from the most recent wave of refugees.

THE BATTLE FOR
THE TOWN

The sound of infantry fire coming from the south caused total panic. A battle for the town was raging just a few kilometres away.

I climbed up the slope opposite the house to the ruins of the fortress to see how close the Chetniks were. I realized that not only was the sound growing louder but I could actually see the muzzle flashes. *That's* how close the Chetniks were!

I turned back, frightened and anxious, but at the same time feeling a strange sort of relief that is not easy to describe. It was like awaiting the last episode of a television series on death, suffering, hunger, isolation, siege, everlasting uncertainty . . . I was as afraid as anyone else of a bloodbath, afraid as every man, woman and child in Srebrenica, but some sort of conclusion was at hand. In some strange way I couldn't wait for the final battle, and I naturally imagined a better and safer place for those who survived it. Somehow I was almost certain that Srebrenica would not fall, that our fighters, seasoned through many battles, would fend off the Chetnik attack.

My head was full of confused thoughts. Certainly none of it depended on me, so I decided to go with the flow. In this way I also managed to overcome the fear. Back on our street I went to see my two new friends who'd arrived in town after Konjević Polje and Cerska had fallen. One of them had a wounded foot, so I often went to see him in the room where the two of them were staying. There was a guitar there. It only had four strings, but I used to play it sometimes. This was one of those moments.

As the shells exploded and bullets whistled around the house the three of us played guitar and sang. We kept the back door open. Our plan was to run should we see any Chetniks coming down the street. The shelling didn't stop all day. It seemed the Chetniks were getting closer. Someone mentioned the date, 15 April 1993, and it suddenly occurred to me that two weeks earlier I had turned twenty-five. Nobody, including me, had remembered my birthday.

All hell broke loose the next day. Nothing we'd been through up to that point compared with the shelling that day. Not even close. Shells of all calibres were falling incessantly all over the town. Sometimes several explosions went off at once. We were frightened speechless, but even if somebody could master the overwhelming fear their voice couldn't be heard above the infernal noise.

They shelled us the whole day without a break. This wasn't the first time our street had been shelled, but it was the first time nobody ventured outside to see what was happening. There were about twenty people in the basement of our house.

Panic intensified when we heard the sound of small-arms fire on Guber Hill; it was coming closer and closer, right towards us. The Chetniks had decided to enter the town along our street.

Some of the men in our basement were armed. Unsure of what to do they nervously fingered their rifles with expressions of fear and confusion on their faces. A few times it seemed they had summoned up the courage to go out shooting, but then a shell would fall somewhere near by and they would change their minds. The rest of us hoped that, should the Chetniks approach the house, these men would shoot through the small basement windows and defend us.

Throughout the afternoon we argued about whether we should stay in the basement or try to reach the town centre. Most of us opted to stay in the basement, which offered some sort of protection at least. Going out into the street was tantamount to suicide. We were convinced that the entire population of Srebrenica was hidden in their basements, but that was not actually the case. I would learn later about the details of the battle. Several hundred fighters were moving from the town centre in order to repel the enemy attack. But we couldn't know that sitting in our basement; we thought that all our men had dispersed and that nobody was defending the city.

At one point we heard fierce machine-gun fire and bullets hitting the wall of the house.

'I'm going upstairs to see how far the Chetniks have got. If we wait for them to approach the house they'll slit our throats right here,' I shouted out to my mother, father and Braco, who stayed in the basement with everyone else.

I ran upstairs and through the house to the veranda and quickly glanced up and down the street. Luckily, at that moment the shells were falling on the steep hillside behind the street. There was no one about, but I could tell from the sound of the gunfire that the Chetniks were very close. Bullets were flying everywhere. After seeing a barrage of bullets hit the house just across the street and rip off chunks of its façade, I ran back down to the basement.

'There's no way we can escape from here,' I said to everyone. They looked at me with dread. 'I'm going upstairs. I'd rather stand on the veranda than be in the basement when they reach the house.' I went back up. I thought that this way I could at least warn them all if I saw the Chetniks approaching. If that were to happen we could all run towards the town. I preferred to take my chances with the shells than be taken alive and tortured by the Chetniks. I think everyone in the basement felt the same way.

Watching the street from the veranda I suddenly caught sight of three of our fighters moving forward under a hail of bullets. They were bent low to the ground, but they moved up the street quickly. All three were dressed in neat uniforms, and each held a machine gun. I recognized them from Naser Orić's unit. I stood watching for just a few seconds, but it felt like time was standing still. I was overjoyed to see them, and I was, so to speak, fascinated by their bravery. These three men seemed to be resisting the torrent of bullets the way a swimmer resists a current. Bullets whistled around their heads as they ran from cover to cover, advancing along the street.

I rushed down to the basement again, but I was so excited that I hardly managed to get the words out. 'It's our . . . it's our . . . it's our fighters! They're coming from the town, advancing towards the Chetniks.'

Everybody raced to the basement windows; I rushed back upstairs. From the veranda I saw another group, about ten of them, running up Crvena Rijeka Street through the stream of bullets, rifles at the ready.

A few minutes later the gunfire became deafening. Evidently our fighters had collided with the Chetniks or the Chetniks had collided with them. Either way, the real battle had begun, face to face with the enemy. Soon the sound of infantry weapons receded. Our fighters were repelling the enemy. The bullets stopped whistling along the street and around the house.

A few others joined me. One of them brought a radio. We heard the BiH Radio announcer speaking about a meeting of the UN Security Council currently being held in New York. The announcer said that it was expected that Srebrenica would be declared a safe area protected by the UN and that a resolution was to be passed.

It is impossible for me to describe the feelings or the expressions on the faces of the people around me. For a start everyone was in a state of disbelief. 'Did we hear that right? What did he say?' we asked one another. 'Did he say we are a UN-protected zone? Did he really say it?'

We stood around the tiny transistor radio hoping that the events being held on the other side of the planet would stop the Chetniks, the shelling, the gunfire as if with a magic wand. I imagined a giant hand descending from the sky to prevent the Chetniks from entering the town.

But that was not what made the Chetniks stop two hundred metres from our house. Our brave fighters, including Naser Orić, who was injured while chasing the Chetniks up a hill for three kilometres, had driven the Chetniks back. Our guys forced the Chetniks to retreat after inflicting heavy losses on them. That's why they retreated, not because of the UN resolution adopted in New York.

Several years after the war a television station would air the conversation between Mladić and another Serb officer that was intercepted and taped probably at the very moment we were listening to the radio. *'Just go ahead . . . Onwards! Onwards! They have nothing but a few toy rifles and a couple of RPGs . . . Shell the town . . . Let the sniper do his job . . . Aim at the flesh . . . the flesh,'* Mladić said.

Mladić personally commanded the attack. He also commanded the attack that would start two years later in July 1995. But on 16 April 1993 Mladić and his Chetnik troops were repelled. The next day the UN resolution came into force; Srebrenica was declared a safe area.

Later, in Sarajevo, Generals Mladić, Halilović and Morillon signed an agreement for the demilitarization of Srebrenica. And with that, the ceasefire began.

'We're saved. We're saved!' we kept repeating day and night, night and day. We kept repeating it to ourselves as well as to each other, not believing our own eyes and ears.

We were saved.

CLINTON FEEDS WHILE CANADA SHIELDS

Over the next few month I would meet many of those who had fought in the battle. Among them was Alija Delić, the commander of the cannon crew. His 105-millimetre cannon was the only artillery weapon those defending Srebrenica had at their disposal. They positioned it on a hill near the village of Bajramovići from where it could zap the Chetniks most effectively. I was surprised to hear that our cannon had fired several dozen shells, mostly towards the area between the village of Zalazje and Divljakinje Hill. This was where the Chetniks had broken into our trenches, but they were driven off as soon as our shells started landing on them. They had genuinely believed that the town's defenders had, as Mladić put it, 'nothing but a few toy rifles and a couple of RPGs', but when the Chetniks finally discovered what it felt like to be shelled they jumped out of their trenches and ran for their lives.

I find the cannon story one of the most interesting details of the battle. The cannon had, of course, been captured from the Chetniks in an earlier action. It was captured along with some ammunition, most of which was expended on 16 April. Had the attack lasted a few days longer our stocks would soon have been exhausted. The Chetnik death toll would have been much higher in that case, but then, given that our fighters had no way of obtaining additional ordnance, it would have been only a matter of time before they broke through our lines and entered the town.

The shooting stopped altogether. As 17 April dawned thousands of people took to the streets. For the first couple of hours we moved along in disbelief, twitching at every sound. As the day progressed, however, people started coming out of the houses and shelters more freely. In the morning the word spread quickly that a Canadian UNPROFOR unit had arrived and that their vehicles were parked in front of the clothing factory on the far side of town. I went there immediately. The sight was unforgettable. About twenty white APCs and ten white jeeps and trucks with UN markings were parked next to each other. Most of the crewmembers were sat on their vehicles, while a few stood near by. It seemed like they were awaiting further orders. All of them kept their weapons at the ready. The first thing I noticed was that almost every APC was equipped with a rocket launcher or, to be more precise, an anti-tank rocket system, which seemed to be a very powerful weapon. We were relieved to see the well-armed protection force, and we felt we could place our trust in them.

Both sides respected the ceasefire. Shooting and shelling stopped in the town, although we could still hear the distant sounds of sporadic rifle fire. We needed time to get used to the new order, both physically and mentally. Having lived in a constant state of fear for a whole year, it took days, weeks, even months for our bodies to relax, muscle by muscle. The permanent grimace of anxiety slowly disappeared from our faces as we realized we were allowed once again to live relatively carefree lives.

When the Canadians arrived the winter was giving way to the warmer days of spring. The shelling had stopped and food convoys would now be able to reach us. After the 'UN Safe Area' sign appeared at the entrance to the town people eventually started to thaw out and communication became more normal. The swearing, which for months had been almost our sole means of communication, gradually diminished, as different words, gentle and pacifying, returned to our vocabularies.

The Canadians set up several checkpoints around the town, with one APC and five or six soldiers at each. They'd brought rolls of barbed wire and fenced themselves within it. What we didn't know at the time was that these were units from the Canadian UNPROFOR battalion located in Visoko, in central Bosnia, and that Canada had agreed only to the temporary detachment of about two hundred soldiers to Srebrenica. Their headquarters remained in Visoko, and the soldiers took tours of duty in Srebrenica. Their Srebrenica base and headquarters were established at the Vezionica clothing factory, which was a much smaller factory than the battery factory in Potočari that would become the military base for six hundred Dutch troops ten months later.

At the time we were, of course, unaware of these arrangements. For us, each of the Canadian soldiers was, through the United Nations, a direct representative of the world itself, the world that had finally decided to protect us from slaughter. The food convoys started arriving almost immediately. While eating wonderfully delicious bread made from flour freshly unloaded from the enormous UNHCR trucks, we thought: We've been saved. We won't starve! There were other foodstuffs in the humanitarian-aid packages besides flour – not too many but enough to give us hope.

My family calculated that we could survive for a month with the flour the four of us received. That sounded very promising given how unimaginable it had been just a short while ago, so I agreed with my mother that we should engage in some form of trade. She made a loaf of bread. I put it fresh from the oven into my backpack and took it to the UNPROFOR checkpoint at Klisa at the town's southern entrance.

The Canadians were very wary of everyone, especially of men and boys. As I approached the checkpoint I noticed how cautiously they sized me up. There were five of them there. One stood in front with the other four behind him with their rifles at the ready. Maybe this was standard practice for intercepting uninvited visitors. They obviously found my little backpack suspicious and appeared nervous when I began to rummage inside it.

I had the advantage of being able to communicate in basic English. My English wasn't good by any means but better than most of the others who stood there gesturing and pointing at things in order to express themselves. I realized just how bad my English was, though, as soon as I attempted to reassure the soldiers of my good intentions. It was difficult enough to understand what they were saying to me, but when they talked to each other I could hardly understand a word.

I'd always believed that Westerners didn't eat as much bread as we did. It must be because as a child I would hear Bosnian *Gastarbeiter* back in Yugoslavia on holiday saying, 'No way a German would ever eat this much bread.' As I was taking the loaf out of my backpack this suddenly came into my mind and made me even more confused. I started to doubt the success of my potential trade, so I took the bread out and just held it in my hands. After several attempts I managed to explain, partly in English and partly through gestures, that I wanted each of them to give me a cigarette for the loaf. They exchanged their views on the matter. All I was able to understand was, 'He wants five fucking cigarettes for that loaf of bread!' The reaction surprised me. For some reason I was expecting friendlier faces and a warmer welcome. The rest of the locals were obviously very interested in what was happening. I could see that all of them were now closely following the developments, mainly because they were astonished that I could communicate with the Canadians in their own language. Over the following days as I walked along the street I heard several locals say that I was 'the one who can speak Unproforian'.

In the end three of the five soldiers gave me a cigarette, and I gave up the bread. They liked fresh bread as much as we did. Meals for soldiers in the field consisted of the very same MREs that the planes had been dropping for us. After our trade was concluded one of the soldiers immediately took his knife, cut off a slice of bread and spread it with peanut butter. The others readily followed suit. The people standing around the checkpoint started to laugh. This exchange had probably made them realize that the UNPROFOR soldiers were people just like us, people made of flesh and blood, people with needs and habits just like ours and probably with the same good and bad qualities.

I hurried to the market and sold my three cigarettes for twenty Deutschmarks. It was the first money I'd earned in the war, and I was very proud to present it at home since we had very little money left.

After I told my father about my entrepreneurial act he wouldn't stop badgering me to go back and ask the soldiers for a cigarette for him. Although he never actually said 'Why did you have to sell all three cigarettes instead of keeping one for me?' I knew that that was exactly what he was thinking. So the next day I went to the UNPROFOR main gate at their factory base and asked the guard for a cigarette. He gazed at me for a few moments.

'You can speak English,' he said finally.

'A little.'

'Just you come with me. Our officers are desperate to find someone who can speak English.'

And so I entered the UNPROFOR base. The guard brought me to a room. He left, but soon a Canadian officer arrived. He introduced himself as Captain Little, and I unkindly thought to myself how well this name suited him. But that was about all I understood from what the captain said, as he was under the impression that I really could speak English. I grasped every third word but kept nodding enthusiastically.

And so my mental torture began. Over the next few months my brain would desperately try to make some sense out of the sounds I heard from the soldiers' mouths. I succeeded more often than not, but when it came to my speaking skills that was a completely different matter. I struggled to form sentences, and who knows what those poor Canadians thought of me. I soon realized that I had a much easier time understanding non-native English speakers and that they had fewer problems understanding me. I kept wishing that my Canadians were from a different part of Canada and that English was their second language, but unfortunately that was not the case.

So while Captain Little talked I nodded and said, 'Yes, yes, OK', totally bluffing. At one point he called in another soldier and told him something. The soldier asked me to follow him, and we boarded one of the UN vehicles. It seemed that I would start assisting the UNPROFOR soldiers that very day, but I had no idea with what.

The soldier was a tall man with a moustache. He kept his helmet on at all times and his rifle over his shoulder. On the way into town I understood that we were to buy some framing timber to build bunkers. During the drive he commented on the girls we passed, and I was surprised that he liked girls that I would never have given a second look.

'Look at that one. Gorgeous, huh?' he said.

'But she's got a big nose,' I said, amazed.

'I like girls with big noses.' He laughed loudly. He had an infectious laugh, as if he didn't have a care in the world.

It crossed my mind then that foreigners might actually be indifferent to our suffering. Later, working alongside them, this would come into my mind many times. There were occasions I even despised foreigners for being able to laugh despite all the suffering they witnessed, despite the thousands killed, despite the slaughtered and the camps they had known about or seen with their own eyes. It took some time for me to accept the fact that I cannot despise people who laugh only because *I* don't feel like laughing.

The tall laughing soldier and I found the wood we needed, and I was once again surprised: he paid for it in cash, no receipts, just a handful of Deutschmarks he took out of his pocket. I helped to load the timber on to the truck. I was expected to do that as well apparently.

For three days I went to the headquarters to assist in this capacity, although I had no contract and wasn't paid. But that was all right with me. I just wanted to stay as close to them as possible in case the Chetniks attacked again. I did hope they might give me some food or a cigarette or two. I also hoped my English would improve enough to have a decent conversation.

In the case of the former, that was a naïve hope. What food I was given was what they didn't want to eat themselves. I could only dream of being offered a cigarette, and if I asked for one they often swore at me – in English, of course. I started collecting cigarette butts from their ashtrays in secret and taking them home. My father was very happy with that, as you could extract a lot of tobacco from those cigarette butts and, if you had cigarette paper, roll a new one.

On the third day Captain Little invited me into his office. 'We don't require your services any more,' he said, and I felt sick to my stomach, 'but I'll have a soldier accompany you to the United Nations Military Observers headquarters in the post office.'

That was only two hundred metres away. There I found two more local guys: Senad Alić, now a civilian, and Emir Suljagić, whom I had seen on our street a few times. With ten days on the job, the two of them were seasoned workers compared with me.

That was to be my first working day with the UNMOs. From then on until the fall of Srebrenica in July 1995 I would not have a single day off, no weekends or holidays. I would work with them every day, 365 days a year, from half past eight in the morning until eight o'clock in the evening. The three of us were not paid anything at the time. There were no contracts to sign, and no one so much as mentioned it.

Emir now lived in Srebrenica all by himself. His mother and sister had managed to reach Tuzla with the Danish UNHCR convoy in March after Emir's father had been killed by a shell. Emir reminded me of Rock Hudson, not that I ever told him that, but, as I've mentioned, I was in the habit of comparing people with Hollywood actors. He was never without a small yellow dictionary in his hand. He had studied English at school for four years, which meant that his English was much better than mine. I'd studied only Russian. When it came to English I could sing the two Beatles' songs I'd learned by heart pretty well – 'Let It Be' and 'And I Love Her' – but I had little idea what the words meant. Through exposure to native speakers Emir had perfected his English in no time, while I struggled, literally, in every new situation and with every sentence.

My need and wish to master English was so strong that I sometimes even hallucinated: I had the impression that everybody in the street was speaking it. I sometimes dreamed in English. But I was learning on the fly, and my vocabulary grew by the day. And the vocabulary was not what you'd find in any ordinary dictionary: 'recoilless cannon', for example, was typical of the sorts of linguistic challenges I had to overcome. Once mastered, the numerous military terms we had to deal with made us feel like experts, not only in military matters but in areas of politics, diplomacy and conflict resolution.

Operation Parachute continued during April and May, delivering food aid by air as the two or three weekly food convoys proved not to be enough to feed the starved people of Srebrenica. The hunt for food delivered by parachute thus continued for a few more weeks, but people were happy because food was still falling from the sky as well as being delivered by land. They would run up to the hills singing, 'Clinton feeds while Canada shields'.

They say you've mastered a language when you start thinking in that language. In my case that happened relatively quickly, in a matter of months, and by the autumn I was thinking in English. We were all very busy that summer. Usually there were three interpreters and six monitors in three jeeps patrolling three different sides of the UN Safe Area. We worked hard and non-stop.

The weather was getting warmer. My jeans were getting too hot for the season, so for ten cigarettes I had a local tailor turn a parachute I'd found in the bushes into a light pair of trousers. I wore them right through the summer.

Several weeks after UNPROFOR arrived an artillery volley fired from the direction of Bratunac landed in the vicinity of Fojhar. That village had rarely been hit, even during the fiercest bombardments prior to UNPROFOR's arrival. The role of the military monitors was to go to the site, establish who had opened fire and from where and record any victims. Their reports were sent first to Tuzla and from there on to Sarajevo. Some kind of a summary of the reports went all the way to the UN headquarters in New York, I guess.

After the incident four monitors went to the Fojhar site in two jeeps. Senad, Emir and I went along with them. We were accompanied by the UN police (also unarmed), whose offices were in the same building as the UNMOs, and the three of us acted as their interpreters, too.

It was a sunny day. We'd heard that there were casualties. This was one of too many occasions that I had to visit places where somebody had been killed either by a shell, a sniper or a machine gun. The Chetniks halted the shooting for a while, but they continued shelling the edges of the safe area. I guess this flouting of the ceasefire was down to there never being any formal sanctions in response to their actions.

We arrived at the village by an overgrown gravel road. The villagers took us to the meadow where several children had been playing when a shell exploded near by. One little girl had been blown up. When we reached the crater the monitors used a device to measure the calibre and trajectory of the shell; they established that it was an artillery (not a mortar) shell, which could have been fired from Kamenolom, a quarry in Serbia that could be seen with the naked eye from where we were standing.

Senad and I both noticed something white in the grass and went to see what it was. It was a piece of the little girl's brain. Senad immediately turned and vomited, and I started swearing at the Chetniks while the monitors wrote in their notebooks.

Throughout the summer of 1993 I went all over the Srebrenica protected area, visiting every imaginable site, village, road and path within its boundary. It was hot, and we drove with the windows rolled down. No matter where we went children would run out to greet us putting their little fingers on the frame of the car window and yelling, 'Mister, a sweetie! Mister, a sweetie!'

At first, the military monitors had two-week tours of duty, but these were later extended to several months. We met people from different parts of the world: Africans, South Americans, Asians, Arabs. Major Hope Fugar, a Ghanaian, was among those who came later and stayed longer. He was generally very calm, poised and friendly. To Emir and me he was so amazingly protective and kind that we nicknamed him Mother. On one occasion, when Major Hope Fugar and I went to visit the Swedish Shelter Project, the refugee camp in Slapovići, there was a three-year old girl who started weeping as soon as she saw us approaching. She hid behind her mother and screamed, 'A Chetnik, Mother, a Chetnik!' She had never seen a black man before.

At the beginning of autumn 1993 I went to Zeleni Jadar with a Swedish captain called Thobi. Zeleni Jadar was the edge of the safe area, and the Chetnik bunkers were only a few hundred metres away. Thobi was driving.

'Payday is approaching,' he said.

'Tell me about it. We don't get any pay.'

'What do you mean you don't get paid?' He was astonished. Thobi had been assigned to Srebrenica after spending several months in Tuzla. The military observers in Tuzla were stationed at the Dubrave Military Base. Dozens of interpreters as well as other local staff were given regular UN contracts and, in addition to a salary, various benefits. It's not like we didn't know about it, but there was nothing we could do to change our status. By then we'd already been volunteering for five months, and during that time a contract had never been mentioned to any of us. But we had worked hard nevertheless; we were true professionals. Sometimes a military observer would offer us each a lunch pack, but that was an exception not a rule.

Thobi was infuriated. He swore at the UN administration and said it was absolutely unacceptable. 'I'm going to Tuzla in a few days, and I'll see to it that you are given contracts. I'll discuss this with the administration.'

In ten days he returned from Tuzla, not with our contracts but with official UN language examination papers. It was the standard English test that all prospective UN translators in the former Yugoslavia had to take. Mark Foster, a British naval officer, also happened to be there when Thobi returned with the news. Mark was the team leader and one of our favourites. He took us to a room on the second floor and, giving us a piece of paper and a pencil each, said that we had forty-five minutes to finish the test. It was by no means easy. We had to translate one piece from English into Bosnian and another from Bosnian to English. We were allowed to use dictionaries.

We asked Mark for more time, saying that nobody could see us and that the people in Tuzla didn't care about us anyway. Our contracts depended on this test, and our salaries depended on the number of points achieved. But he wouldn't have it. He entered the room forty-five minutes later and took away our papers.

'Time's up, guys,' he said. 'We'll send your tests to Tuzla with the first officer heading there.'

The UN examiners took a few weeks to mark our papers, but eventually we were informed that Emir had received a grade three and I'd achieved a grade two; two being the lowest score the UN accepted for interpreters.

MY FIRST ENCOUNTER
WITH THE CHETNIKS

By the summer of 1993 more than seventeen months had passed since I'd last spoken to my girlfriend. She didn't know whether I was still alive. I was spending most of my time at the UNMO offices in the post office building and had befriended the local radio operators who worked on the second floor and who were tasked mainly with operating the only amateur radio in Srebrenica. Thousands of people were waiting their turn to speak with their families in Sarajevo, Tuzla or further afield. Our radio operators had reached agreements with other amateur operators, even those in Serbia, to link radio connections to telephone lines to enable communication between Srebrenica and the rest of the world. The system functioned well enough, but even today I have no idea how all the telephone bills were paid. The waiting list was extremely long, of course, and I was ecstatic when I learned that a conversation between Mirza and myself had been permitted. I was given the date and the hour, and I was waiting anxiously to hear her voice.

However, on that very day I was ordered to accompany two Norwegian military observers to Observation Point Echo at Zeleni Jadar. A Canadian detachment was stationed there. My colleagues and I refused to cross the demarcation line into Chetnik territory, for we still had no contract or UN accreditation cards. The Chetniks might arrest us or kill us – nobody could guarantee they wouldn't.

The two Norwegians drove across the line while I waited for their return with the Canadian crew. About three hundred metres of paved road led to the Chetnik bunkers. There were minefields on either side of the road. I had asked the UNMOs to return quickly because the radio link for my conversation with Mirza was scheduled for 2 p.m. I politely pleaded with them to return before one thirty as we needed at least fifteen minutes to reach Srebrenica. But I waited in vain. Realizing that I was going to be late I asked the Canadians to contact the Norwegians on their walkie-talkies, but they couldn't establish a connection. It was almost two o'clock, so I was definitely too late for my radio rendezvous with my girl. I was sad, disappointed and livid with the two Norwegians. I would have to wait several months before getting another chance. I felt totally depressed.

Then finally the jeep appeared. It wasn't driving in a straight line but weaving along the road. They pulled up beside me, and as soon as they rolled the window down I knew they'd had a few drinks. Great, I thought, they've drinking with the Chetniks while I was desperately waiting for their return. Then one of them showed me a folded note and asked me to translate. I took the note, unfolded it and read: 'We'd be glad if you could come and interpret our conversation.' It was signed Colonel Vuković.

I looked at the two tipsy, grinning Norwegians. When I asked, 'Do you have any idea what you've done to me?' they laughed, saying, 'Hasan, c'mon. Enough about you and your girlfriend . . . Let's not talk about it now.' They guaranteed that nothing bad would happen to me were I to come with them and interpret.

I have no idea what came over me. I got in and said, 'OK. Let's go then.'

I came to my senses halfway down the road. I thought I'd just made the biggest mistake of my life. I wanted to get them to turn around and drive back. But the Norwegians were paying no attention to me anyway, and all of a sudden I saw ten uniformed Chetniks sitting around a clearing in the woods. The officer approached us, all smiles. He wore a proper JNA olive uniform with his sleeves rolled up.

Now this is no joke, I thought. I'm visiting the Chetniks that I've been running from all this time. It's all over now.

We got out of the car, and as we walked towards the officer I felt like I was on another planet. I noticed that the rest of the Chetniks were watching me with great interest. It must have been quite a sight, a *Baliya* walking in their direction. All eyes were fixed on me.

'Colonel Vukota Vuković,' said the officer, extending his hand.

'Hasan,' I said, shaking it.

I knew he would rather kill me than shake my hand; I was 100 per cent sure of it. As we shook hands he winked in a way that only I would understand. The foreigners had no idea what was happening and would never have comprehended anyway. But I knew it, and the colonel knew it. I only hoped the he, having invited me personally, would not act on impulse.

A table had been set, and the colonel invited me to sit. The Norwegians beside me, the colonel across from us, while his men stood around him with their weapons. The colonel reacted very sharply to this and ordered his men to put them down immediately. 'What have I told you? What's wrong with you?' he snapped. His men set their rifles against a tree. To my surprise, Vuković insisted on addressing me using the formal pronoun, although I was half his age.

Thoughts were spinning around my head. How should I behave in this situation? Should I try to be casual about the whole thing? Should I put on a macho act and come across as the 'brave Muslim'? Should I pretend that I was more afraid than I actually was? I opted for number three. In order to leave the desired impression I started stammering on purpose. The Chetniks laughed their heads off.

'You know what,' I said as if attempting to explain myself to them, 'ever since the beginning of the war I've never seen you alive, in the flesh.' What I'd meant to say was that I'd only ever seen their side on television. What they understood, I guess, to judge by the way they abruptly stopped laughing and how grave they looked all of a sudden, was that I'd seen a lot of dead Chetniks. They glowered at me, colonel and soldiers alike. The conversation abruptly ceased. The Norwegians were clearly puzzled.

'I mean I've only seen you on TV,' I added quickly, but their expressions did not change.

Then one of the soldiers said, 'Hey, leave him alone. Wouldn't you be afraid to go down to Srebrenica?'

That seemed to do it. They relaxed and started chuckling again. That was close, I thought.

The meeting lasted for half an hour, but it seemed much longer to me. I couldn't wait for it to end. All the time I was interpreting I kept thinking: Never again. If I come out of this alive I'll never do anything like this again.

At the end we all shook hands with the colonel, who walked us back to the jeep.

As we passed a machine-gun post a soldier called out to me, 'How's Naser?' There was a note of apprehension in his voice.

'I wouldn't know. I've seen him once or twice but never met him,' I said, which was true enough, for only later would I get to know him better, when he would occasionally attend the UN's official meetings in the post office.

'The Muslims have inflicted a lot of evil upon us,' Colonel Vuković said, 'but let's not speak about it now. Have a safe journey. We will meet again.'

Not if I can help it, I thought, and we sped off towards the demarcation line.

But after we interpreters received official UN passes in September meetings with Colonel Vuković were introduced as a regular UNMO activity, as the Norwegians used him as a liaison between UNPROFOR and the Drina Corps of the Republika Srpska forces. My colleagues refused to work across the demarcation line, so for the next two years I would be the only interpreter to have that duty. These meetings with Colonel Vuković would take place on Tuesdays at ten in the morning at the same location.

Almost three years later, in March 1996 after the Dayton Agreement had been signed, I was the first Bosniak survivor of the Srebrenica genocide to re-enter the town. My fellow travellers were four unarmed UN officials – an American, a New Zealander, a Swede and an Israeli, Illana Betel – who organized and undertook that journey for my sake alone. They knew I was searching for information about my mother, my father and my brother, who had last been seen at the gates of the UN compound in Potočari on 13 July 1995. After the Canadians, a Dutch battalion had assumed responsibility for the UN Safe Area in 1994, and they were safe-guarding Srebrenica when the final Serb assault was launched that led to the fall of the town and the mass execution of thousands of Bosniak men and boys.

By March 1996 the International Commission on Missing Persons had registered over twenty-seven thousand missing people in Bosnia and Herzegovina, of whom over eight thousand were from the Srebrenica enclave.

Like most of the Srebrenica survivors I had ended up in Tuzla. I continued working with the UN; accompanying UN staff on their occasional tours was the only way I could cross into the Serb-held half of Bosnia. Indifferent to the risks inherent in these trips, I was driven by an intense need to learn anything about my missing family.

By some freak coincidence, the day I went back to Srebrenica I saw none other than Colonel Vuković. He was sitting in a yellow Ford parked on, of all places, Crvena Rijeka Street, our street. I couldn't believe my eyes. I shouted to the driver to stop the car, but I jumped out before he actually came to a halt. I ran over to the yellow Ford and opened the driver's door. Vuković was astounded to see me. He sat there clutching the wheel. Perhaps he thought those in the UN vehicles were from The Hague Tribunal sent to arrest him. If only that were true!

I demanded he tell me where my family was. He stammered something about not being in Srebrenica at the time, of having moved to Belgrade. I went completely berserk. He attempted to close the car door, but I wouldn't let go of it.

I demanded he give me his phone number. He swore he didn't have a phone.

'Hasan, let him go,' a voice said from one of the jeeps. Exasperated, I slammed the car door shut, and Colonel Vuković's yellow Ford quickly disappeared out of my sight.

I looked up and saw some people sitting on the veranda of Razija and Veljko Bašić's house, the same house we had occupied during the siege. They were probably refugees from Croatia's Krajina region. I'd heard they'd settled in Srebrenica even before the Dayton Agreement was signed.

I went over to them and asked, 'Did you by any chance find any photographs when you moved into that house?'

'No, nothing was here but rubble and wreckage. Everything was in ruins when we arrived.'

'Hey, comrade,' said an old man with a moustache, 'you don't happen to have a cigarette for me, do you?'

'No,' I told him, although I had a packet of Marlboros in my pocket. 'Let's go to Vlasenica,' I said to the driver.

Over the next few years I would spend every waking hour putting together the pieces of the puzzle of my family's last days. I would travel thousands of kilometres in my quest for information and talk to hundreds of individuals. I would beg and pay for pieces of knowledge. The smallest details would haunt my dreams. During that time I could never drive by an old warehouse without looking at it suspiciously, nor could I pass a meadow in eastern Bosnia and not wonder if its undulations were concealing the bones of the missing.

Ten long years would pass before I could finally bury my father at the Potočari Memorial. A further five years were needed before I could lay the remains of my mother and brother to rest.

To be continued